Patrick Geddes and Town Planning

Patrick Geddes is considered a forefather of the modern urban planning movement. *Patrick Geddes and Town Planning: A Critical View* studies the various, and even opposing ways, in which Geddes has been interpreted up to this day, providing a new reading of his life, writing and plans.

Relying on Geddes' extensive writings, the book also provides scholars of planning and related subjects, for the first time, a much-needed, long overdue model of his urban theory. Rebutting earlier appreciations of Geddes' sensitive planning, the scheme is presented as a formative and a deterministic paradigm in which City and Society became the subjects of a mutual transformation towards a predefined "ideal" city and "civilized" society. Current perspectives in geography and post-colonialism are used to examine the practice of this theory through Geddes' greatly celebrated – yet hardly studied – work in India and in Palestine. Studying Geddes' plans for such different cities as Edinburgh, Calcutta, and Tel Aviv, the book suggests a critical reading of Geddes' colonial work, offering a valuable contribution towards the concretization of the theoretical frameworks and to local historians as well.

Geddes' scrutiny is finally presented as a case study for town planning as a whole. Tying together for the first time key concepts in cultural geography and colonial urbanism, the book proposes a more vigorous historiography, exposing hidden narratives and past agendas still dominating the disciplinary discourse. Written by a cultural geographer and a town planner, this book offers a rounded, full-length analysis of Geddes' vision and its material manifestation, functioning also as a much-needed critical tool to evaluate modern town planning as an academic and practical discipline.

Noah Hysler-Rubin is qualified as a town planner and holds a PhD in Geography. She teaches history and theory of town planning at the Bezalel Academy of Art and Design, Jerusalem.

D0219362

Patrick Geddes and Town Planning

A Critical View

Noah Hysler-Rubin

Taylor & Francis Group

LONDON AND NEW YORK

First published 2011
by Routledge
2 Park Square, Milton Park, Abingdon, Oxon, OX14 4RN

Simultaneously published in the USA and Canada
by Routledge
270 Madison Avenue, New York, NY 10016

Routledge is an imprint of the Taylor & Francis Group, an informa business

Typeset in Univers by
Pindar NZ, Auckland, New Zealand
Printed and bound in Great Britain by
TJ International Ltd, Padstow, Cornwall

British Library Cataloguing in Publication Data
A catalogue record for this book is available from the British Library

Library of Congress Cataloging-in-Publication Data
Hysler-Rubin, Noah.
Patrick Geddes and town planning: a critical view / Noah Hysler-Rubin.
     p. cm.
   Includes bibliographical references and index.
   1. Geddes, Patrick, Sir, 1854–1932. 2. City planners—Great Britain—Biography.
3. City planning—Great Britain—History. I. Title.
   HT169.G7G434 2011
   307.1'216092—dc22   2010026346

ISBN13: 978-0-415-57866-0 (hbk)
ISBN13: 978-0-415-57867-7 (pbk)

For Yoel, for Evyatar and for Yotam
With all my love

Contents

Contents

Illustrations

Acknowledgments

This book started many years ago out of love to the city and its builders. Many people have walked with me various strands of the way and to them I am grateful. My journey started in Jerusalem, at the Historical Archives of the Jerusalem Municipality. Menahem Levin assisted me greatly in my search into the earliest files of British planning in the city. My work in the historical archives of the Tel Aviv, Haifa, and Tiberius municipalities was also very significant as well as my work at the Central Zionist Archives and also at the Israel State Archives. In England, my earliest sojourn was at King's College historical archives in Cambridge, as I was tracing down the work of Geddes' predecessor in Jerusalem, Charles Robert Ashbee. It is a pleasant duty to thank the devoted archivist and my host at the Centre for History and Economics, Gareth Stedman Jones.

Over the years I have spent many blissful hours at the British Library, delving into the Oriental and India Office Collections. It is there also that I got priceless lessons in historiographical research, tracing down as much as I could from what had been written about Geddes along the years. Many archivists and librarians assisted me greatly in my research possibly without ever knowing. I would also like to acknowledge my work at the Public Records Office at Kew. My initial visit to the Geddes collections at the Strathclyde University Archive in Glasgow set the course of my research. I am grateful to many archivists who assisted me along the years, especially Anne Cameron. Finally, the National Library of Scotland, where I consulted Geddes' manuscripts, and from where I could take daily visits to the Outlook Tower and walk up and down the Royal Mile. I would also like to mention the great assistance I have received over the years at the National Library of Israel, and my friend, Smadar Bergman, who was very generous with her time and put much effort into editing the figures.

Many generous grants I received over the years made my work possible. Grants from the Cherrick Center for the Study of the State of Israel have supported me during various stages of my research. The Rachel Yanait Award of the Yad Yitzhak Ben-Zvi and the Hebrew University of Jerusalem joint research center and the Levi Eshkol Institute for Social, Economic and Political Research in Israel enabled my early venture to the British archives. A research support grant from the Paul Mellon Centre for Studies in British Art and a generous Harold Hyam Wingate Scholarship have eased my stay. Finally, the Shlomo Glass and Fanny Balaban-Glass Foundation Scholarship for doctoral students and a postdoctoral grant from the Hebrew University facilitated the final writing.

I have learned so much from many teachers along the years but will mention only a few. Yehoshua Ben Arieh, whose books it was that I initially followed in my search for the modern history of Jerusalem, eventually led me to the study of its British origins. His generosity and his devotion have given me much courage. The late Arie Shachar, in his fascinating lectures and endless kindness, lured me into the captivating world of town planning. Ruth HaCohen taught me so much more than music appreciation and enhanced my study in various cultural aspects. And finally, my PhD supervisor, my guide, my teacher, my friend, Ronnie Ellenblum, has been by my side almost from the very beginning. He had shared with me his knowledge, his thoughts, his beliefs and his doubts, and had inspired my own. He supported me in every path I had chosen to take and accompanied me on every step. I am lucky to have him by my side.

Many teachers who have also become colleagues inspired me during my stay in England, many of whom I had met at the London Group of Historical Geographers at the Institute of Historical Research and who made me proud of being one of them. To my hosts at the Department of Geography at Queen Mary, University of London, who played a crucial part in the long, British part of my research, and especially my teachers and my friends, Catherine Nash, Miles Ogborn, and Alison Blunt. They taught me much of what I know about cultural geography and postcolonial readings. It was at the University of Edinburgh where I was exposed to the Scottish Empire and led down another fascinating trail. My local host, Jane Jacobs, assisted me greatly in my work in the Scottish archives and opened my mind to read about colonial cities from without and within. Helen Meller, who I was lucky enough to get to know at the very beginning of my work, had generously shared with me her vast knowledge about Geddes and modern planning, eventually trusting me with the handling of some of the most precious of Geddes' reports. It was her blessing for the road that pushed me into Geddes' infinite theory and work as deeply as I did. Volker Welter, who had previously followed in Geddes' footsteps, was kind enough to share with me many of his fascinating findings. I found Leonie Sandercock's writings immensely influential from the very beginning, helping me to outline many of my sporadic thoughts and giving a clear direction to my multidisciplinary readings. Later on, her personal advice encouraged me to believe in my target. Finally, the warm support I had received from Zeynep Çelik and Anthony King, two precious teachers I met at the final stretch of the journey, helped me turn my research into a book.

My parents' everlasting belief that I could do whatever I set my heart on enabled me to undertake this venture without ever thinking of the consequences. My father took me along his long walks about Zion, taught me to look up and to the sides and encouraged me to imagine the story behind the buildings and their inhabitants. My husband's parents joined the journey wholeheartedly and helped us in every possible way. Thank you; I know we could never have done this without you. My sons, Evyatar, who was born in Jerusalem not long before my original research plan was approved, and whose lessons in mothering made me a better researcher; and Yotam, who was born in London only six months before the first draft was completed, made the final stretch especially enjoyable. I love you both very much. And finally, to Yoel, my tireless companion night and day, who endured my travels and my moods and who believed I was right even when I had my doubts. I am forever indebted to your humbleness and devotion. You have taught me so much; this book is as much yours as it is mine.

Introduction

Interpreting Geddes, a Contemporaneous Task

I. Geddes today, a disputed pioneer

Patrick Geddes (1854–1932), one of the better known early British town planners, is a popular subject of research, whose legacy attracts renewed scholarly attention.[1] Geddes was born 2 October 1854 in Ballater, Scotland. He studied natural sciences in London and Paris, and finally became Chair of Botany at Dundee College in 1889. Geddes' social aspirations led him to be involved in piecemeal rehabilitation of the urban environment in his city of residence, Edinburgh, where he purchased and rebuilt several properties along the dilapidated Royal Mile. His more educational endeavors included the city's first students' hall and especially the Outlook Tower, a unique museum that hosted various educational, social, and environmental activities. In 1897, Geddes worked abroad for the first time, helping Armenian refugees in Cyprus to regain their livelihood through a local agricultural endeavor. He then became involved in various urban plans in Scotland, his first major work being a suggested park for Dunfermline in 1904. Geddes' major debut as a planner was at the Royal Institute of British Architects (RIBA) Town Planning Conference of 1910, where he presented an urban planning exhibition. Having later displayed the exhibition in Dublin, Geddes instigated the first international planning competition for the city in 1914. On the same year he embarked on his imperial career, having been summoned to present his exhibition in Madras. The exhibition traveled throughout India, bringing Geddes numerous planning commissions, mainly for local independent rulers. He also suggested plans for Aden and for Ceylon. The vast majority of his plans, however, were never implemented. Following his celebrated plan for the University of Indore in 1918, Geddes was invited to Palestine to plan the Hebrew University in Jerusalem. Geddes returned to Palestine several times, suggesting more successful plans for various cities including Jerusalem and Haifa, finally creating the first master plan for the city of Tel Aviv. At the same time he also served as the chair of Sociology and Civics at the University of Bombay while still pursuing his local career as an independent planner. Geddes' final major educational endeavor was the Collège des Écossais in Montpellier, France, where he died on 17 April 1932.

All of Geddes' biographies (the first published already in 1927) emphasize his contribution to planning. Numerous works, written by both British and local researchers throughout the former British Empire, describe his work as a planner. Others discuss his theories regarding city and society or consequential practical means.[2] Nevertheless, in spite of Geddes' recognition as an important member of the town planning movement and of his great influence upon it, he has always been considered to be an outsider to it; explanations to this phenomenon, as well as to his apparent failure as a practitioner, relate to Geddes and his work, as well as to his general acceptance.[3] Notwithstanding, Geddes' uniqueness is emphasized and he is celebrated for being sensitive to both the environment and the community, his work studied as a tool for raising public awareness for the built environment. Geddes' work for the Zionist Commission in Palestine especially had received great attention in Israeli history and geography, generally reflecting his popular perception. Patrick Geddes is thus regarded as a representative of the well-meaning British Mandate over Palestine (1922–47) and of the modern discipline of planning. Thus, his plans for Jewish neighborhoods, agricultural colonies, and public buildings, including the Hebrew University of Jerusalem, are described as successful local manifestations of modern planning and celebrated as the proper enhancement of old and new for a reviving nation.[4]

Original intentions of the present research

Being educated as a planner in Jerusalem, I set out in research under the impression of the prevailing appreciation of Geddes, in order to learn in what ways Geddes was different from his planning contemporaries, thereby strengthening his place as a unique, albeit forgotten, planner. By studying Geddes' work comparatively, examining his work in Palestine against similar work in India and also his earlier work in Britain, I strove to reveal the ways in which he tended to the needs and the aspirations of the local community. I expected to uncover inherent differences in Geddes' plans by tracing the adaptation of his planning theory to each unique locality. As Geddes' writings are practically endless, including theoretical papers, lecture syllabi, planning reports, extensive correspondence, plans, and several personal collections, I planned to use the various researches and examinations written about Geddes as a theoretic basis upon which I could advance to a comparative examination of his practical work. I thus intended to rely mainly on secondary sources for discerning Geddes' planning theory, preparing to focus at a later stage on the material which had hardly been studied, that is, documenting his work in the colonies.

From a very early stage of my work, however, I found my task unfeasible. In spite of all that had been written about Geddes since his early days as a planner and until this very day, I could not work out and word Geddes' theory of town planning; I still didn't know how Geddes planned. I could not bridge the gap between Geddes' general theories and the selective account of his planning tools, as in spite of the long-lasting and contentious discussion of Geddes as a town planner, the historiography of his work lacks a basic attempt to trace his overall planning system. What was Geddes' much-praised planning paradigm? Similarly, there seemed to be a gap between the appreciation of Geddes as a thinker and as a practitioner. Geddes' biographies generally describe his achievements and relate them to his life story; works dealing with his planning usually discuss only elements from the overall theory, neglecting his full vision of an urban ideal, while those bestowing Geddes' philosophy are not usually concerned with his practical urbanism. Accordingly, other than anecdotal justification for Geddes' absence from mainstream planning, there was little criticism of Geddes' work and no comparative basis for its examination within different contexts.

Most important of all, though, was the fact that the accumulated secondary sources regarding Geddes seemed to yield an uneven picture, changing considerably with time: Geddes as a town planner was appreciated differently in 2007 than he was in the 1960s or even during his own days. The inevitable conclusion was, that the perception of Geddes as a planner today is a new one, and even that not as monolithic and as united as assumed. The prevailing comprehension of Geddes today reflects a general conception which had amalgamated since the 1970s only, and strengthened since the 1980s mostly by planning historians. The laborious literature review brought me to ask new questions about the gap between what I knew about Geddes as a town planner, in Israel and elsewhere, and the uneven, incomplete, and generally uncritical corpus of historiography, questioning the actual appreciation of Geddes as a town planner, its focal points, and its changing modes. Additionally, I ventured to compile a critical reading of Geddes' theory and practice throughout the British colonies, composed out of his vast writing and analyzed through current theoretical prisms.

My eventual conclusions brought me to regard Geddes' historiography as a case study for the turbulent history of the discipline. The general positive outlook upon Geddes as a planner of good intentions, and the commonly positive approval of his plans and treatment of society, are slowly changing with new readings of his work from more critical perspective, although generally not those of planners. Thus, the present research calls for an updated evaluation of town planning and its historiography, arguing the intersection of postcolonial theories and cultural geography in particular as offering challenging opportunities to explore the ideological and practical roots of modern town planning and its practice, providing much-needed critical tools for exposing hidden narratives and past agendas still dominating the disciplinary discourse.

II. Reading planning histories

The subfield of Planning History has emerged as part of the discipline of planning only in the past 30 years, being formalized in 1974 with the establishment of the Planning History Group (later, the International Planning History Society). Most investigations stretch back approximately 100 years, concentrating mainly on institutional, statutory town planning which has developed since the beginning of the twentieth century. They reflect an agreed periodization of three major eras of modern urban planning, which can be categorized generally as the evolution of town planning, a modernist highpoint, and the humanist revolt.[5]

The history of town planning is currently condemned as a unified, monolithic, and consensual reading, chronicling "the rise of the profession, its institutionalization, and its achievements."[6] Planning history, as described by Leonie

Sandercock, has adopted a descriptive approach in which planning is presented as part of the Western project of modernization and of the rise of liberal democracy with its belief in progress through science and technology.[7] Revisiting planning history seems to be revealing an official story, the story of planning by and through the state, part of a tradition of city and nation building;[8] historical studies emphasize success over failure and the neatness of theories and design intentions, rather than the messiness of actual outcomes and lived experiences of planning activity.[9] Planning itself emerges a hero, its role unproblematic and its opponents reactionary; planners are believed to know, or able to divine, "the public," possessing an expertise which must prevail over politics: equated with progress, planning has no flaws.[10]

Reading the history of town planning, as claimed by planners themselves, has great significance for the discipline, its development and its aims.[11] Disciplinary history creates a composite sense of solidarity and pride, making the recovery of one's history a first step in constructing or reconstructing professional identity,[12] as the contemporary culture of the present discipline is inevitably molded around memories of past struggles and triumphs.[13] However, as inquiries tend to be conducted on internal concerns of the profession and its practices,[14] the past is often changed and even twisted in the course of the disciplinary mission. "Successive generations of scholars do not so much rewrite history as revisit it and re-present it," claims Sandercock, "investing it with contemporary meaning"[15] and the history of planning is determined in the first place by the prevailing definition of planning.[16]

Unavoidably, omissions as well as systematic exclusions occur. Events which do not accord with the chosen image are forgotten, expediently writing out material of a non-conforming nature[17] while more conforming memories are enhanced,[18] leading eventually to the repeated presentation of grand models that dominated the field in previous decades.[19] Critics also condemn historians' tendency to focus on details (individual agents, projects, or codes) as the constituting elements of planning histories, which provide only glimpses or partial views of cities and planning. Planning monographs as narratives are accused of replicating the original political role of their objects.[20]

Planning biographies, initially suggested as case studies "in the belief that they will provide a more rounded understanding and explanation of events"[21] are now seen as the history of planning itself. According to this new reading, certain individuals were thus elevated to the status of social phenomena of exceptional importance, whose actions personify the era in which they lived and whose innovative contributions are profound and enduring. The milestones that they have embedded along the highways of history have become points of reference and orientation to the profession.[22] These chosen planners are crowned as undisputed heroes, their lives are turned mythologies.[23] Planners' biographies are also understood as presenting two selves, where it is suspected that the author reveals not the least about himself than he does about the planner whose life he is describing.[24] Thus, while the past can be perceived as the parent of the present, the present can equally be conceived as the creator of the past, the "facts" of history not existing for any historian until she or he states them.[25]

In need of critical theory

In *Making the Invisible Visible* (1998) Leonie Sandercock acknowledged the importance of theory for the history of planning, urging to inject it by a series of critical themes, theories, and methodologies, exposing and reclaiming systematic exclusions and revealing stories of marginalized and oppressed groups. Sandercock suggested using different categories of analysis, acknowledging forgotten or repressed contributions through feminist, postcolonial, and other critical frameworks.[26] In this process, traditional narratives should be broken down, turning to individual, sensitive, and holistic stories, and revealing physical and social urban complexities, the challenge being to deconstruct and reconstruct them again, using new theoretically defensible interpretations.[27] Similarly, by understanding personal myths and studying their components, pleads Krueckeberg, the individual planner would be revealed; the myth would be disbanded; and the making of that myth, and the components of the planner as well as his own motives, could be better understood.[28]

III. The historiography of Patrick Geddes

Geddes' recognition as a planner has been a debated matter from the very days in which he practiced as such. Since then, a controversial figure, the professional appreciation of Geddes had known many changes. Part I presents three major periods in which the appreciation and discussion of Geddes changed considerably. Chapter 1 describes the ambivalence towards Geddes' role in formulating town planning, as during his own days Geddes was generally not described as a planner, certainly not by planners. Chapter 2 describes how Geddes was largely forgotten by the world of planning in the days of modernist and comprehensive reconstruction; his planning diagrams, however, served modernist architects and planners as device for a comprehensive worldly analysis.

Chapter 3 is devoted to Geddes' revival as a representative of good planning, occurring simultaneously with the rise of the history of town planning. The 1970s writings about Patrick Geddes are abundant, ranging in genre, places of origin, and disciplinary attribution. Various works celebrate personal and professional landmarks, from a collection of essays on urbanization published following the Golden Jubilee of the Department of Sociology of Bombay University (1969) to the latest symposiums conducted upon Geddes' 150 years birth centennial in 2004.[29] New biographical accounts are accompanied by discussions of Geddes' theories and their individual components. Geddes' contribution to various disciplines is explored, including history, geography, sociology, and not the least, planning. It was at this age that many present-day planning merits, including public participation in planning and sustainable development have been associated with Geddes, and his name became synonymous with attentive communal planning. Chapter 4 describes the accumulating research regarding Geddes' work throughout the empire, first and foremost by British and Israeli historians, geographers, and planners, celebrating his practical work and lasting impact on the urban landscape. The discussion in Chapter 5 finally claims that the changing status of Geddes as a town planner is a clear reflection of the contemporary status of town planning, its perceived strengths and its weaknesses. This chapter also analyzes the apologetic explanations given along the years as to why, Geddes has remained outside mainstream planning, and finally, sums up the problematic evaluation of Geddes' overall contribution to planning.

IV. Geddes' planning paradigm and its geographical evaluation

In order to facilitate a comparison of Geddes' work in various locations, I next set to propose an overall Geddesian planning theory. Going back to Geddes' own writings and plans seemed at first to be an incredible task, due to multifarious writings from the 1880s to the 1930s encompassing different and varying themes, including history and geography, education and evolution, culture and civilization, society and world peace, relating also to Geddes' practical tools and techniques, including surveys and parks, the Museum and the Outlook Tower. Slowly, though, I began to realize that Geddes' theoretical themes were constant, as all his subjects were related to each other in one complex, yet well-thought-of paradigm, exposing different but consistent sides in his worldview. The themes from which Geddes drew represent his wide scientific interests and involvement in contemporary discourse, including biology, economics and sociology, and of course, town planning; the focus of Geddes' writings shifted from time to time, initially concerning theoretical themes; later, accentuating their relevance to the practice of town planning; and finally, addressing matters of war and peace. However, Geddes' theory, tools, and expected outcomes all seem to have remained constant since their initial inception, composing an overall urban scheme which can be defined and traced throughout his various endeavors.

Chapter 6 presents the role Geddes assigned to modern day planners as emanating from his comprehensive urban theory, aiming at complete, urban and social, transformation. It was a regulative scheme, designed to enable a mutual process of urban design and communal education, representing popular notions of natural evolution, civilization, and modern urbanism. The analysis of Geddes' comprehensive worldview is elaborated in the Appendix. Chapter 7 describes Geddes' practical tools and known institutes: the survey, the museum, the exhibition, the Outlook Tower, the university, and the civic center, all based on popular geographical notions of the time, as elements in his comprehensive process of urban improvement.

Critical readings into Geddes' theory and practice have nevertheless developed over the years but never incorporated into the appreciation and analysis of his work. Chapter 8 opens with Lewis Mumford's unknown rebellious writings, accusing Geddes' way of thinking as a closed system which allowed no input or criticism from without. Geddes, Mumford claimed, became imprisoned in his own thought, refusing to incorporate any voice other than his. The result, claim later writers, was in fact a false concept of evolution, in which Geddes "had little intention of following Darwin into the unknown."[30] According to this critical reading, Geddes ended up selecting as tendencies, as indications of what the future will bring, those activities that he favored.[31]

A growing corpus of critical discussion in Geddes' theory and work rises today from the subfield of cultural geography, where many of Geddes' educational endeavors and related tools are discussed in relation to geographical concepts prevailing in Britain at the end of the nineteenth and the beginning of the twentieth centuries. Labeled an imperial science,[32] geography's alleged objectivity regarding the representations of the world has long been tied with complex relations of knowledge and power; its visual appliances and products no longer considered innocent but rather linked to critiques of a totalizing gaze. Critical geographical readings of Geddes' "survey," the Outlook Tower, and the schematic Valley Section serve as case studies for larger concerns in cultural geography, and highlights the imperial traits of Geddes' theory, incorporating him within contemporary postcolonial readings.

V. Patrick Geddes, town planner in the colonies

Between the years 1914 and 1925 Geddes worked mainly in the British colonies and the colonial endeavors constitute the bulk of his practical work. It is generally agreed that Geddes practiced in India (and later in Palestine and elsewhere) the theory he had amalgamated at home, and also that in his first stop in India, Madras, he devised a basic practice which he was to carry throughout his work.[33] India and Palestine were both important elements in Geddes' global scheme: India, as the fascinating representative of the traditional oriental civilization; and Palestine, as a constituting phase in Western civilization which must recuperate its ancient glory. This part discusses the practical manifestations of Geddes' theory, tools, and urban outcomes through his work in the Colonies, under British administration, local Indian elite and the Zionist Commission. Chapter 9 describes the travels of Geddes' traveling exhibition, which was designed to improve the local planning procedure by comparison to chosen examples from great cities and civilizations far and wide, and demonstrates its great success in India alongside its failure in Palestine. Chapter 10 describes Geddes' surveys, a means to study the city and discern its evolutionary trend, which resulted in arrays of local elements chosen to represent the traditional Indian culture on one hand, and the biblical Hebrew city on the other. Chapter 11 traces the regional analysis of Palestine as it was assigned the role of a leader in the renewing Mediterranean basin. Chapter 12, "The Garden in the City," describes Geddes' urban and social work in Indore and in Tel Aviv through the concept of physical and moral nurture. Chapter 13 discusses Indian and Palestinian museums and outlook towers which presented the local findings of Geddes' surveys, set within his worldly scheme. Finally, Chapter 14 discusses the proposed university for Indore and the suggested Hebrew University in Jerusalem as modern-day cloisters, hosting intellectuals in their task to analyze local past and project an incipient future.

VI. Patrick Geddes as a colonial town planner: a scrutiny through geography and planning

Due to Geddes' standing appreciation as a planner without political inclinations or intentions, his work had scarcely been discussed through the prevailing postcolonial urban discourse. This part suggests reading Geddes as a colonial town planner, one whose theory represents shared imperial notions and whose work had inevitably been affected by various colonial circumstances. The evolution of the sub-discipline of colonial town planning and its main themes are discussed in Chapter 15, which also provides an initial analysis of the imperial networks through which Geddes had operated and their inevitable implications upon his work for the British, Indians, and Zionists. Chapter 16 proposes a new paradigm for the examination of colonial town planning through geography by joining together geographical imperial scrutiny with the current study of colonial cities. A critical analysis of Geddes' urban paradigm as a colonial gambit is offered, presenting his planning as a direct manifestation of imperial geography. Finally, Chapter 17 discusses the uses made of Geddes' regulating urban paradigm by the British, the Indians, and the Zionists. However, since Geddes' paradigm was inflexible and his colonial perspective unchanged, Geddes' local planning is again presented as a direct reflection of his own personal perspective, ultimately disappointing his employers. Analyzing the more applied plans for Jerusalem and Tel Aviv shows the actual implication of Geddes' geographical notions upon the landscape, finally calling for their re-evaluation as "success" or "failure."

Part I

The Planning Historiography of Patrick Geddes

Chapter 1

The Town Planner as a Miracle Worker

Patrick Geddes, 1854–1932

I. Early endeavors

Three biographical sketches were published about Geddes during his lifetime, all tending to his role as a town planner or at least a re-maker of the environment.[1] But during his time, Geddes was more commonly applauded for other accomplishments; his role as a planner and his overall contribution to town planning were not clear.[2] Geddes' early urban work and related activities in Edinburgh were described by his colleagues and friends as part of his overall approach to the city and its dwellers, and considered as part of a social, cultural, and physical revival.[3] Geddes' early work in London was reported only by his supporters.[4]

Many of Geddes' achievements were related to the Outlook Tower, described in 1927 in the *American Journal of Sociology* as the basis for "the Edinburgh School" of British Sociology.[5] Yet to many, the carefully linked exhibits seemed a random jumble.[6] Amelia Defries, Geddes' disciple and first biographer commented sadly, "the pity is that few of his fellow-citizens and sometimes even of his collaborators – have yet understood the Tower or its work; and scanty means and membership thus leave it but a beginning of what it seeks to be."[7]

II. Doubtful turning points[8]
Beginnings in Britain

Reviews described Geddes' first official task of planning in Dunfermline as comprehensive beyond precedent, acknowledging the planning report's imagination and enthusiasm and marveling at its specificity as a utopia.[9] But, as Helen Meller claims, the popular press tended to misunderstand the work. Moreover, many of Geddes' colleagues were baffled.[10] T. C. Horsfall, "despite his record of being a campaigner for bringing Art and Beauty to the city," refused to review it.[11] Ebenezer Howard was highly appreciative, "though there may have been a barb," says Meller, "in his comment that a copy of the report should be in every public library," presumably thinking it was inspirational rather than practical.[12] Charles Booth and Walter Crane highlighted the artistic value of Geddes' suggestions and the importance of conservation raised in his "charming volume."[13] Another critic simply asked to see the extension of the projects to the population itself.[14]

Patrick Abercrombie described the first International Town Planning Conference held by RIBA in 1910 as Geddes' first town planning emergence into public after having "long been subterraneously at work."[15] The *Town Planning Review* marked out Geddes' unique contribution amongst many other participants.[16] According to Philip Boardman, the London newspapers recognized that in Geddes' gallery lay the keynote of the whole international exhibition: *The Standard*, for example, told its readers to head straight for the Edinburgh room if they would understand what town planning was all about.[17]

Yet Geddes' approach was ambivalent and somewhat problematic. In a later account of the exhibition Abercrombie described how Geddes, in "that nightmare of complexity, the Edinburgh Room," shattered the idea that town planning was a simple thing, composed of basic elements. In an often quoted passage Abercrombie accuses Geddes of torturing his crowds.[18] Following the conference, Geddes had secured support from the leaders of the British town planning movement for his exhibition; but invitations from large cities were not forthcoming and it was only displayed in Edinburgh, in Dublin, and in Belfast.[19]

The exhibition in Dublin in 1912 was mainly an impetus to the competition of the planning of the city in 1914. The plan and later exhibition were followed closely by the *Town Planning Review*, mentioning the prize offered by Earl of Aberdeen, Lord Lieutenant of Ireland, and naming Geddes as one of the three adjudicators. Geddes' great Housing and Town Planning Exhibition was described as part of the overall Civic Exhibition.[20] The Irish experience, claims Meller, was crucial in establishing Geddes' position in the British town planning movement not the least because of his association with Raymond Unwin and Patrick Abercrombie.[21] When the exhibition was lost in sea, Defries wrote: "Many of us considered that this would be the end of Patrick Geddes. His name was so little known to the general public that it had never occurred to me that he had any real following . . . to whom did it matter that Geddes' Exhibition of his ideas was destroyed?"[22]

Town planning in India and in Palestine, 1914–25

Geddes' work in India received great local press coverage, reporting mainly about the town planning exhibitions and accompanying series of lectures and calling the public to take advantage of the great and unique occasion, as in "a carnival of fine speeches . . . Professor Geddes unravels the town-planning mysteries to an admiring audience."[23] "Geddes has come out to India to give us the benefit of his experience of towns and cities and men in Europe, America and Asia, and the huge collection of photographs and drawings . . ."[24] In Britain, many articles in the new planning magazines were devoted to town planning in the colonies in general and in India in particular, describing work of local improvement trusts and municipal committees; none of these mentioned Patrick Geddes or his work.[25]

In Palestine Geddes' work was celebrated by magazines for bringing modern ideas into the building of the old–new homeland.[26] Unlike his work in India, though, it also drew attention in Britain, where Geddes was reported as working "to plan toward the development of Palestine as a land flowing once more with milk and honey,"[27] introducing the newest innovations in town planning into Palestine while also preserving its unique traits.[28] "They who hesitated to follow his suggestions for rebuilding Edinburgh, Dundee, or Aberdeen," claimed Boardman, "heartily approved when it was a question of Jerusalem."[29] The *Garden Cities and Town Planning Journal* described the Jewish settlements in Palestine as an ideal return to an agricultural mode of life, a perception later strengthened by others.[30] The *Egyptian Gazette* described Geddes' vision of Haifa as a Town Beautiful.[31] Flattering and enquiring letters came also from Charles Zueblin in America and Thomas Adams in Canada.[32] The planning of the Hebrew University was closely followed and its opening ceremony described as an event arousing unusual interest, "not only among Jews but also among all civilised people's."[33] Amelia Defries later wrote of Geddes' work in Jerusalem, "do I exaggerate when I say that . . . it seems that Patrick Geddes is helping to lay the foundation of living faith – based upon the realities of science – and elastic for development and discovery?"[34]

III. Geddes' controversial theory and tools
General theory and publications

Geddes' "Draft Plan for a National Institute of Geography," published in 1902, was received with much interest and sympathy; yet it was also thought to be impractical and possibly redundant.[35] Between 1904 and 1906 Geddes introduced his overall theory of Civics.[36] Booth and Howard, claims Meller, completely misunderstood it.[37] Civics was declared not inclusive, ignoring the effects of the inequality of wealth as well as the rights and duties of citizens; a regional survey was not enough.[38] Geddes was accused of neglecting to consider the formation of cities in new countries and disregarding the implications of modern industry.[39] On the other hand, Civics was criticized as too detailed and too burdening for the sociologist.[40] Many protested against Geddes' implied environmental determinism, calling out the danger of confusing resemblance with relationship or the lack of reciprocity between the society and environment.[41] When Geddes later introduced his "charming diagrams," his arguments were apparently even more problematic, and confused his audience.[42] The Valley Section was accused of outright determinism and the practical outcome of Civics was, again, not clear.[43] When the Museum plan was introduced in 1907 Geddes was commended for paying attention to the future by supplying an institution for urban conservation.[44] Giovanni Ferraro claims that the unease that professionals felt towards Geddes' suggestions can be seen in the response to a paper he read in 1921 at the Town Planning Institute.[45]

When *Cities in Evolution* was finally published in 1915 it was received as an interesting sample of writing about town planning, yet not necessarily a very useful one.[46] "Prof. Geddes would make the study of regional geography fundamental with a view to town planning, but he does not attempt to show in detail how by this means the end is to be achieved . . . he has not distinctly asked himself how much wider than mere regional survey must be the outlook of one who would explain the past and forecast the fortunes of cities . . ."[47] In 1915 Geddes also started editing, together with Victor Branford, the series *Making of the Future*, elaborating many of his ideas as tools for peaceful social reconstruction. It was not considered to be related to town planning. *The Coming Polity* (1920) was thus described: "the authors seem to move in a dream world under the guidance of a science and a history of their own invention . . . This is not science. The book might be described as the result of an effort on the part of belated mystics to create a 'regionalistic' religion."[48]

Geddes' immediate influence on planning

During Geddes' many years of absence from Edinburgh, the Outlook Tower had fallen on difficult times and Arthur, his son, was working to keep the legacy alive.[49] Finally, in 1927 Patrick Abercrombie noted that Geddes, "the magician of the enchanted Edinburgh Tower," is being recognized as the practical man who showed how to build town planning on a sure foundation, admitting that all the leaders of the planning movement base their practice on his theory.[50] The regional approach and the Survey were often referred to by the leading planners of the time, giving Geddes due credit as a pioneer but generally portraying a very practical, straightforward approach.[51]

The main discussion concerning Geddes' Regionalism and Survey was held by the regional survey movement of the 1920s, but, according to Meller, this was not a meaning that was accepted by all geographers.[52] The same could be claimed about the mainstream of sociology, as Meller shows how in America Geddes won no support; the Chicago School studiously avoided any mention of him.[53]

Geddes' obituaries: lamenting an idea

The many obituaries published after Geddes' death celebrate his personality and his life, as he stood alone "in the quality of his spirit, his piercing wit, his luminous expressiveness, the light and laughter of the blue eyes that took in everything within their range."[54] Geddes was described as a practical genius, bold and ambitious, a precise observer and of penetrating insight.[55] Acclaimed as a Messiah, Geddes was also a prophet and a social reformer, a dreamer, the true interpreter of his age.[56] He was a guide, an inspiration, even his physical appearance was that of a spiritual guru.[57] Unfortunately, though, Geddes' extraordinary range of intellect led him to develop relations and analogies very hard to follow and thus "to the average mind the vision was liable to be obscured in a maze of detail"[58] and he did not have the direct appeal to the public his ideas deserved.[59]

Geddes' Outlook Tower and other educational projects, as well as his work in Edinburgh, were hailed as the deeds of a conservationist improving social and sanitary conditions.[60] Yet "it would have been better if the example set by Geddes had been more clearly understood and followed," many schemes being often more notable for their vision than for practical qualities;[61] even the Outlook Tower was described as only a vague symbol of what it was intended to be.[62] Many recalled Geddes' description of his function: "ring the bell and run away," agreeing that he was better at realizing problems than offering solutions.[63] The failures were excused by a variety of causes.[64] "It was said of him, and the compliment was as great as the irony, that he failed in everything he undertook," wrote Charles Robert Ashbee.[65] Yet

Geddes' lamenters were optimistic, as he was always greater than the momentary achievement; he worked for the future.[66]

Geddes' name was claimed to have been most closely identified with town and regional planning work.[67] His listed contributions included the concern with saving of life and beauty, securing conditions for the development of cultural life through his uniqueness of regarding cities as complex organisms, "humanizing" town planning and harmonizing man and surroundings;[68] Geddes' greatest input was a preliminary "survey of the communal life."[69] The Town Planning Institute wrote, "his works and observations gave the philosophical and sociological key to planning work and revealed its underlying purposes."[70] American planners claimed to be sharing his heritage.[71] Frank Mears' obituary reads like one final attempt at explaining Geddes' town planning, rationalizing the whole of his activities.[72]

The Dunfermline report was hailed as Geddes' greatest work "yet it only partially embodies the Town Planning ideas which filled his mind at the time."[73] The Irish builder and engineer lamented Geddes, "the town-planner who saw visions and dreamed splendid dreams."[74] Marjorie Pentland described Geddes' summons to India due to his enthusiasm and interest in his surroundings;[75] Geddes was praised as having associated between the Mohammedan and the Hindu.[76] *The Times of India* described the Scottish origins of the Bombay exhibition.[77] Radhakamal Mukerjee, Professor of Sociology at Lucknow University, described Geddes' contribution to the science of sociology, but claimed that most of work in planning is not widely known even in India.[78]

Many of Geddes' designs for the reconstruction of Indian cities are listed as "Magnificent failures," although hope was expressed that India might some day rediscover them and that the rich results of an Indian career "may yet be reaped when India's days become less stormy."[79] *The Times of Ceylon* wrote about the death of the expert who "was paid a handsome fee for his report on the possibilities of laying out the city of Colombo" yet who came in for a good deal of criticism, "ringing the bell and running away," leaving the elaboration of the scheme to the authorities.[80] Lanchester explained Geddes' uniqueness in India against the background of British procedures.[81]

The creation of Tel Aviv was celebrated by D. M. Stevenson, describing his recent visit to the city which evolved "by the brain of a fellow countryman of mine."[82] In Palestine, Geddes "threw down the glove to Jewry in his plans for a university; but he was before his time."[83] The Hebrew University was described as part of Geddes' continuing failure to reform and vitalize the universities of the world.[84] David Eder summarizes Geddes' deeds and accomplishments in Palestine, providing a glimpse into his disappointments of the fate of his work and concluding that these must be blamed on the authorities.[85]

Chapter 2

1940s–1960s

Geddes' Role in Reconstruction

Arthur Geddes, Edward McGegan, and Frank Mears lectured and published several papers concerning Geddes between 1933 and 1940, calling planning professionals to adhere to his advice.[1] Lacking historical documentation, Boardman's first biography (1944) relied heavily on Geddes' obituaries and earlier descriptions, the result being a very personal account and a very poetic one.[2] Howard Odum of the University of North Carolina described Boardman's as a long-needed volume, it being a duty to learn Geddes for his contributions to sociology and town planning, concerning the unity of nature and completeness of the individual, community, and nation, and the structure and function of regionalism.[3] Generally the discussion of Geddes in this period is not very wide and restricted to periodical circumstances or local professional discussion of his work.

I. 1947, Cities in evolution and the revival of the "region"

In 1947, Geddes' Cities and Town Planning Exhibition was brought to Britain and Arthur Geddes became the president of the Outlook Tower Association, which was meant to be an active center of thought, visual education, planning, and social activity.[4] In 1947 also, the Town and Country Planning Acts were published in England and in Scotland.

Arthur Geddes, together with Jacqueline Tyrwhitt of the Association for Planning and Regional Reconstruction published an edited volume of Geddes' Indian reports: *Town Planning in India*,[5] incorporating "passages that clearly illustrated the practical application of those town planning principles for which Patrick Geddes stood."[6] In the introduction to the book, Lanchester discussed Geddes' unique and efficient techniques which were brought by his ability to identify with the mental outlook of varying social and racial types.[7] The themes highlighted in the book include the diagnostic survey, the importance of rural surroundings, problems of overcrowding and social segregation, "conservative surgery," planning for health and open spaces.[8] Geddes' original text was illustrated using contemporary photos. The book was described as giving a good indication of Geddes' ideas and methods, and claimed to be of value to all planners.[9] Geddes was praised for recognizing the elements which made Indian ways of living different from Western ones, such as family sense, traditionalism, and ample supply of fruit and vegetables; "This little book is a helpful contribution to the discussion of Indian social policy in these days of hopeful expectancy."[10]

The Outlook Tower Association further commissioned a group of planners to produce a revised edition of *Cities in Evolution*.[11] Tyrwhitt claimed that much of the book was out of date almost as soon as it was written, since Geddes' intention was to write a political tract; yet while his thesis of "survey before plan" has become planning dogma, his own organic and interrelated methods of investigation and interpretation were far in advance of current thought.[12] Special attention was directed towards Geddes' thinking machines which, as claimed, have often been dismissed as vagaries or simply incomprehensible. "Perhaps it is only now – in the period following the Second World War – that the time is really ripe for the reprinting of this book."[13]

II. 1954 centenary retrospection: in search of Geddes' legacy
New biographies
Towards Geddes' forthcoming centenary and upon the discovery of new material, Arthur Geddes believed a new biography would be beneficial to a new generation of planners.[14] Philip Mairet, the chosen biographer claimed that Geddes' generation failed him by paying so little attention; he therefore highlighted important contemporary issues. Thus, he protested, the earlier accounts of Geddes' work in Edinburgh naturally disregarded its modernity and universality, while Cyprus constituted a clear case for survey and an experiment in reconstruction.[15] Similarly, the finest qualities of Geddes' Dunfermline report are the historical sense, the grasp of economic factors and working-class needs, and the wealth of practical detail, portraying "what may be called . . . *futurism*, meaning . . . the optimistic spirit with which P.G. viewed the opportunities of the future."[16] Geddes' Indian reports were "invaluable as revelations of what could be done given adequate time and power to act in a specific case."[17] Jerusalem was a scene of reclamation and rehabilitation ("and above all, of colonization"), an almost ideal sphere of action for the civic and regional scientist; but only few realized Geddes' harmonization of social customs and religious ideals with the work of modern reconstruction.[18]

Yet Mairet's book was criticized for failing to assess the general influence of Geddes on the development of town planning, "perhaps because the evidence wanted is folk-lore."[19] Boardman's biography which was only then published in Britain was accused by the same reviewer for not having much in it to guide the reader, which is unfortunate, "because regional planning has suffered so much from lip-service . . . the loud proclamations which Geddes continually made are in sad need of repetition."[20]

Centenary celebrations
A symposium held in Edinburgh as part of the centenary celebrations of Geddes' birth in October 1954 produced a 37-page report.[21] Planners and others took the opportunity to retrospect on and re-evaluate Geddes' legacy, believing "the further we move away from him the clearer stands the great scaffolding which he erected for others to climb on."[22] Geddes was accredited for the actual existence of the

Town Planning Institute as well as the London and Liverpool departments of Town Planning. William Holford mentioned the university as one of Geddes' greatest points of relevance for a period of great university building, both colonial and foreign. He also accredited Geddes with a true sensitivity for mixed communities.[23] Patrick Abercrombie reviewed the important phases of Geddes' work and marked the study of Dunfermline as a fundamental book for teaching.[24] H. J. Fleure praised the regional survey techniques as valuable to rural and urban planning, and summed up: "The papers read at this centenary celebration have given a sketch of a very active imaginative observer with so many facets to his mind that we can hardly visualise the whole . . . when we talk of Geddes we may think that if at times he seemed almost to fail, yet his work is going on and going on most nobly."[25]

Other contributions read as belated obituaries, although much less informed. For example, the Lord Provost of the City of Edinburgh commented: "I am glad to learn that much of his life was spent in this city of Edinburgh . . . to men of vision and courage such as Geddes . . . we must express our indebtedness."[26]

At the same time, the *Journal of the Town Planning Institute* published three articles of sponsored research students at the Outlook Tower regarding Geddes' contribution to planning.[27] One noted that although Geddes' mantra of "Survey before Plan" had been accepted and written into the planning process, its natural corollary, the exhibition, with its possible contribution to citizenship has strangely been ignored.[28] Another examined the resemblance between Geddes' approach and modern planning, showing the similarities between the work which took place in the Outlook Tower and the current process of survey, analysis and production of the plan, also claiming that Geddes' fostering of the public interest is echoed in the present call to engage the attention of the citizen.[29] In a special issue of *Town and Country Planning*, marking its 50th year, Geddes was quoted as one of the earliest supporters of the Garden City movement and suburbs in general.[30]

A year later, George Pepler proclaimed it an immense advantage to the development of town planning that Geddes' ideas were forthcoming at the time of legislative sanction, as "Geddes' great construction to town planning was in ideas rather than in actual plans."[31] Pepler marked out many of Geddes' ideas as foresight, such as the need to plan cities orderly and to solve housing and congestion problems, as well as his preaching for adaptation rather than destruction in India. Geddes, he claimed, also worked the term "public relations." "It may be affirmed today . . . his philosophy still pervades the members of the profession of town planning, and, in my judgement, will continue to do so one hundred years hence."[32]

III. Three disciplinary outlooks: Geddes recalled
Geddes and the genesis of town planning: regionalism,
a contribution missed

Upon its 40th anniversary, the *Town and Country Planning* journal claimed that although many plans proposing reconstruction are graced by an the introductory phrase "folk, work and place," they must also embrace Geddes' notions about organic development and also recognize town planning as an educational, citizenry process.[33] R. N. Rudmose Brown claimed, "To many who lacked the wits to understand him Geddes was dubbed unpractical,"[34] naming his greatest contribution as the idea and use of regional survey preliminary to any constructive work. Phipps Turnbull, who assisted in editing *Cities in Evolution*, traced different interpretations given along the years to Geddes' idea of *conurbations*, concluding that the current conception of regional planning was more comprehensive than Geddes' original meaning.[35] Finally, an article in *Town and Country Planning* in 1949 described Mears' *Regional Plan and Survey for Central and South East Scotland* as being symbolic of Geddes and his methods, making it a unique plan worthy of close study.[36]

In 1954, William Ashworth supplied "the first attempt to trace . . . the development of planning during the nineteenth and twentieth centuries."[37] He described Geddes as a leading figure with most original and comprehensive approach to the subject, stressing mainly the influence of environment. Of all the enthusiasts for town planning, Ashworth claimed, Geddes was the one whose attitude was most truly social; yet for many years his suggestions remained unfulfilled as they were drastic, and his lines of thought less known to others. Ashworth concluded that Geddes' influence was to cause people to think of urban problems and treat them, less to act upon his own suggestions.[38]

Modernism and Geddes: synthesis and comprehensive schemes

Ian Boyd Whyte illuminated how some of the propagators of Congrès International d'Architecture Moderne (CIAM), who realized the dichotomy existing between spiritualism and rationality in the late 1940s, searched for reconciliation in Geddes' words.[39] One of those responsible for "feeding back Geddesian arguments into the discussion of the postwar city" was the Association for Planning and Regional Reconstruction, and Jacqueline Tyrwhitt in particular.[40] At the 8th CIAM congress in 1951, integration and synthesis were the main strategic themes, as it was believed that within the newly defined Urban Core there existed "the natural condition for the organic synthesis of modern architecture, technology and the plastic arts as instruments and expressions of society."[41]

Another appeal of Geddes to the modernist imperative might be a more expected one, as his techniques were used as suitable vehicles for a comprehensive worldview. Boyd Whyte explained that in his thinking machines, portraying "a progressive or meliorist view of history, Geddes anchored his mystical view of human progress in a rationalist, mechanical universe . . . [also] in a grid based on his observations of the tangible world, Geddes inscribes a utopian 'frame' that invokes our nostalgia for the lost totalities."[42] One such use of Geddes' "frames" is illustrated by Eric Mumford, who showed how in 1956 several suggestions to improve CIAM administration were based on Geddes' settlement hierarchy embodied in the Valley Section. A project presented on the adjacent meeting showed grids based on Geddes' notation, examining relations between size of population and architectural forms.[43]

Similarly, Arthur Glikson, as described by Volker Welter, not only propagated Geddeian ideas, but also developed Geddes-style diagrams in order to elaborate his own approach to planning.[44] Glikson apparently searched for inspiration for a planning approach which would reflect the totality of mankind's environment, finally finding the necessary comprehensiveness in Geddes' *Notation of Life*.[45] He developed a number of "pyramids of regional occupations," changing a few of Geddes' suggested layers to suit modern occupations, inevitably extending their original conception to the modern division of labor in cities and "filling in a conceptual gap in Geddes' theoretical model."[46] Glikson also offered a theoretical outline of Regional Planning by suggesting variations to Geddes' *Notation of Life*, further incorporating his diagram into a larger one, interpreting the regional process as one single movement and culminating in planning, an analysis upon which he relied while working in Israel. Eventually, as Welter shows, Glikson omitted Geddes' intertwining evolution of citizen and city. Welter claims that through his interpretation Glikson lost some of the dynamism of the diagram as well as actually eliminating its main characteristics.[47]

In 1972, in an edited volume by Tyrwhitt and Bell, Geddes' diagrams were analyzed along with those of Le Corbusier's. They were both described as encompassing the totality for analysis of urban problems and setting the framework for new developments, allowing the creation of programs for present action and planning for future growth. Geddes' grid served to check that all necessary details had been considered. The scheme suggested by CIAM, though, replaced Geddes' spiral by static columns, thus eliminating its characteristic eternal movement.[48]

Geddes' absence from social urbanism

In 1956, Ruth Glass examined Geddes' role in the formation of social urbanism, concluding that Geddes and his planning partners left hardly any trace and accusing him for actually detaining the development of the sub-discipline. For town planners, claimed Glass, Geddes' "sociology" as interpreted by Lewis Mumford remained the only sociology, taking little notice of other traditions and developments in the social sciences, while surveys of towns and regions have not been sufficiently systematic to make a cumulative contribution to the knowledge of urban environment and society. Town planning, she claims, thus became a field of anti-urbanists, trying to shape the town in terms of idealized rustic images.[49] In a later article, Glass attributed this anti-urban bias to the nineteenth-century utopian view of society, "imbued with nostalgic notions about the virtues of the small-scale, balanced and self-contained community," the ambivalent term "regional planning" connoting an arbitrary entity.[50] Later, J. Halliday used Geddes' terms to illustrate his claim that for town planners, the improvement of the race complemented the improvement of occupations and the improvement of surroundings, as the ideal of the planned City was for the biologist "the full realization of racial potency."[51]

IV. Geddes abroad

Geddes' work in India and in Palestine was reviewed at this period mainly upon the preparation of local master plans. In Jerusalem, the last British town planner, Henry Kendall, described Geddes' plan in 1948 as one of the most influential British plans for the city.[52] The plan was reviewed again in 1968 as a first Israeli master plan for the city was published, and claimed to be determining the major spatial development patterns for the city.[53] In India, a new master plan prepared in 1965 for the city of Lahore included reference to the observations of Patrick Geddes, claiming his techniques as relevant as before. Its review in *The Geographical Journal* stated the importance of the publication of anything that resulted from Geddes' work due to the current relevance of his plea for conservative surgery as "positive and enlightened improvement" relating to grandiose schemes for complete clearance, followed by gridiron or drawing-board development plans. "The editors have done a great service in making available this fifty-year old report, contributing an elegant and economical demonstration of how modern planners might apply Geddes' principles in the area centred on a 17th century mosque."[54] A similar notion was raised by Kenneth Gillion, describing Geddes' sensitivity to the existing urban fabric as he opposed the removal of Ahmedabad's walls. Gillion claimed that Geddes' report reflected great respect for tradition, for history, and for local customs which had hitherto been lacking in the improvements carried out in that city and elsewhere in India.[55]

In Tel Aviv, great plans made on a large scale during the 1960s were invested with great imperatives such as improvement of large urban areas and characterized by mass housing, vast transportation networks, and mass urban renewal.[56] None of those related to Geddes' plan. Twenty-five and fifty-year anniversaries of Tel Aviv which were marked, celebrated, and written about made no mention of Geddes, including a book describing Dizengoff and his work in the city.[57] A unique mention in 1959 by Nathan Dunevitz, a local journalist, supplies a sarcastic account of both Geddes' plan and its aftermath, describing the plan "for which today every driver curses the streets [. . .] ever since then, the municipality brings on urban planners and traffic experts to fix the distorted plan, but it is too late . . ."[58]

Chapter 3

The Humanist Perspective

The Return of Geddes, 1970s Onwards

Writings on Geddes since the 1970s present a unified perception of a pioneer of town planning and one of its constituting fathers, a displaced prophet whose work was never fully appreciated. Geddes, it is claimed, had unfortunately remained outside the mainstream of the movement, the extent of his influence never clear and his ideas having little impact on the course city planning took after his death; Geddes' legacy is considered to be only a shadow of what he sought it to be.[1] The nature of his discoveries has been but rarely discussed, leaving subsequent generations puzzled as to their true importance.[2] But today, it is almost unanimously claimed, Geddes is more relevant than ever, having dealt with many subjects and raising many questions which are as contemporary today as they were in his own days. His theory and planning are finally being realized and addressed; his legacy is greater than might be supposed.[3]

I. Geddes' planning theory: three outlooks
Peter Green: a practical lesson in town planning
In 1970 Peter Green studied Geddes' planning reports outside Britain and concluded that Geddes' basic theories were already developed by the time he embarked on his first experiment in regional, social, and economic planning in Cyprus in 1897. Reports produced later, in India and in the Middle East, claims Green, indicate that his methods remained virtually unchanged.[4] Relying on this assumption, Green introduced Geddes' planning philosophy and practice by a series of sub-headings which he then demonstrated with lengthy quotes from the reports.[5] Green treats town planning as a creative and a positive science, being responsible for the total environment and the confidence of the community. His approach to Geddes' work is that of a practical planner, pointing out Geddes' tools for planning to be utilized in the present day. Green's proclaimed point of departure is the problem of citizen participation in planning, "the quest for participation" being the most difficult task, which had been envisaged by Geddes to bring about a successful culmination of the planning process.[6]

Thus, Green elaborates upon the high moral professional stand that Geddes demanded from the planner, making himself professionally independent of any sectarian interest or influence by tending both to the mass of the people and the individual citizen and encouraging active participation by promoting skilful use of the tools of planning practice through education.[7] It was also the responsibility of the planner to advocate alternative planning forms and objectives, according to Green, making this Geddes' most revolutionary aspect of planning.[8] Similarly, he claims, Geddes asked for maximum publicity for planning data, fighting against the emergence of a remote bureaucratic system.[9] He thus came to shape the minds of many administrators towards a humanistic attitude in the use of power.[10]

Green described Geddes' planning theories, such as the relationship between place and people, survey before planning and the Valley Section as defining a basic planning unit, grasping "the essence of the place, its raison d'être" and promoting change "by influencing the behavioural environment" via an effective environmental regional regeneration.[11] Similarly important is the quality of the visual environment, produced by accentuating focal points, introducing a diversity of urban features, emphasizing specific characteristics of community, morphology or design and refraining from inserting alien elements.[12] The conservative surgery is presented as a positive tool, supporting the creation of amenity standards and successful economic rehabilitation.[13] The third publication of *Cities in Evolution* in 1968, claims Green, came to show how a society can come to fashion a quality environment, seeking optimal use of resources within a continuing state of environmental balance.[14]

And yet, Green concludes, the considerable responsibility of the individual planner appears to be an unrealizable attainment; Geddes himself could not live up to these stringent requirements and the means to achieve "public involvement" is left vague or unsaid. This, he suggests, was perhaps the attribute which was to result in the lack of acceptance of Geddes' work and ideas; "It may well be that Geddes was temperamentally fitted for this role but it was somewhat naïve to assume that others would be."[15]

Helen Meller: the cultural evolution of the environment

Helen Meller relied on Geddes' earlier development as a social evolutionist to explain his approach to planning as a cultural endeavor, exposing and promoting the mutual uniqueness of people and place as the result of their interrelated cultural evolution. "Culture" thus determined the form of social and urban change, imprinting itself on the cityscape; improving the place went hand in hand with improving the human cultural environment.[16] Geddes, Meller claims, stretched the term to encompass his entire approach, offering a philosophical and a practical understanding of the complexity of modern city life.[17]

Thus, according to Meller, Geddes' initial survey of Edinburgh and its region gave hope of an integrated approach to all aspects of planning, indicating also the crucial connection between nationalism, cultural identity, and social endeavor.[18] Geddes emphasized the organic nature of urban growth, later becoming an emotional inspiration to environmental groups;[19] artistic symbolism and Greek mythology were also acknowledged as components of his holistic and sometimes metaphysic approach to life.[20] As the form and the history of the built environment was considered to be encapsulated in regional identity, Geddes advocated the region as the natural unit for environmental planning, a notion which composed both as his greatest achievement and his most damaging failure.[21]

Possibly the most important practical component of Geddes' approach, according to Meller, was that of urban conservation. He commanded the preservation and the enhancement of the environment in order to give people a sense of belonging and to allow re-interpretation of cultural traditions in a modern context. The objective of the regional survey and of Civic Reconstruction was accordingly to find ways of implementing modern techniques and knowledge within the framework of the existing culture. Geddes wished to find the means to enable those within a specific cultural tradition, ensuring fullest potential development.[22] His work in Edinburgh, claims Meller, gave him experience of what was becoming a key planning problem: the need to renovate and rejuvenate historic city centers.[23]

Meller believes that having the individual as the focus of policy placed Geddes above politics, which he regarded irrelevant for planning. Thus Geddes managed to plan in spite of foreign political imperatives, allowing just representation even for those removed from centers of power.[24] As such, Dublin provided Geddes with a favorable setting for planning, "since as a colonial city, the free play of social and political factors was stifled and Geddes, with his non-political approach, was welcomed by all"; India, politically and economically underdeveloped, offered him a chance for an even more fertile response.[25] The conscious direction of evolutionary forces would be achieved through education, a matter of self-awareness and also the link between Geddes' assorted activities.[26]

Giovanni Ferraro: the spiritual planning game

Giovanni Ferraro also drew on Geddes' Indian reports for inspiration for solving current planning problems, searching Geddes for the key for re-starting town planning on a higher level, not dogmatic or authoritative.[27] Departing too from the issue of public participation, Ferraro used theories relating to business management and public policy to describe Geddes' planning process as a dialogical strategy or "a planning game," in which the planner performs a transformation of the unfathomable urban maze into a chess board for the citizens.[28]

The main object of the planning game, according to Ferraro, was to enable all players to play well. This could only be achieved by establishing cooperation between citizen and planner, mutual agreement and freedom of the will, and avoiding excessive authority. The planner thus must be flexible, cautious, and patient, always prepared for the gentle discovery of the citizens' alternatives; the game is infinite and winning means only persuading the component to accept the best collective solution. Hence, the result of town planning is unpredictable and its effectiveness measured by gaining the inhabitants' trust and by making them planning allies.[29] For Ferraro, Hope is the key element in Geddes' plan, representing the willingness to enter into the planning process.[30] The effectiveness of the plan is also measured by the ability of the inhabitants to educate themselves into efficient citizens, making re-education a political redemption.[31] The object of the survey in this sense is not only to collect data but also to make it available to all players, as well as to expose the planner to critiques and sometimes even to mute resistance.[32] The report is just the beginning of the process; "Where the text ends the game begins."[33]

Ferraro claims India a spiritual revelation for Geddes, where his positivist work found support through religion and tradition.[34] In India, planning was turned into a religious challenge, presenting planning as elongation of the vital, evolutionary, and voluntary Indian culture.[35] Ferraro thus terms the process of planning "re-religion," which equates with re-education.[36] Thus, claims Ferraro, although conservative surgery started out merely as a cheap alternative, Geddes eventually realized its important role in respecting the past, working in widening circles around the religious center of collective life. In the process of Conservative Surgery as an action of practical, as well as political, intervention,[37] planner and community are educated together to choose and revive past elements within the present; the planner must shed Western prejudices;[38] respect is a basic element.[39] Unfortunately, Ferraro concludes, since it is difficult to assess the effectiveness of a plan – its main intention being to do as little as possible – it is almost impossible to appreciate Geddes' success.

II. Additional themes in Geddes' theory: community, politics, and sustainable development
Administration, politics, and society

The discussions of Geddes' work today repeat in various ways the ideas suggested by Green, Meller and Ferraro. A consistent theme is strengthening the community while decentralizing power and planning. Thus, it has been claimed impossible to understand Geddes' social thought without viewing the various activities in his life as an attempt to create a new sense of community from the particles of a modern society, as he used community to stress the importance of the social structure.[40] The drama which Geddes enabled through the pageant of the city, claims Wheeler, was rediscovered and described by Jane Jacobs in her plea for the return of diversity of people and occupations to the city street.[41] Wheeler thus suggests an "updated" aspect of conservative surgery, one which would avoid the disintegration of much of inner-city life, and the dissolution of many urban communities and the imposition of inhuman planning ideas;[42] Conservative Surgery in this sense meant giving priority to housing and neighborhood needs, rather than to transportation or purely aesthetic considerations.[43]

Sophia Leonard claimed that planning, for Geddes, was "the gentle but purposeful guiding . . . Public Participation is not the 'icing on the cake' but is at the very core of planning."[44] Geddes, it was also argued, promoted planning as a public activity rather than mere legislation;[45] the greatest contribution of *Cities in Evolution* was to allow a better relationship between planner and community.[46] Similarly, the regional survey constituted an opportunity to involve as many people as possible in decision-making[47] and a revitalized Outlook Tower would serve as a visitors' center or a Community Forum, bringing together the planners and the planned.[48]

Geddes' approach to urban management altogether, claimed Colin Ward, adopted a completely decentralized standpoint.[49] Colin Mercer claimed that Geddes' work could assist in managing imperatives of contemporary governance, as he himself provided a point of contact between planning as a governmental, technical capacity and the human sciences, the Outlook Tower allowing distinctive ways of representing and intervening in the relationship between cities and governmentality.[50] The Valley Section portrayed the need for inter-disciplinary tools for a regional analysis as the many different professions involved must work together as a team.[51] Geddes' work envisioned an open and liberal era which today can be appreciated.[52]

Urban and environmental sustainable development

Another contemporary theme is Geddes' protection of the environment. Robson claimed that Geddes' work revealed greater concern for existing cities than was customary among new town advocates, preaching small-scale rehabilitation and accommodation of existing environment rather than resorting to large-scale plans.[53] Peter Hall claimed that the development of the concept of conservative surgery, "or in latter-day jargon, urban rehabilitation" was done in reaction to the Corbusian city of towers, suggesting the escape from mass industrialism.[54]

The starting point for the discussions in *Think Global, Act Local* (2004) compiled upon Geddes' 150 birth centenary was an environmental search, as it was found that the original phrase was being used mainly by those dealing with sustainable development.[55] Geddes' concern with cities was thus considered a forerunner of present day activists coping with ugly and unhealthy environments, emphasizing the need for environmental sensitivity through visual awareness. As such, Geddes is regarded a precursor "of our own growing environmental awareness,"[56] concerned with "what now we would call environmental management"[57] finally arriving at "a broad integrative viewpoint."[58] Geddes is thus claimed to constitute the intellectual link between Darwin and today's "green" movement, being the first to specifically connect the concept of city regions to units of sustainability.[59] The Valley Section, the more environmental side of development, offers insights for both the environmentalist and the educator.[60]

Chapter 4

The Appreciation of Patrick Geddes as a Planner Today

I. Geddes' work in Britain: representing the genesis of town planning

Geddes' newly discerned merits are reflected in the accumulating descriptions of his practical work. In Edinburgh, writes Sophia Leonard, "like an old testament leader, Geddes set about galvanising his neighbours into individual and community action to achieve similar ends."[1] The Halls of Residence were described as revolutionary residential projects.[2] Geddes' long involvement with Crosby Hall in London was discussed as part of the evolving consciousness of tradition in Chelsea[3] and the museum planned for Dunfermline described as the place where the synoptic view of the sciences allowed new analysis and administration of society.[4]

Geddes' work in Dublin was described by Michael Bannon in a series of works examining the genesis of modern planning in Ireland. "It was inevitable," claims Bannon, "that the wandering Scot would turn his attention to Dublin"; being Scottish, it was not surprising that the Aberdeens were familiar with Geddes, and conscious of his potential to generate local enthusiasm.[5] In Dublin, Geddes, "one of the evangelists of the founding fathers of modern town planning," sought to understand the local relationships and to educate both the general public and the power elite, and to devise sympathetic and realistic proposals for social and environmental improvements.[6] This was also the main value of all entries to the Dublin planning competition, described as educational tools regarding the nature of town planning.[7] Personally, claims Bannon, Geddes preferred Ashbee and Chettle's plan to the winning entry submitted by Abercrombie, being more in his conservative tradition.[8]

II. Geddes in India: a positive outcast

Geddes' work in India is considered as best revealing both his theories and their use, India described as an extraordinary laboratory for his social experimentation.[9] The profound social and political changes, the local society still holding bonds with its past, interlocking traditional practices and modern techniques, and still mainly rural all created an atmosphere in which Geddes' enthusiasm could meet with some response.[10] In India, Ferraro wrote, Geddes found new hope;[11] cut off from Europe, according to Toppin, he was able to flourish.[12]

Since it is generally agreed that Geddes' approach and techniques hardly varied, the analysis of their practice in India is commonly achieved by a small selection from the reports.[13] A recognized founding father of the discipline, Geddes is considered to have introduced modern town planning ideas into India;[14] but as an exceptional planner, Geddes' work is also described as a direct result of his unique cultural, holistic appreciation of community and environment, which assisted him in understanding and appreciating the spirit of the place, standing outside all major trends and concepts.[15] Visiting India in the 1990s, Sophia Leonard marveled at the proposed suburb in Lahore which was built and had turned into one of the most desirable places to live in town as "a classic garden suburb layout with wide avenues and generous garden spaces";[16] unfortunately it was only available now for well-to-do or high-ranking government officials' families. Similarly in Lahore: "how right he was . . . the avenues . . . would not look out of place in any leafy suburb of a European city."[17]

In India more than anywhere else, claimed Ferraro, a profound gap opened between the plan, on one hand, and the material and cultural condition of society, on the other.[18] Thus it is generally agreed that in order to fully appreciate Geddes' work in India it is necessary to compare and mainly to contrast his approach and his methods with those of his fellow colleagues.[19] Geddes, too, addressed urban deficiencies; but the India he was able to see, as Douglas Goodfriend maintained, was "surely closer to the indigenous experience than any India of the sanitation engineers and imperial planners."[20] With religious tradition as the starting point of planning, according to Ferraro, Geddes gave different meanings to Western-defined ails.[21] Geddes was in a unique situation in which a non-member of a tradition acted to preserve and renew it, linking two cultures and talking to Indians as his equals.[22] The conservative surgery, "the logical corollary against engineer considerations of demolition"[23] was described as having aimed to repair "the damage inflicted by British cultural domination."[24]

The conservative surgery, claimed to have been conceived in India, is considered a direct manifestation of Geddes' aspiration to combine the old with the new, protect existing elements and incorporate them within the new plan.[25] In 2004 Narayani Gupta appreciated Geddes' unique role in India as nurturing an additional aspect of the nationalist revival: the built urban environment. "If Geddes had not happened to India, we would have had little sense today of the old Indian discourse on architecture and planning."[26] Today, she claims, the relevance of Geddes' philosophy and his suggestions for conservative surgery acquire a new relevance.[27]

Finally, criticizing planning as early as 1969 for being inflicted upon traditional, incremental planning and contradicting with the local socio-economic structure, T. G. McGee propagated the use of Geddes' conservative surgery as means for creating a better urban environment and allowing for inhabitants' approval of the changes.[28] McGee attributed Geddes' success in India to the fact that his intervention came at an early stage of the integration of local and foreign economic systems, and for Geddes' understanding of the dualism of the Asian city, finally crowning his Indian planning reports as early manifestations of Jane Jacobs' approach.[29] Geddes' call to revive and to nurture relevant customs and traditions, expressing his belief in the continued applicability of traditional methods to contemporary challenges was also related to the need to involve the population in the planning operations.[30]

III. Geddes' work in Palestine: an account of Zionist revival

Peter Green described the main component of Geddes' planning in Palestine as the development of the primary rural base of activity.[31] In the urban sphere, his primary objectives included the centralization of urban functions into specific and accessible areas, linking together internal re-housing and rehabilitation policies with a positive programme of suburban and overspill settlements.[32] Green claims that the Jerusalem report, in particular, revealed a threefold approach, consisting of environmental control and rehabilitation in the built-up areas, the creation of new garden suburbs, and the promotion of a controlled economic base for the city as an emerging cultural and regional center, capitalizing on a considerable tourist potential.[33]

Most of the accounts of Geddes' work in Palestine nevertheless follow Meller's cultural interpretation. The major work describing Geddes' work in Palestine is part of Benjamin Hyman's PhD, "British Planners in Palestine, 1918–1936," analyzing his work according to a set of ideals and tools which he compiled relying on previous research and portraying the local use Geddes had of the established ideals.[34] Geddes' summons to work in Palestine seems a most natural idea to Israeli and other contemporary writers highlighting Geddes' consideration by the Zionists as a "first class man" who could bring world-class planning standards to create new settlements and suburbs.[35] A common notion is that Geddes' belief in the relationship between the social and cultural structure of the community and the physical environment enabled him to offer "clues to the returning Zionists on how to resettle their homeland and to return to the essence of their culture."[36] Geddes, as often described, easily complied with the Zionist project, his planning ideals matching the notions of rural reclamation of the land, on one hand, and of bringing in the most progressive planning of the day, on the other. This is embodied, for example, in his commitment to the Garden Cities Movement.[37] However, Geddes' appreciation of the key importance of agriculture in social evolution made him also particularly sensitive to the important issue of conservation.[38] Thus, after quoting Eder's reasons for employing Geddes, Herbert and Sosnovsky concluded: "there is, in this definition, Eder's implicit but unspoken planning ideology, which embraced all the physical design fields . . . together with their underlying social goals. This was the comprehensive, holistic philosophy he ascribed to Geddes."[39]

Relocating Jerusalem

Meller claimed that Geddes viewed Jerusalem much in the same way as he had seen India in 1914, in the sense that he saw himself "as being above the wrangling of sect and creed and thus able to direct the emotional resources generated by such allegiances into channels which could produce results."[40] Geddes' work in Jerusalem is generally discussed as part of the British effort to conserve the city and develop it.[41] An important element of Geddes' plan, the green belt around the Old City serves to underscore and to preserve its special character.[42]

The plan for the Hebrew University (which never materialized) was described by Mordechai Shapira as part of the enhancement of the genius loci of Jerusalem itself, although the Zionists, he explains, had much more restricted goals.[43] The actual planning of the building and its symbolic architecture were interpreted as a direct outcome of Geddes' sensitivity to the place and to the people "as a cultivator of humanism and respect to the environment."[44]

Geddes in Tel Aviv: the celebrated Israeli Garden City

Since the 1970s there seems to be no better match than Geddes and his plan for Tel Aviv; accordingly, no other city in which Geddes has worked has so tightly been associated with his name. Quick urban changes which took place in Tel Aviv since the end of the 1970s, coupled with the lack of historic depth of the young city, brought forth a great need for historical urban anchors.[45] Geddes was immediately recognized as the key planner of Tel Aviv, the first Hebrew city in Palestine.[46] Thus, when a new urban vision was created of a reviving city, attracting a young population and developing a new urban lifestyle, Geddes' Tel Aviv has come to be admired for promoting a great sense of community, a pedestrian-scaled city of neighborhoods and supportive of an active civic life.[47] The 1925 plan for the city was praised as an adaptation of Geddes' modern garden city idea within existing circumstances, geographic and climatic as well as social and cultural;[48] Geddes' City, claimed an architecture journalist, came to represent the city as many would have liked it to be.[49] Clearly, Geddes' original planning ideas were found to be quite useful in the current planning of Tel Aviv, according to the present-day planning notions listed by the municipal engineer.[50] No doubt, for its "level of pedestrian friendliness, spatial integrity, functional variety, and neighbourhood feel," Geddes' plan offered an early prototype of contemporary urban notions which even "advocates of the 'New Urbanism' could applaud."[51]

The newly discovered appeal of the city and its unique merits culminated with the official recognition and declaration of UNESCO of the older parts of the city as a World Heritage Site in July 2003. The site, which consisted of the original Geddes' plan area and an area adjacent to it, was found to contain a unique ensemble of over 4,000 houses built by architects who studied in the established Bauhaus school and practiced mainly in the newly developing city. Considered the largest urban concentration of the Early International Style, "The White City" as it was officially termed was described as an experimental arena for the basic principles of modern architecture.[52] An immediate connection was made between Geddes' plan and the White City which became inseparable terms in describing the celebrated city. It was now claimed that Geddes represented both Zionist idealism *and* the neutral targets of the modern movement, embodying the urban affinity between the Garden City Movement and the Modern Movement through Zionism.[53] This notion was echoed by writers around the world who displayed sudden interest in Geddes and his work in Tel Aviv, now described as a city of opposites, a transitional place between the overpopulated European cities and rural Palestine.[54]

Chapter 5

Discussion

Geddes' Historiography as a Reflection of the History of Town Planning

I. Patrick Geddes, a planner through the ages

Reviewing the writing about Geddes as a planner over more than a century yields an uneven picture of his work and his legacy. The appreciation of Geddes is ambivalent and in many cases there seems to be much left to explore, as many predicaments and contradictions remain to be settled. Moreover, many of Geddes' periodical advocates neglect to fully explore dilemmas which their own assumptions arouse, holding on to their prescribed conclusions, sometimes even risking internal contradictions.[1] Along the years, Geddes acquired many interpreters, and at times it is difficult to differentiate between his own thoughts, which were confused to begin with, and their explanations, sometimes claimed better than the original.[2] In any case, it has often been claimed that it is hard to trace Geddes' contribution, as much of his ideas have been adopted from others, his own creations having later received various interpretations.[3] As a result, it seems that several strands of descriptive genealogies have been established, in which Geddes' early descriptions were incorporated into later writings; Helen Meller's convincing interpretation seems to satisfy many who use it today as a handy scheme to explain Geddes' work. "As often in such cases," claims Hebbert, "he is more referred to than read."[4]

Perhaps it should be expected to find that the appreciation of Geddes has changed over the years: The quality and the quantity of material available to research changed from time to time, as did the number and the identity of the writers. Different perspectives rise, and so do needs and expectations of the writers, finally affecting their conclusions. Geddes' biographies tell one story while his plans' analyses tell another; sociologists would emphasize a trend which town planners might overlook. Different themes in Geddes' theory are highlighted at different periods, different sources are used to describe his practice, and different accomplishments arise. Yet the correlation between Geddes' history and the periodization of the history of town planning is quite clear, and it is here suggested to read Geddes' historiography as a town planner as representing the history of the discipline itself.

The genesis of town planning: Geddes as a non-planner

While planning was formulating as a discipline, Geddes' role was more than ambivalent. At this time Geddes was generally not described as a planner, certainly not by planners; Geddes' name as a planner is hardly known. The partial success of the Exhibition somewhat changed that and in the event, some of Geddes' earlier projects were related to the rising discipline. In general there seems to be a clear division between the appreciation of Geddes' theory and his practice, his theory having been discussed mainly by his closer friends, and even they did not always understand Geddes nor agree with him; even geographers were not so sure. Planners' accounts of Geddes tend to be uncertain, hardly referring to his theories, not to mention his diagrams.[5] Geddes' theory was only partially reviewed and received; only clear and straightforward ideas were commented upon. Even then, criticism soared. Planners apparently found it hard to utilize and to contain even Geddes' most practical ideas. His actual work is hardly discussed, including his proclaimed success in Dunfermline or even in Dublin. Several of Geddes' grasped and embraced ideals turned into catchwords and were eventually incorporated into the planning vocabulary, but he himself was generally regarded eccentric in relation to the constituting mainstream.

As Geddes moved away from Britain he was almost completely forgotten. There is scarce discussion of his work throughout the British Empire. His work in Palestine is described in the same way as he had regarded it, a biblical mission of resurrection, and related mainly to the Holy City. In the colonies he was received as a planning hero, representing modern urban planning. In his obituaries, Geddes is on one hand acclaimed as a planning forefather and his value as such rises; on the other hand, his work is assessed, for better and for worse. The obituaries seem to be a great opportunity for Geddes' admirers to discuss his accomplishments, but it seems there is not much to talk about. Here too, Geddes' work in Palestine and in India is described mainly by locals. His failures are counted and some blunt criticism is sounded. While being described as a prophet, his planning theories are still obscure and his legacy undefined.

Geddes' descriptions as a planner, a representative of the discipline, are related accordingly to aspirations and successes in rural rehabilitation and urban renewal, urban congestion, the organic and natural evolution of the city and the need for historic conservation. As a sign of a constituting discipline, the discussion either relates Geddes to the successful line of planners or removes him away from it.

High modernism: Geddes forgotten

In the second period, the modernist highpoint, Geddes was largely forgotten by the world of planning. His humanist and sensitive planning premise, which inserted ambiguity and uncertainty into the planning process, was not at all appropriate for an era of modernist and comprehensive reconstruction; in an age of decisive determinism, there was no place for Geddes' locally orientated, historically differentiated, incremental evolution. Most of those who discussed his legacy were former students and colleagues, recalling old sentiments. Otherwise, Geddes was discussed for two main correlating reasons: the popularity and the need of regional planning in Britain and the survey, his planning scheme regarded, under various interpretations, as a tool for civic and regional reconstruction in the period between and immediately following the World Wars. These received different interpretations according to varying and sometimes competing needs. The discussion about regionalism seems to reflect the split between England, busy with local and regional reconstruction, and modernism elsewhere.[6] Although there is hardly any discussion of Geddes' projects, the Empire and its dismantling did provide an influential context for discussion, as Geddes' work is hailed as a lesson for the future or a further means for differentiation between first and third world countries, mainly in correlation with the second edition of *Cities in Evolution*. The scarce description of Geddes' work in India and in Palestine echoes either the sense of accomplishment on the side of the British (Kendall, Tyrwhitt) or the strife for independence and local traditional reclamation (later local accounts in India and Israel).

Surprisingly, though, modernist architects and planners did not neglect Geddes altogether, finding his diagrams a device for a comprehensive analysis, thereby adapting his theory and changing it according to their needs, sometimes actually sterilizing them in the process.[7] The periodical Geddes-based terminology varied accordingly. On one hand, it included anything concerning regional surveys and planning, while on the other it echoed what eventually found its way into CIAM discourse such as holism and synthesis, pragmatism, rationality, and economy, standardization and urban quality of life, social problems and psychological imperatives.[8]

Humanism revived, Geddes rediscovered

The third period, the humanist revolt, witnessed a great revival of Geddes' memory, legacy, and research; was it Geddes' prophecy finally being realized? Geddes was embraced as a hero forgotten and happily revived as a misinterpreted prophet of the constructive and blissful practice of town planning. His name stood for anything that was considered sensitive, human, and small scale and taken in opposition of the previous mechanistic and inclusive era in planning. Geddes was similarly held to be the precursor of public participation, the importance of the community and the return of its history, as well as of environmental awareness. Practically, it seems as if Geddes was there to justify town planning in its present, successful stance. This includes culture and religion, less rationality and more spirituality, emphasizing "place" rather than mere "space," achieving rehabilitation within context and reconciling tradition and modernity while not neglecting issues of environmental awareness.[9] This is joined by the administrative side of planning and includes public participation and advocacy, alternative planning and general political sensitivity.

This humanist period is a long one and can be split into sub-eras, the general trend easy to discern: Initially, Green signified a blunt rejection of modernist values, finding in Geddes some needed remedies; his straightforward account of Geddes' urbanism reads like a simplistic morphological description by Kevin Lynch. Reference to Jane Jacobs seems obvious (although she herself did not regard Geddes very highly). Meller's corpus and later yet Ferraro's unique approach signify a softer embrace of Geddes' cultural and also spiritual, even metaphysical points of departure, manifesting careful open-mindedness towards the discovery of Geddes' various disciplinary resources. These portray sensitive readings of the interconnection between physical and social environments and more delicate approaches to the elusive relationships.[10]

A major contribution to this period regards the actual description of Geddes' work, generally embraced as something forgotten and happily revived. The description of Geddes' work throughout the Empire is that of the only representative of the locals who disregarded imperial circumstances by turning only to the needs and the aspirations of the native population. Notwithstanding, he is also considered to be representing modernity and all its wonders. Both in India and in Palestine, the rich yet selective descriptions highlight Geddes' practice of conservative surgery and his insistence upon local styles, promulgating national revival and its varying manifestations. Strangely, Geddes' work in Britain received the least attention; the main contribution regards the modernist planning of Dublin as detached from England. In India, Geddes is described almost entirely as representing the opposite of the British government's aims, disregarding his imperial role and turning only to the needs and the aspirations of the local population. And yet, maybe excluding Ferraro's mainly theoretical work, there is no meticulous description of Geddes' work in India, repeatedly analyzing the same projects. Other than a few notable exceptions, Geddes' work in India is described by British while his work in Palestine (as well as his work in Scotland and in Ireland) is mainly described by local writers. In Palestine, Geddes similarly represents various strands of modernity, yet the dichotomy between the British and Zionists is none existent; on the contrary. Here, too, the description tends to be selective, highlighting Geddes' contribution to the Jewish revival. Geddes' overall adoration in Tel Aviv bluntly obscures all contradictions since his plan became to represent the city's merits in almost every direction. In all three stances, the nationalist imperative is evident, as Geddes seems to have represented in each the most innate aspirations of the local population.

II. Geddes out of mainstream: apologetic explanations along the years

Many explanations have been given along the years for Geddes' ongoing estrangement from the mainstream of town planning. Many blame the incomprehensiveness of his vast writings, being often unclear and confusing and always in need of personal explanation or mediation.[11] Geddes' schematic thinking machines are also considered problematic, their content questionable and concepts ill-defined.[12] Others emphasize his unfortunate absence from Europe during the critical years of the formation of town planning.[13] Otherwise it is claimed that Geddes' controversial ideas about planning, as well as his unique and outstanding social perceptions[14] contributed to the obvious lack of communication between him and the town planning movement.[15] Geddes, it is thus asserted, tended to rely on his imagination or intuition, his interpretations often being too personal, turning him into an optimistic, unrealistic, dreamer.[16] Philip Boardman, one of Geddes' earlier biographers bluntly denoted Geddes' tendency for "discovering and spelling out in black and white the errors and stupidities of other people, academics and officials in particular."[17] Thus, Geddes' work has been accused as idiosyncratic or too original,[18] too scientific and empirical, while his overall model being too dynamic and theoretical.[19] After all he remained outside conventional frameworks, institutional as well as academic, a fact which prevented him from laying claim to any particular body of knowledge and which Ferraro called "the paradox destiny of Geddes' legacy."[20]

Another set of apologetic, or rather reproachful, explanations for Geddes' absence from contemporaneous planning discourse relates to the status of town planning or other disciplines, the main claim being that Geddes was simply well ahead of his day[21] and therefore misinterpreted, also causing his work to be falsified and trivialized.[22] Some relate the early lack of interest in Geddes' work to disciplinary need for certainties and legitimatization, while Geddes, who promoted an anti-authoritarian perspective, made the status of the planner ambiguous;[23] all the same, Geddes' message has also been claimed to be too conservative for the new progressive activity.[24] The professionalization of the discipline, naturally narrowing its cultural horizons[25] and barring alternative ideas[26] apparently caused further displacement. As a result, planners took what they liked of Geddes' teaching and abandoned his practical planning, having no use for involved or understanding citizens;[27] geography abandoned the development and incorporation of social theories, and planning neglected to realize its responsibility to educate the public.[28]

Finally, justification has been attempted for periods during which Geddes was better known and admired. Helen Meller explained his initial attractiveness to the world of planning by the attempt to illustrate gradual human evolution rather than progress; additionally, she claims, early planners relied on Geddes' vision to validate their work and their methods.[29] Geddes, claimed Gordon Cherry, gave early town planning the rudiments of a theoretical base which went beyond the disciplines of the built environment.[30] Geddes suggested a philosophical and a practical understanding of the totality of modern city life in all its complexity at the formative period in the social sciences.[31] Another recurring theme justifying Geddes' importance to town planning is his emotional commitment to cities and civilizations.[32]

The organic integration of society and environment, the enlargement of the planning scale from the city to the region and the development of the regional survey are still regarded as Geddes' main contribution to town planning, being mentioned by the majority of writers. However, "Town Planners today," claims Ferraro, "think that they have completely assimilated Geddes' legacy once they have mentioned the organic image of the city and recalled the necessity of the preliminary knowledge of the town."[33]

III. Evaluating Geddes as a planner: a critical view?

In spite of the seemingly unified portrait of Geddes' planning theory, it has not been completely spared of criticism accumulating piecemeal along the years. In every period there seems to be a different outlook, a hidden criticism, sometimes silenced, sometimes not quite developed. Nevertheless, already in 1980 Geddes' planning was denounced by Michael Hebbert as an "overblown historicist theory of urban growth and decline, as popularized by Mumford."[34] Additional critical readings in Geddes' planning, curiously contributed in a symposium conducted in Dundee upon the 100 centenary of Geddes' work there, point to flaws, inconsistencies and inner contradictions, as not once or twice to be conflicting with his own theory.[35] Geddes' avoidance of matters of the day and crucial rejection of terms had been questioned;[36] substantial criticism pointed to flaws in his philosophy and the irrelevancy of his tools to modern society.[37] Geddes' disregard for politics had been considered curious, on the verge of complete social misunderstanding.[38] It had also been claimed that Geddes' practice proved repeatedly that his demands from the planner or the sociologist were too much for anyone to perform, even for Geddes himself.[39]

Geddes' contribution to planning debated: the "region" and the "survey"

Even Geddes' most acknowledged and lasting contributions to planning, the Survey and the Region have been greatly contested. Both have been accused of lacking full description and implied practicality, never really developing into a method.[40] The Survey had been criticized as a ritual, a mere collection of information;[41] Regionalism had been condemned as aiming at the re-establishment of the preindustrial man–environment equilibrium, proving to be of doubtful validity to both planners and social scientists.[42] Geddes' regionalism, "propounded as a general panacea" was accused of diverting political energies from more central and structural issues.[43] Even Geddes' most faithful admirers, says Hebbert, would be hard-pressed to discover any merit in his attempts to interpret the World War and the general strike from a regional planning perspective.[44]

Geddes, it was claimed, did not succeed in transmitting his ideas of the Survey to subsequent town planners, as in practice the public was eliminated from the process by skilled experts.[45] Those who later argued for surveys to be made compulsory, argues Hebbert, did so as part of an enthusiastic vision of social reform, which usually encouraged aimless empiricism.[46] In fact, a recurring claim is that what are considered Geddes' ideas of regional planning and surveying were actually developed by others, in accordance with local needs and practical experience.[47] A comparative analysis of Geddes' writings and of Abercrombie's plans shows that the latter does not correspond with the former.[48] Even the "Survey-Analysis-Plan" mantra, which is still the major idea associated with Geddes, was traced by Michael Breheny to the late 1940s and the beginning of the 1950s, suggesting that the phrase had originated with an active group associated with Tyrwhitt, then the Director of Surveys for the Ministry of Town and Planning. It was stressed heavily in her introduction to the 1949 edition of *Cities in Evolution*, and the "catch-phrase of the early 1940s" finally appeared as a concept only after 1951.[49]

Regarding the overall plan, Harvey Simmons claims that Geddes was eventually left with a series of metaphors that soon proved of little value.[50] Welter claims that Geddes never really had an ideal urban plan, having never discussed practical implementations of Civics.[51] Michael Hebbert bluntly states that Geddes had no urban theory at all, his insights being "inherently flawed" and his baffling writing a sign of the uncertainty of his message.[52] Geddes' failure to finally put his "bits and pieces" into a grand coherent system perhaps sprang from the realization that the task was impossible, Hasselgren concludes.[53] More theoretically, Meller is concerned over the fact that Geddes' contributions to the academic social sciences were at best marginally illuminating and at worst, counterproductive.[54] Worse yet,

claimed Hebbert, for too many years Geddes' notions (or their interpretations) isolated planning from the mainstream of developments in the social sciences; Geddes'
amateurish sociology, as detected by Ruth Glass, had plagued practical planning.[55]

It is wrong, sums Simmons, to look at Geddes for new insights into
contemporary problems. Geddes, he states, was above all a man of his time, representing many of the traits of his contemporary intellectuals and sharing with their
shortcomings;[56] "muddled, irascible and unhappy, his lifework led logically to the
cul-de-sac of distinctly seedy ventures in the fringe world of international educational
establishment."[57] Geddes' work came to nothing; his life is a chart of what to avoid,
and the more closely we are tempted to share his illusions, cautions Hebbert, the
more closely we should study it, as his interest today lies only in his failures.[58] In
fact, he concludes, Geddes had actually disappeared from the mainstream of social
philosophy and policy, being remembered today only by a close circle of his friends.[59]
Rescued from time to time by one of his disciples,[60] he is abstracted from an ambivalent intellectual background so that the "practical visionary" might be better seen.[61]

Part II

Geddes and Geography

Chapter 6

Geddes' Urban Conceptual Framework

I. Cities in evolution
The art of Civics: treating city and society

Modern cities, Geddes claimed, reflected "the ignorant and hideous, stupefying and degrading monotony of life which goes on in both east and west ends of the modern industrial town."[1] The actual problems he described were no different from those which disturbed his colleagues: Cities were overcrowded and defected, suffering of foulness of atmosphere and squalor of surrounding, thus unhygienic and unsuitable for women and children. Housing was in the state of slums.[2] Society suffered from poverty and unemployment, vices and apathies, crimes and indolence.[3] Like many of his contemporaries, hoping "to live again in the delightfulness of the Hellenic world, the joyous freedom of the Renaissance,"[4] Geddes urged a cleaner and a more efficient industry. He called for improved planning of railways and docklands, cleaning of rivers and the beautification of cities.[5]

However, finding a direct link between the state of the city and its inhabitants, Geddes also described the evils of the modern city as civic and social disease.[6] "Civic Hygiene" described not only physical well-being, but also global social problems such as dirt and disorder, alcoholism, insanity, crime, and vice; cleansing the city, Geddes claimed, would ultimately allow the returning of citizenship.[7] Geddes' comprehensive art of Civics, "the Science of Cities"[8] was described in three consecutive articles published between 1905 and 1907.[9] According to Geddes, treating alike both city and society was the task of the planner: As planners constitute themselves into a profession, Geddes claimed in 1915, Civics and town planning must advance together.[10]

Cities in evolution

Rebuilding the City, being the fullest and most developed expression of the human activity, was no simple task. Geddes regarded the built environment as physical inheritance and described the city as the place where "past phases of evolution" lie lingering as fossils.[11] Thus, acting as a "specialized organ of social transmission, the vehicle of acquired inheritance,"[12] the city portrays past ideals and constitutes the best place to pursue and accomplish present ones.[13] Since an ideal city was believed to be latent in every town, Civics was designed "To discern [. . .] the ideals which build cities and which keep them"; "To interpret them"; and finally, "to renew them, city by city."[14] This was the art of the evolution of Cities. However, since an ideal society was to be rediscovered as well, resting accordingly on ideal citizens, Geddes suggested complementing Civics with eugenics, "the re-nascent art of human evolution"[15] as an equivalent cure for human degeneracy. Planners were thus given the role of renewing cities by discerning past ideals, interpreting them and renewing them, and also the equivalent role of recuperating the failed evolution of citizens by similar processes of "preservation, selection, ennoblement."[16]

II. The successful city: recurring types

Geddes' definition of a good Civilization embodied his notion of the totality of the environment and the mutual effect of the Place and its People upon each other.[17] It was therefore first and foremost a geographical definition. Geddes used the Region, "a representative section of the universe," as a basic geographical unit, claiming that it embraced all possible modes of human life and symbolizing comprehensiveness in the order of nature.[18] He represented the Region through a typical Valley Section which he believed to be a characteristic unit for much of the familiar world, embracing all forms of human occupations, social compounds and types of settlements, from the smallest hamlet on top of a mountain to the great city at the bottom of the valley.[19] A peaceful harmony in the Region could be achieved by ensuring the success of each of the components in the Valley Section.[20]

The Valley Section, a typical definition, could be related to places throughout the world and across time, and its overall success or failure could thus be

THE NATURE OCCUPATIONS (cf. p. 182)

6.1
The Nature Occupations in the Valley Section.
Originally published in: P. Geddes, "A Rustic View of War and Peace," Sociological Review *10(1), 1918, 5. From A. Defries,* The Interpreter Geddes: The Man and his Gospel, *foreword by Rabindranath Tagore, introduction by Israel Zangwill. London:* George Routledge & Sons, 1927, p. 73.

discerned throughout history; therefore, the peaceful harmony, or the resulting Civilization, was also a historical recurrence. Indeed, Geddes defined a succession of such historical peaks, in which a successful regional harmony was achieved, comprising a historical schematization which was based on occidental history.[21] *The Masque of Learning*, an educational pageant devised to be performed by the community, presented different phases of successful civilizations according to Geddes' interpretation.[22]

A graphic representation for the progression of the worldly civilizations was provided by the *Arbor Saeculorum* or the Tree of History.[23] It was a comprehensive symbolic representation of the major historical eras based on "the common nineteenth-century understanding of mankind's history as a succession of highly developed cultures"[24] and their main characteristics. Within those, Geddes accredited three main civilizations for manifesting close to perfect integration of the social and geographical components. The earliest one was what Geddes considered as the first stage of the Western civilization, Israel, symbolized by the hexagonal Star of David and the term for the Hebrew God, יהוה. *Hebraism* or the Hebrew culture, being developed in a period of settled greatness, resulted in moral unity, synthesis, and justice.[25] The Mediterranean region, the cradle of the Hebrew civilization, constitutes a model region;[26] Jerusalem an ideal hill-fort.[27] Next, the Greek civilization symbolized by sea-bearing and by Wisdom, manifested fine harmonization, resulting in proper evolution of body and mind.[28] The Greek Polis portrayed perfect balance

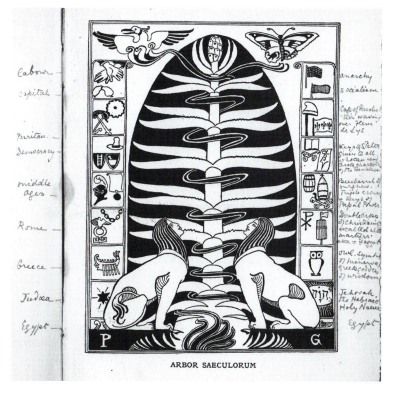

6.2
The Arbor
Saeculorum.
From The Evergreen:
A Northern Seasonal,
1895, Part I,
Strathclyde University
Archives.

ARBOR SAECULORUM

between country and city; the ideal unison was expressed in the real city of Athens, an acropolis of idealism and perfected art.[29] Finally, the medieval city was described as being close to perfect.[30] It was also the home of a model society, a notion represented by the ideal division of society into four major groups representing the basic roles of individuals in society.[31] The ideal division was reciprocated in the perfect arrangement of buildings in the city, as each of the four groups was hosted in its proper institution.[32]

Although Geddes' model was taken from the Occidental civilization, he nevertheless claimed that it is "deeply interwoven with that of the Orient."[33] However, in opposition to the ever-evolving, ever-improving, Western civilization, Geddes characterized the Eastern ones as traditional, agriculturist and rather primitive, and portraying hardly any development. The main contact points of those with the Western civilization were described at the primal, initial stage, at which point they have contributed important notions such as spiritualism, faiths and religious hopes.[34] Representing several Eastern cultures, India is described as an empire of "vast philosophies and comprehensive symbolisms."[35]

The recurrences of the urban and social ideal

While acknowledging that every age faced new challenges, Geddes claimed that each phase of civilization is recreated by reference to earlier ones.[36] The procession of civilization was thus arranged as a spiral, making each phase a reincarnation of an ever-existing ideal and constituting "some fresh variant of the sphinx riddle."[37] The *Masque* is accordingly characterized by multiple parallels and variations: Traits of prominent historical figures are inherited and individual types are repeated, finding expressions in leading figures across time and space. Thus, Geddes drew a direct connection between Homer, Moses, and Zoroaster, and found parallels between the empires of China, Rome, and Canada; he compared Buddhism and Christianity and traced the origins of similar myths and shared philosophies, and this on many planes. "These parallelisms of activity and mentality, and with this even of individual career, from land to land, age to age, are often so close and striking to have been imagined as literal individual rebirths."[38]

And thus, although each city is unique, evolving according to its local features[38] Geddes' urban ideal was defined on a global scale, and the target was universal: "Olympus, Parnassus or Zion are not merely elements of the social heritage; but as respectively the expression of individual, cultural and spiritual evolution; and hence no less realisable than of old."[40] In Geddes' scheme, each city and its society were examined as parts of a worldly system, and judged against ideal types of worldly significance: the re-incarnation of the ideal city, East or West, inevitably necessitated knowledge of great past civilizations.

> Hence each antecedent type of city must be studied before we can really understand our own. Hence it is that we explore the ruins of Nineveh, excavate Babylon, Jerusalem, Athens, Rome; hence we search the written records of all these past civicisms which we too vaguely call civilizations, too often practically forgetting the literal meaning of that word,

vitally civics as it was, and as it must ever be . . . We must go through all this to construct that full concept of our city throughout history . . . Nor can we pause with the scholar specialists who confine themselves to the city cultures of the ancient or the classic world; we have to deal in the same way with mediaeval cities, from Byzantium on through the Mediterranean, and thence by way of Venice and by Florence to the north; and again through Germany and the Hanseatic towns, through the antique cities of the Netherlands and of France to those of our own islands. Once more we have to renew our journey with the Renaissance, starting from Constantinople once more, traversing Italian and northern cities also . . . We thus readily arouse a fuller interest in visiting these great collection, and in making more complete use of them, towards building these up not only into our own personal education, but into the living presentment of the past of the great cities . . . to represent our rich and varied heritage from all the civilizations.[41]

III. The modern town plan
Directing urban evolution

Geddes employed terminology of the perfect medieval city to describe the process by which the residents of the local *Cloister* reflect upon their *Town* and refine it. The new ideal which they conceive is eventually projected back into reality, thus creating the new and improved City; "a principle of transformation from rustic to civic, and from townsman to citizen."[42] The Medieval Cloister was used as an archetypical institute representing the place of the contemporary intellectuals, where "the Greek thinker, the mediaeval schoolman, the modern investigator or the artist" are occupied "in elaborating some kind of inner life for themselves apart from the activities of the town, apart from its established and authoritative schools."[43] It was the role of the cloister to direct the evolutionary process by reflecting on the past, supplying "a continual and critical selection among the ideas derived from experience."[44] Thus, opposing his contemporaries' definition of evolution as purely natural and deterministic, Geddes claimed that evolution could, and should be directed through conscious decision and collective action.[45] The absence of the cloister could abrupt the chain of urban evolution, leading to stagnation or even regression of city and society alike.[46]

Directing the process of urban and social evolution via means of modern town planning was the main theme of Geddes' *Cities in Evolution* (1915), giving the town planner the task of the mutual urban transformation. Geddes argued that present-day planners failed to view and plan the city as a synthetic whole,[47] neglecting to provide a re-interpretation of the city's history and uncover its highest past moments. However, Geddes insisted, it was their task to coordinate arts of utility and of beauty alike, of health and of education, of material and of moral progress.[48] He described the process of urban improvement as a comprehensive evolutionary cycle, representing progression from "the individual's activities" to "highest deeds in City."[49]

The true plan, the only one worth having, is the outcome and flower of the whole civilisation of a community and of an age. While starting from

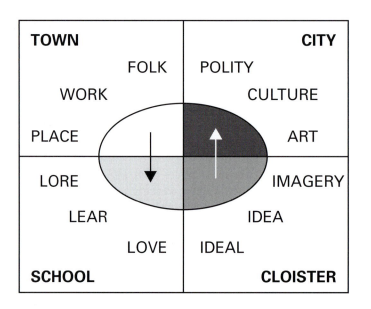

6.3
The schematic
transformation from
Town to City.
*After various sources,
e.g. "Civics: as
Concrete and Applied
Sociology, Part II,"
Sociological Papers II.
Published for the
Sociological Society,
London: Macmillan &
Co., 1906 p. 90.*

its fundamentals, of port and road, or market and depot; and from its essentials too, of family dwellings worthy to be permanent and hereditary homes, it develops onwards to the supreme organs of the city's life . . . Now in our day we have again to develop the equivalents of all these.[50]

The planners of the modern age were thus ultimately given the role of present-day intellectuals. "Leave us at peace in our cloister," said Geddes to his colleague, Amelia Defries, in 1913, "to think out and prepare the better city."[51] However, what would be the shape of the City, the aspired result of the urban transformation, upon which the planner was set? Geddes did not give a definite answer. The suggested ahead, based on his writings, is divided into three: the rehabilitation of the city's region; the improvement of the old city; and finally, the new city, a modern creation.

"It takes a region to make a city" [52]

In Geddes' geographical analysis as portrayed in the Valley Section, the city was one component only of an overall regional system. Calling for "a revision of our traditional ideas and boundaries of country and town"[53] he addressed urban recon-struction in the country as well. Geddes claimed that regional neglect leads to the evolution of deserts, a cosmic process strengthened by the mischief of ages of war and destruction of irrigation work.[54] In his quest to rehabilitate the components of the Valley Section, he advised extensive aforestation;[55] works of irrigation and the construction of damns to prevent swamps and malaria;[56] the preservation of moun-tains and moorlands, and the provision of bettered agriculture.[57] He also called for the rehabilitation of deteriorating villages by means of education, conservation, and rehabilitation of local crafts.[58]

Geddes claimed that the country encapsulates the historic development of the city and its inhabitants, also supporting bodily and mental health;[59] detachment from nature and village life would lead to symptoms of decay, both of society and of the city.[60] He thus supported education for the love of Nature and involving the public in caring for it as a direct means for citizenship enhancement.[61]

New cities: Garden Cities

In *Cities in Evolution* Geddes suggested country-like solutions within the city, changing the basic perspective of planning: "Make the field gain on the street, not merely the street gain on the field."[62] The solution he adopted for the incorporation of the country within the city was the popular Garden City paradigm.[63] In cities designed as such, cities which were "characterised by electricity, hygiene, and art, by efficient and beautiful town planning and associated rural development, and by a corresponding rise of social co-operation and effective good-will," Geddes apparently found the solutions he was seeking.[64] Garden Cities provide "swifter and cheaper communications," helping to "loosen out the crowded city, and so serve all its interests most efficiency in the long run;" they offer low housing density.[65] Garden Cities are "of hygienic orientation"[66] providing essential healthy conditions, like medieval Westminster, for example.[67] The connection between physical well-being and personal growth was a given; "It will be for this coming generation of child-gardeners themselves to make the Garden City. Each oasis, once begun, may grow; some day they may even meet."[68]

Old cities: cleansing and conserving

The improvement of ancient cities was based on the preservation of the town's worthy monuments and buildings, defined as such by the planner and put into current and future use through the incipient plan.[69] The city itself is to be treated as an educational document, its buildings being remnants of past glorious eras manifested in a limitless exhibition,[70] "old time streets and houses [. . .] conserved as the very nucleus of the city's material heritage."[71]

> In historic cities and in commonplace towns . . . there still remains for us from the past . . . enough to constitute for us and for our successors an Open-Air museum of the Centuries – a series of surviving buildings which would have something characteristic . . . at least of each great period of culture, each great phase of social and civic life, each type and stage of national and European culture.[72]

The actual practice Geddes devised for improving the urban environment while preserving worthwhile buildings, the conservative surgery, was developed through his practice in India.[73]

Chapter 7

Geography and Education

The Planning Tools

I. The merits of geography

The planner, according to Geddes, had the complicated role of studying the city and its society, discerning their unique hidden inheritance, and ennobling these through comparison to past achievements; it was a parallel transformation, aiming at the creation of both proper City *and* Citizenship. Education was thus an indispensable part of planning, serving the goals of both Civics and eugenics by promoting personal improvement and by enabling the community to be aroused to its urban past and preparing for its study.[1] Geddes found geography to be the most appropriate discipline for his stated goals, basing both his planning and his educational conceptions upon its axioms. Geography was a synthetic science, representing the universe as a whole[2] while also allowing to understand the city as a microcosm.[3] As such, geography would aid civic consciousness to rise from the city to the nation and even to larger geographical units such as the British Empire;[4] this would be geography at the service of world peace.[5]

The study and practice of geography of the time were based on popular visual means which allowed, according to Geddes, the interpretation of all phenomena "as parts of an orderly unity."[6] Geddes related to visual power as a natural capacity, childlike and untamed, and standing open to all men.[7] Notwithstanding, the power of observation could be trained and enhanced;[8] he therefore propagated education as an outdoors, physical activity, allowing direct experience with nature, promoting popular activities such as surveying, rambling, camping, scouting, and nature studies.[9] Those, he claimed, would also connect between "the child's enjoyment of nature around him" to "the geographer's maturity in visualising the world."[10] Geddes' tools designed for planning were all such visual, educational, means. They were comprehensive, correlating concrete observation with general views, as well as synoptic, addressing as many aspects as possible. They were practical, combining "various levels of thought" with "respective fields of action."[11] Finally, they were claimed scientific and methodic, based on orderly description and classification.[12]

II. The survey

In a series of articles published in the first three issues of *Garden Cities and Town Planning* (1911) Geddes provided a practical guide for local surveys, promoting the practice of "survey before planning."[13] The survey is be based on first-hand, direct observation, practiced outdoors and preferably from a high and commanding place.[14] Allowing to record the material buildings of the city and to study its life and its institutions, the survey would enable the appreciation of past development and present evils.[15] Geddes compared "civic diagnosis before treatment" to a surgeon's thorough physical examination[16] and bestowed the responsibility for surveying upon all those involved in local town planning, starting with the citizens and ending with the city architect, recommending the creation of a local "Cities Surveys Committee."[17]

A comparative analysis, requiring a complimentary general history "from the earliest beginning of civilisation,"[18] would enable the surveying planner to record local tradition, recover past glories and mark material heritage for conservation. Identifying local qualities and defects, and, moreover, discerning potentialities would be determined by the overall chosen narrative as dictated by the planner: "This selection is done by the surveyor-planner, giving a renewed interpretation to the historic facts, ending in a renewed narrative; for this sociological utilisation of the wealth of narrative history, we need not merely its facts and dates, but an orderly arrangement of them."[19]

Considering the regional survey as the natural extension of rambling and childlike gathering of nature samples,[20] Geddes advocated it also as a pure educational tool toward the improvement of both body and mind[21] and also toward citizenship, reminding the individual of his relative social formation in the civic whole.[22] Geddes thus encouraged the formation of local groups to aid in the process of planning and to associate in "endeavours of citizenship,"[23] incorporating society in the mutual process of city and citizenship improvement,[24] eventually extending personal commitment by expanding "vital interest and love from the home region to national trust and beyond."[25]

Finally, a systematic survey, with "the heads of such a regional, civic, and local survey, in its various elements of past, present, and suggested future," will result in a systematic report, where the planner's conclusions will be translated into a practical plan of local renewal and reconstruction.[26] Geddes often practiced the science of the Survey on Edinburgh – a recurring example was Geddes' survey of Edinburgh.[27]

III. The Civic Museum: index to the world

The findings of the survey would constitute the beginning of a Civic Museum, incorporating also existing collections of local libraries or museums and providing a comprehensive representation of the city. The museum is described in Geddes' third article of Civics, "A Suggested plan for a Civic Museum" (1907). A year later, Geddes elaborated upon the suggested contents of the museum and the galleries devoted to describing the city, past and present.[28] A separate gallery would be devoted to the city's future, presenting current plans, formal and alternative:[29] "I do not know of any way more likely to interest people in their city," said Geddes, "than to put facts, criticisms and projects for improvement before them; they all fight over these, and thus their civic consciousness is awakened, their interest thus increased."[30]

The roles of museums in education and planning were listed in a letter in which Geddes applied to be a museum curator. Geddes described his experience as an improver of physical environment and urban hygiene, being involved in planning and rehabilitation as well as in artistic decoration.[31] It was clearly a role for the planner: "Now the modern Town Planner, for whom Greek citizenship is not a mere learned reminiscence or a moral wonder, but a working conception once more, is in these days actually designing, for the bettering cities of the opening future, their veritable 'Museion'."[32] As an important public center,[33] Geddes' museum in Edinburgh hosted summer meetings and held such activities as a Current Events Club for shared reading of local, imperial, and global news.[34]

If the survey was the advanced version of a boy's wanderings, the incipient museum was designed to host the accumulation of the boy's findings.[35] As yet unarranged and unlabeled, those must be described, classified, and interpreted.[36] The museum's collection thus compiled would comprise a reference collection, in which all objects are related to the world at large,[37] each local collection representing global phenomena locally. As an "Encyclopaedia Civica,"[38] the museum would aid in revealing the relations between local objects and "general civilization" in total, comprising "a type collection, an Index museum to the world of culture."[39]

IV. The exhibition: the comparative dimension

Geddes promoted a traveling Cities and Town Planning Exhibition to accompany and enrich local planning endeavors through additional educational and comparative means. The Exhibition was initially compiled for the RIBA conference in London, 1910, and described in length upon its presentation in 1913 at the Ghent International Exhibition.[40] The traveling exhibition offered suggestive examples of surveys of characteristic cities, expanding upon geographic and historic origins and developments of civic life and thought. Geddes hoped that each city would lend a small exhibit of its own essentials. While selecting from the large collections, such material may be of service to itself, as a good example for the future or a warning [of dire developments in the past/pitfalls in the past].[41]

The exhibition was composed of various galleries of civic exhibitions with plans, elevations, perspectives, pictures, and models, including also a reference library and a cinema of cities. The main part presented typical cities and recurring schemes of development, a comparative study of cities and their evolution. Examples of the Past included Classic Cities such as Athens and Rome, Babylon, and Jerusalem. Edinburgh provided a key to the study of medieval cities, illustrating elements such as castles and cathedrals and the correct relation between country and town. The city of Rothberg illustrated healthy democratic civic life, well-planned streets and open spaces, roomy dwellings, private and public buildings, public monuments, towers and fountains, town hall and belfry.[42] Important cities of the Renaissance such as London, Vienna, Rome, and Berlin exhibited war, overcrowding, material dilapidation and fortification, alongside new forms of town planning, parks and canals. Illustrations of Paris, Versailles, Washington, and Chicago furnished the gallery of the "great capitals." These displayed modern railways and telegraph lines, administrative and economic centralization and intensification of powers; they also housed "all the apparatus and resources of the complete civilisation of their time," the great museums.[43]

THE GHENT EXHIBITION

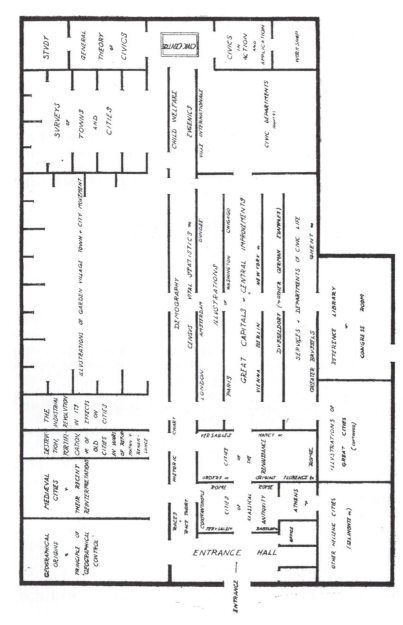

7.1
Floor Plan of the Ghent Exhibition, 1913.
From "Two Steps in Civics: Cities and Town Planning Exhibition and the International Congress of Cities, Ghent International Exhibition, 1913," from Cities in Evolution: An Introduction to the Town Planning Movement and to the Study of Civics, *London: Williams & Norgate, 1915, p. 271.*

Another part of the exhibition introduced the town planning movement, illustrating how various problems were being met and handled by town planning and portraying typical civic developments.[44] A major gallery was devoted to Garden Suburbs, stressing the way development and extension "gain completeness and value from each other and from the city's past."[45] The exhibition also illustrated various related sciences dealing with society, corresponding with the development of the citizen and presenting new Civic sciences, some of which were invented by Geddes, such as *Racial Anthropology* and *Civic Demography*. Also presented were the new-born Eugenic Movement and a selection from recent Child-Welfare Exhibitions.

Geddes meant the visit to the exhibition to be in itself a directed, trans-formative process. As viewing the exhibition could be done in many ways, he suggested several routes which allowed tracing the evolution of cities from different points of view. The route following the historical narrative traced the evolution of cities, culminating at the Garden Suburbs gallery.[46] The geographical narrative traced the development of regional character and activity.[47] The presentation of the exhibi-tion was accompanied by public lectures and even courses which developed those themes on local basis.

V. The Outlook Tower: observation in widening circles

The Outlook Tower, "a little tower of synthetic studies"[48] was designed to link social effort and urban activity. It was to form in itself a local type museum, described also as an embryonic school and college.[49] Geddes' scheme for the Outlook Tower, which was based on his most successful endeavor in Edinburgh, had been extensively described in five public letters Geddes wrote "to an Indian friend" in 1901 and in 1903.[50] The tower contained five floors of exhibits and an open-air roof, in which an optical device, camera obscura, provided a synoptic view of the city and its region from above. The tower was actually meant to allow observation outwards and inwards as well as a personal place for spiritual contemplation.[51] Thus, next to the observation point stood a Cell of Unity, a small room with only a chair in it, allowing personal meditation: "To see life clearly, we must see it whole."[52]

"The Outlook Tower is being arranged as a type museum and observa-tory, alike of physical and of political geography. This is comparatively arranged, as far as may be, through its descending storeys."[53] The arrangement of the exhibits along five floors allowed one to examine a specific locality on expanding scales in a growing cycle, proceeding from the top of the tower downwards, and from the locality outwards. Starting the visit at the Tower, the visitor would be descending "storey by storey, through City and Province and Region or State to Nation and Empire, and thence again to the larger Occidental Civilisation, of which these form a part, and finally to the Oriental and Primitive sources."[54] The top floor, devoted to the city, was to act as a local museum. The next storey, devoted to the country or state, provided the regional outlook. The next storey, in Edinburgh's case, was devoted to Britain or more generally to "the English Speaking world."[55] Finally, the ground floor provided the global outlook, where also the Oriental civilizations and the general study of Man were displayed: "from the European level we descend to a still

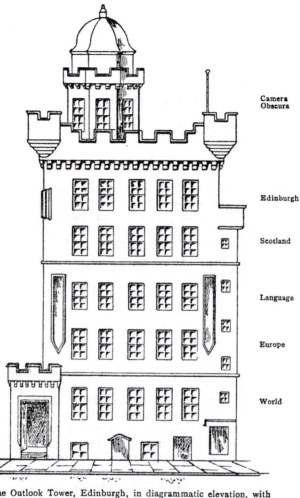

7.2
Diagrammatic
elevation of the
Outlook Tower.
*First published in
1906 in "A First
Visit to the Outlook
Tower" (Edinburgh:
Patrick Geddes and
Colleagues) p. 4,
from: A. Defries,* The
Interpreter Geddes:
The Man and his
Gospel, *foreword by
Rabindranath Tagore,
introduction by Israel
Zangwill. London:
George Routledge &
Sons, 1927, p. 92.*

Camera
Obscura

Edinburgh

Scotland

Language

Europe

World

The Outlook Tower, Edinburgh, in diagrammatic elevation, with
indication of uses of its storeys—as Observatory, Summer School,
etc., of Regional and Civic Surveys, with their widening relation,
and with corresponding practical initiatives (from *Cities in
Evolution*, by P. Geddes. Williams and Norgate, Publishers).

wider outlook – that over the Cultured Orient – the Culture-Orient . . . recognising
at least the need of an outline of the civilisations of India, China and Japan."[56] This
arrangement left the ground floor to the study of "the simpler races" and of the
basic regional components, of which "all our cultures – Occidental or Oriental – are
but more complex developments."[57]

VI. The university and the city: the modern Cloister

Geddes' university symbolized the current incarnation of Wisdom.[58] The modern
cloister of reflection and research was given the important function of urban and
social transformation.[59] The fullest account of "the incipient university" is provided
in the letters mentioned above; however, Geddes' best description of a university

anywhere was provided only in 1918 upon the planning of a university in India.[60] Within the university, individual energy is fused with others, causing a collective genius to emerge.[61] The university would have its foundations on local tradition; nevertheless, as "a fortress of ideas, regional, civic and humanist"[62] also demanded of it were "solidarity of civic and national spirit, with openness and hospitality to the larger world – English, colonial, American, Continental . . ."[63]

Consequently, the *Masque of Ancient Learning* (1912), describing the historic procession of education and civilization, culminated with the union of University and the City, the Alma Mater of knowledge working together with Alma Civitas of greater civilization, "Enthroned, side by side as type of influence and of authority, spiritual and temporal . . . Thus the masque which began with a humble schoolboy ends with a student-citizen, who will later in life be a citizen-student"; citizens and faculties merge, "creating the latest and greatest of faculties, that of Citizenship."[64]

Geddes regarded the Outlook Tower in Edinburgh and its many activities as an example for the cooperation between University and City, a model for the new academic type, the Incipient University.[65] One way in which he recommended achieving unity and collaboration between the City and the University, interacting between higher education and the life of cities, was through the tradition of university residence, advancing "the interests alike of culture and citizenship."[66] Geddes resembled this social union to other social movements such as University Extension lectures, their lecturers being "a new type of preaching friars."[67]

VII. The Civic Center: a modern cultural Acropolis

> We need some shelter into which to gather the best seed of past flowerings and in which to raise and tend the seedlings of coming summers. We need definitely to acquire such a centre of survey and service in each and every city – in a word, a Civicentre for sociologist and citizen.[68]

The urban institutes described above, including the Museum, the Outlook Tower, and the University, were to be incorporated in the Civic Center, "a clearing-house of social science with social action, of vital interaction of thought and deed."[69] The physical center of the city was designed to also include existing cultural and civic institutions, all meant to enhance and propound local civilization, a modern day Cultural Acropolis, the most important element which differentiates between towns as mere "dwelling places" and as "true cities."[70] Placing the Acropolis in a central, high location would allow it visual domination.[71]

Geddes' elaborate plan for Dunfermline (1904) was an early attempt to plan a civic center. Although the plan was never realized, the report could be viewed as a catalogue of the many suggested urban institutes of the urban Acropolis, including historical and geographical museums of various sorts, art institutes and technical schools, music halls, and numerous specialized parks.[72] The Civic Center was also to include a city hall and various historic houses adapted for new uses, including, for example, a library and meeting halls, "[. . .] a literal Athenaeum, a home of social and intellectual life, a radiant centre of educational, civic, and moral activities."[73]

Chapter 8

Geddes' Planning Theory

Critical Evaluations

I. Directing the process of evolution

Geddes assigned the modern planner the role of a motivating force for urban trans-formation, relating to the improvement of both city and society. Although he insisted that the improvement must be unique for each and every city, it should also be guided by means of comparison, by a uniform global scheme. Geddes' interpreta-tion of history and civilization were based on the conventional periods of European history as defined by his contemporaries. Describing local histories worldwide as comparable made it easy to analyze any history by discussing its European equiva-lent;[1] thus, parallels to Geddes' typical Western-based schemes were to be found everywhere. As a result, Geddes saw no difficulty in striving for full implementation of his theory almost anywhere, finding simple and straightforward correlation for his ideas wherever he searched for them. This notion, nevertheless, has become the topic of some critical assessments of Geddes' work, so far overlooked.

The Geddesian Gambit, or the Disciple's Rebellion

Giovanni Ferraro discussed Geddes' planning theory and practice, as manifested in India, as a planning game, in which it was the task of the planner to lay out a playing board for the local community to participate in, a successful game yielding a commu-nal planning process.[2] Yet a closer analysis of the components of Geddes' planning scheme raises a picture which is more suitable to Lewis Mumford's late description of his work, referring to *The Geddesian Gambit*. Mumford is generally viewed as a mediator of Geddes' ideas into practical urban analysis, making him a natural addi-tion to almost any major book published about Geddes for many years.[3] Mumford was evidently convinced of the importance of Geddes' ideas and of his relevance to the present and promoted them.[4] Yet, even in the early years Mumford claimed that Geddes was naïve in disregarding politics and in overestimating the direct effect of modern technology upon social life, concentrating instead on education. In *The Disciple's Rebellion* (1966) Mumford claimed that as a man who relied so heavily on the spoken word, Geddes couldn't be followed without the greatest difficulty.[5]

Eventually Mumford became blunter. In *The Geddesian Gambit* (written in 1976 but never published) Mumford claimed to be breaking down "the wall of silence" by doing "what no one has so far adequately done, or even attempted: namely to make a close critical examination of Geddes' achievement as a systematic thinker," considering his own earlier presentments of Geddes' life and work as idealizations overlooking personal faults and intellectual defects.[6] Mumford's greatest attack on Geddes relates to his way of thinking, accusing it as a closed system which allowed no input or criticism from without.[7] Geddes, Mumford claimed, became imprisoned in his own thought, believing that his skill as a simultaneous thinker enabled him to map, as an ideological mapmaker, every human culture; but synthesis, he argued, could not be a goal in itself, and any attempt to produce a single synthesis good for all times, all places, all cultures, and all persons actually meant to reject the very nature of organic existence. This, Mumford concludes, turned Geddes' theory into a "close-ended" game, which rules were set only by their planner:

> The game of intellectual chess Geddes had invented could not be played except according to the fixed rules he had laid down, with pieces he himself had carved and given his own special values to. In fact, it had become a form of intellectual solitaire . . . not merely did one have to accept Geddes' private definition of his terms and not question their fitting into this or that compartment: one soon discovered that on this tightly occupied and over-crowded chessboard whole tracts of life had been excluded, if for no better reason than that he had allowed no room for them . . . in short, unless one gave each piece the specific place and function that underpinned Geddes' interpretation, the game could not be played; for Geddes had left no open spaces . . . for manoeuvre or riposte . . . the opponent was checked before he could make the first move.[8]

Finally, Mumford claimed, for Geddes there was only one way of seeing things: his own. Writing about his visit to the Outlook Tower he exclaimed,

> [I]nstead of letting me take in the landscape in my own way, he insisted on my seeing it through his eyes, standing back of me and holding me by the shoulders, almost savagely demanding that I pick out of the panorama what he was seeing, and respond to it in the same way . . . Much as I admired Geddes . . . I would not see Edinburgh or aught else through his eyes.[9]

Arthur Geddes might have consented, as he also claimed that Geddes attempted, consciously or sub-consciously, to shape the work and minds of others; "by 1921 a conversation with PG had become, not a dialogue, but a monologue."[10]

Geddes' failed concept of evolution

It is not surprising that later interpreters of Geddes' work have developed the concept of his failed notion of evolution. Writing in the 1980s, Hasselgren regarded

Geddes' concept of the urban evolution as a deliberate, rather than a natural, proc-ess. To an extent, he claimed, "Darwin's theory of natural selection was the joker in the pack." For Geddes, he described, "evolution-towards-what-one-wished could be projected by careful selection of the evidence in the past and by discerning 'tendencies' in the present."[11] Thus, in his restless search for "the secrets of the evolution of cities" Geddes ended up putting the cart before the horse,[12] creating "a compound of visionary wishful thinking," according to Robson;[13] "but exactly what kind of memories or 'acquired characteristics' does the city pass on?" proclaims also Simmons, "And how? And why?"[14]

Lately, it is Volker Welter who carries on this criticism, relating to Geddes' selective process of evolution. "A process of selection by interpretation is required, followed by the recombination of the selected elements into a vision, which gives rise to the city in deed . . . the inquiry itself is guided by a priori choices."[15] Welter illustrated Geddes' forced process of selection and preservation in Edinburgh, as he emphasized the role of the city as a living museum in which only the Middle Ages were allowed the straightforward application of the concept; earlier and later periods in Edinburgh and Scotland's history became topics of a decoration scheme only.[16]

II. Geddes' geographical tools and the postcolonial critique

A growing corpus of critical discussion in Geddes' theory and work rises today from the subfield of cultural geography, where Geddes' educational endeavors and related tools are discussed in relation to geographical concepts prevailing in Britain at the end of the nineteenth and the beginning of the twentieth centuries. In these, geography is considered to be unconsciously ethno-centric, rooted in European cultures and reflective of a dominant Western worldview.[17] Labeled an imperial sci-ence,[18] geography's alleged objectivity regarding the representations of the world has since long been tied with complex relations of knowledge and power;[19] its visual appliances and products no longer considered innocent but rather linked to critiques of a totalizing gaze.[20]

The most obvious impact of postcolonial studies on human geography has been on the historiography of the discipline, its strategies and its devices.[21] Descriptions of landscape by mapping or through texts are treated as providing cues to memory and signification, consolidating shared meanings and acting as commu-nity builders or representative images.[22] Both the observer and the author are thus believed to be making sense out of the world from their own experiences.[23] In this framework of studies, the popular notions of Geddes' theory and his famous tools are mainly used as illustrations for critical discussion of geography in service of the empire, ultimately incorporating him within the postcolonial critique.

Knowing the landscape: visualization, ordering, comparison, and display

Simon Naylor and Gareth Jones employ Geddes' Valley Section and its uses by his colleagues in Latin America to describe particular forms of representation which have proved especially effective at enforcing and naturalizing power relations, and which had been widely used for the study of the Empire.[24] Their classification of these strategies as *visualization*, *ordering*, and *display* will serve as convenient headings for the geographical discussion of Geddes' tools.

Tools of visualization, including surveys, fieldwork, and maps have been deemed responsible for capturing the world in a gaze and presenting an image of it at home.[25] By asserting difference and distance, they connote means of *othering*, eventually developing into a rhetorical device used also for political means.[26] Thus, Christine Boyer has described Geddes' "variety of optical instruments[27] as connoting power over the landscape, placing the viewer outside the instrumental proposition of daily lives[28] "through which the world/city could be gazed upon, penetrated, analyzed, recorded, ordered and classified, and laid down for proposed changes."[29] Geddes' Camera Obscura, David Matless agrees, endowed the observer also with "a funny, potentially voyeuristic kind of power over the object, deriving from both the nature of the image and its place in the dome."[30]

The same tools enabled viewers' gaze to focus on aspects of the scenery that drew their attention, reaching out to confront the massive amount of data as a necessary first step toward an instrumental control over the future form of a city, or the preservations of what was left of its past. As Geddes conceived of the regional environment as a visual archive and the city's architectural history as revealing its formation, Boyer explains, "the phantasmagoria of material facts . . . had to be mapped and structured in some manner if this plethoric accounting of details was to be intelligible."[31] Naylor and Jones explained how the use of the archetypal device of the Valley Section provided a set of guiding principles lending itself to landscape representation anywhere in the world and used, as in the case of Latin America, for purposes of economic exploitation.[32]

Geddes' Survey, being based on a process of global homogenization as well as local-level groupings and classifications, also enabled a process of *division and ordering*, a strategy which Naylor and Jones described as responsible for reducing diversity into convenient and ordered categories by and for the colonizing imagination.[33] As the key organizational device for the regional survey, the Valley Section represented the natural region in its "purest" form and provided the essential material for study.[34] The survey and the section together therefore provided a set of guiding principles, one particular set of categorizations and orders.

Naylor and Jones employ Bruno Latour's term "cycle of accumulation," describing the process of gathering and ordering artifacts at one site of the imperial periphery and transporting them back to be interpreted at the imperial centers of calculation, to emphasize the value of extraction and subsequent redeployment of things into new knowledge formations.[35] They show how through the survey, information was gathered into manageable and transportable figures, lists, and measurements, which were then effectively transported back to British academic audiences and business interests. Geddes' description of his incipient museum, where finding of the survey were stored, brings to mind the collection of the spoils of Empire: "We bring home . . . spoils, treasures, wonders, beauty-feasts [. . .] each obviously the beginning of a museum-gallery proper. But the specimens are as yet unarranged and unlabeled."[36] His meticulous taxonomy served, once again, for the ordering of his treasures; based on a European-defined taxonomy which classified things into hierarchies it reflected, as Louise Pratt termed, "Eurocentred planetary consciousness."[37]

Finally, the data collected through Geddes' regional survey was intended to be *displayed* in institutes retaining pedagogic and ideological underpinnings. The Outlook Tower and similar institutes constituted, according to Naylor and Jones, devices concerned with imposing an order and an interpretation upon the items collected form the periphery, as means for comparing and displaying. Geddes' Tower, claims Boyer, indeed functioned as an *encyclopedia of memory*, displaying images on which comparisons were made, acting as the stimulus to memory by having the didactic role of resurrecting past ideas; Geddes' Index Museum, she explained, cleverly called on images for arousal to civic action and city planning.[38]

The regional survey was also a form of display in itself, a way of synthesizing and organizing the region.[39] As devices used for the strategy of comparison were capable of establishing the exotic nature of the object, place or people under study, creating a series of appropriate hierarchies. Thus, the final destination of the collected and collated information from the imperial periphery, and the knowledge it produced was often some form of display in popular exhibitions, fairs, museums, botanic gardens, and archives, all concerned with imposing their interpretation and ordering.[40] Geographical education is viewed as yet another form of display which helped to strengthen geographical, and maintain imperial, accomplishments.[41] As such, Geddes' courses, lectures, and various other educational means can be regarded as appropriate representations of the popular custom.

Imperial citizenship and geographical education

Another intriguing discussion in British cultural geography today concentrates on the uses of geography "at home," meaning the imperial core, where efforts were made to strengthen and to maintain existing imperial territories and sentiments. Geographical knowledge of the environment was tied to citizenship on various scales via an enhanced sense of patriotism and responsibility, as common good was believed to be achieved through the principle of citizenship, emphasized as a practice of shared values and obligations.[42] The geographical contribution to the study of the relation between societies and their environments was widely acknowledged by leading imperialists and captured as a potential for international scientific cooperation for international peace.[43]

Morag Bell describes Geddes as a leader of a prominent group of Scottish scientists and public figures, holding views on the contribution of geography to modern citizenship and its potential to transform society.[44] The group's concern with the revival of Scottish nationalism along with social ethics and a local environmental tradition constituted a distinctive combination of civic consciousness with a regional identity.[45] In a series of papers discussing geography as a social practice, Bell and Matless examine Geddes' work as part of the discursive field connecting the learning and the shaping of the environment with social imperatives.[46] They describe a "particular interpretation of nature-society relations which emerged within a political and social context marked by widespread concern over the need to rehabilitate British society, creating visions of nature and the international."[47] They both regard Geddes to be a major source of inspiration, supporting values of harmony and cooperation central to civic responsibility. His synthetic views are described as providing an intellectual basis to the wide knowledge of the world as elementary duties of citizenship, combining a broad outlook with the intensive survey of particular localities.[48] Geddes' Outlook Tower, in this sense, was examined as a direct educational aid.[49]

Morag Bell shows how specific concepts of nature played a powerful role in defining social identities and in strengthening a commitment to places, identifying and connoting particular landscapes with qualities enshrined in "ideal" citizens. Concerns over physical health, rural revival, and eugenics all grew significantly in influence, emphasizing national fitness and the needs of the imperial race.[50] Environmentalism, defined by Felix Driver as "the belief that the environment in which people live constitutes a set of interrelated influences which shape their opportunities and experiences" can be used to explain how mutual social and environmental improvement were believed to be pursuing harmony and complementarity.[51] In this context of examining citizenship as a normative and relational category,[52] the Valley Section was described as providing a scale of moral geography; defining proper social conduct, it ultimately also defined the opposite: "The valley section provided not just a typical social geography but a typical 'anti-social' geography [. . .] Geddes' psychology presented the social and anti-social as two sides of the same coin; the task was to encourage the one to the discouragement of the other."[53]

Emphasizing the close relationship between people and their environment, Geddes thus strove to bring improvement upon improvement, breaking what he regarded as a mutual degeneration of people and their place.[54] Environmental citizenship emerged as a condition to which individuals should aspire through responsible conduct: The capacity for aesthetic judgment, just like the power of vision, was after all believed to be latent in all.[55] The educational devices, including local surveys,[56] models building, field trips, rambling and scouting[57] helped "to build English children's understanding of their individual and collective place as local, national, Imperial or global citizens of the world."[58] Thus, the regional survey movement, a Scottish endeavor, was considered "a geographical articulation of the local,"[59] and rose partly out of "the endeavour to make of the pupil a good citizen – ideally a citizen of the world, but in any case a citizen of his own country."[60] Geddes' various environmental activities, although seldom discusses as such, grew out of these sentiments and represent them directly.

III. Social engineering and city planning

According to Bell, modern citizenship could be communicated, reinforced, and applied most effectively at the local level.[61] Cities offered "places of darkness and concealment," in which fear of social segregation and its consequences was most greatly manifested.[62] Thus, Driver agrees, individual reformation was believed to be achieved through reconstruction of the urban environment and the power of environmental engineering.[63] Studying the relations of citizens to their urban and regional setting closely linked it with a contemporary interest in civic improvement and international urban planning;[64] eventually, as Matless demonstrated, planning agencies adopted similar notions and vocabularies.[65] Michiel Dehaene illustrated the use made by planners of the survey and its related activities. Through constant reappropriation, selection, re-interpretation and re-enactment of a fading past, planners stimulated and directed the conscious and upward development of cultural heritage.[66] This, he explains, allowed the planner to assume the position of a great redeemer, who could transform the great knowledge of the city and society through a creative imaginative project. The emphasis on the pedagogical project, he claimed, can be found in the work of a number of planners, often featuring Geddesian sympathies.[67]

Geddes' urban and social evolution indeed found their utmost representation in the urban plan. The actual plan, however, is rarely discussed, perhaps because Geddes left for the planner to devise according to local evolution. In regards to new town planning, the Garden City paradigm apparently supplied Geddes with best solutions for both Civics and eugenics, although this notion too is never explained in full. Nevertheless, Geddes' focus on the city for the place to cure all of society's ails made the actual plan much more than an official document, but rather a visual representation of the sum of the planner's work. In "Paper Cities: Visual thinking in Urban Planning"[68] Ola Söderström analyzed the actual procedure by which planners process the complex reality which is the City, a procedure which demanded, once again, selection, schematization, and synthesis. Being similarly based on Latour's concept and enabling to pass from one complex reality to its simplified figuration, the process which Söderström suggests recalls Naylor and Jones' analysis of imperial geographical devices; the result, a complex visual construction of the city is the process of urban planning.[69]

Complementing the initial process which Söderström termed *internal efficacy* is *external efficacy*, being the professional's capacity to win over public opinion by using such professional tools as a map or a model. Söderström discusses the geometrical plan, the master plan and the zoning plan as tools which became both metaphors and instruments of power and which enabled total and immediate regulation. The development of an urban cartography during the second half of the nineteenth century, mainly in Britain, increased the perception and visibility of urban space, helping to impose a rational order on a world which had many dark zones made up of unknown territories within large cities. Charles Booth's social map, he illustrates, enabled to reason about the city in terms of homogeneous spatial units; Patrick Geddes was a pioneering user of the above in modern town planning.[70]

Part III

Planning in the Colonies

Chapter 9

The Cities and Town Planning Exhibition

Success and Failure

The traveling Cities and Town Planning Exhibition, initially mounted in London in 1910, apparently marked the birth of Patrick Geddes as a distinguished planner. It then embarked upon a journey across Britain and, from there, the British Empire at large. The exhibition was first displayed in Edinburgh where it was opened by the local Lord Provost, followed by an address of Lord Pentland, then secretary of State for Scotland. It hosted teachers and school children in the mornings and paying public in the afternoons, the evenings being filled with working men and women, and was a notable success.[1] The exhibition then moved to Belfast in conjunction with the Health Exhibition and the Royal Sanitary Congress, and then to Dublin, in connection with the congress of the Royal Institute of Public Health and upon the invitation of its president, Lady Aberdeen whose husband was at the time Lord Lieutenant in Ireland.[2] There it aroused great interest and ended in practical results, including an international planning competition and the beginning of a Department of Town Study in the National Irish Museum.[3] Its success was described in length in the report Geddes later wrote for the city of Nagpur. In 1911, he said:

> The Exhibition interested only small sections of the community, but neither Corporation nor citizens, governing, or working classes as a whole. [. . .] and within less than three years . . . the Cities Exhibition was recalled, as the nucleus of a "Civic Exhibition," upon a far greater scale . . . Dublin was stirred . . . Hence a "neighbourhood Brightening Association" arose, and this largely among the slum people themselves [transforming] the whole aspect of the eleven surrounding streets in a very few weeks. The Corporation mended the streets, and improved its cleansing and watering. Friendly donors saw to the supply of flowering plants for such poor houses . . . help too was given with the removal of the rubbish heaps, and with the levelling of fallen houses, as temporary playgrounds, with the whitewashing of the walls surrounding these . . . But in the main . . . the people of the neighbourhood produced the essential transformations themselves; and set about the cleansing and

brightening of their homes, inside as well as out . . . all concerned, from the Viceroy and his consort downwards, were agreed that the most encouraging result of the Exhibition, was the renewal of citizenship and domestic uplift together; and this in a class and in a neighbourhood at the lowest level of this poorest of Western cities.[4]

I. The exhibition in India: a reinforced European display

In 1914 Geddes was invited to display his exhibition in Madras by the Governor of Madras, John Sinclair or the Lord Pentland, former Secretary of State for Scotland, Scottish born and also the son-in-law of Lord and Lady Aberdeen.[5] However, on its way across the ocean, the ship upon which the exhibition traveled was sunk by a German submarine and the collection had to be reconstructed. From Geddes' letters and the pleas he sent out to his family and friends, it was to resemble the original exhibition, compiled in Britain, as much as possible, as Geddes wrote to his wife: "the material is important in India at least as it was in Europe."[6] It was this renewed exhibition which was displayed throughout Geddes' imperial endeavors, with some local highlights. The exhibition in Calcutta, for example, examined the city as "possessing similar problems to those of all British ports – congestion and confusion; roads too narrow and few; railways in difficult positions, as well as its own domestic difficulties."[7] Besides the regular features of London; Paris from early days; the Romans' Europe; Athens; new Edinburgh; types of houses, etc. Geddes highlighted the urban type fit for Calcutta – the city by the sea – for which, as reported, "one good example of town study he found in Aberystwith, the Welsh watering place . . . and the application of this to Calcutta was that Calcutta University should take its place as the Acropolis to crown the banks of the Hooghly."[8]

Courses on Indian evolution

The lectures which accompanied the Exhibition in Madras, Calcutta, and Bombay were filled with government officials and administrators, advisedly only those who were fluent in English and whose participation fees and expenses were covered.[9] The courses examined various themes related to town planning, emanating from Geddes' own theory and practice, following his established comparative logic and exposing prevailing European preconceptions. A series of courses which Geddes conducted in Calcutta in 1915 introduced cities of antiquity; medieval cities; Renaissance cities; industrial cities. A session was devoted to "problems of Indian capitals." Another series presented European capital cities; garden suburbs and garden cities; constructive citizenship; problems of sanitation, education, and citizenship in Calcutta; and revival of arts and crafts.[10]

Geddes found many similarities between Indian and European cities, and described their decay by using analogical symbolical types: "after the Brahmin Raj of Cathedrals came the Kshatriya Raj of fortresses, then the Caravan Raj of railways and lastly the untouchable Raj of corrugated iron, and advertisements."[11] However, it seems as if most of the "lessons" were to be learned from foreign cities rather than from Indian ones. In one of his lectures, it was reported that Geddes stressed the importance of acquaintance with mythology for the understanding of the pasts;

9.1
Syllabus of
Lectures, Cities,
and Town Planning
Exhibition, Calcutta,
1915.
*Strathclyde University
Archives and Special
Collections.*

CITIES AND TOWN PLANNING EXHIBITION.

TOWN HALL, CALCUTTA.

OPEN DAILY 7 a.m.—6 p.m. (except Sundays).

I.—Guidance and Demonstrations in the Galleries ; by Professor Geddes and Assistants—

(7-30—9 a.m., 10-30—12, 12—1 p.m. ; 2-30—4 p.m.; 4—5 p.m.)

II.—Practical Class in Town Planning (throughout the day).

III.—Reading Room (with examples of Town Planning Literature).

IV.—Lectures, by Professor Geddes, 5—6 p.m. daily.

SYLLABUS OF LECTURES.

Saturday, 20th November, 5 p.m.	Introductory (H. E. the Governor in the chair).
Monday, 22nd November, 5 p.m.	Problems of Smaller Cities.
Tuesday, 23rd November, 5 p.m.	Ditto ditto.
Wednesday, 24th November, 5 p.m.	Cities of Antiquity (Mesopotamia, Greece).
Thursday, 25th November, 5 p.m.	Ditto (Rome).
Friday, 26th November, 5 p.m.	Medieval Cities.
Saturday, 27th November, 5 p.m.	Renaissance Cities.
Monday, 29th November, 5 p.m.	Industrial and Railway Cities ; Ports.
Tuesday, 30th November, 5 p.m.	Problems of Indian Capitals.

yet it was also remarked that "the lecturer had no adequate competence in Indian mythology and so would talk on Greek mythology with which he was more conversant."[12] His lecture about *The Temple Cities* (1919) expressed almost apologetic arguments on behalf of rough-looking temples as well as Indian myths which were more difficult to appreciate, agreeing that the ones which are easier to admire are those with European parallels.[13] The comparison between stages in the development of Indian cities and Jerusalem, Athens or Rome and other medieval, Renaissance and industrial cities, "the basis of the civilization of our present times," was apparent.[14] Similarly stressed in the lectures were the importance of enhancing citizenship via education, as reported following Geddes' appearance in Lucknow: "in India all sorts of methods were being used for the search after the right life, and he believed that citizenship would form the new yoga, and endeavour to prepare from boyhood not only the boy scout but the citizen."[15]

The audience was apparently thrilled with Geddes' treatment of his local findings, as he "was mightily pleased with the temples . . . [and] the irregular confusion of the huts of the untouchables in remote rural spots, the solitary mansion-bungalows of men of wealth rank;" the global comparison was also found to be appeasing: "Another gentle chord that he touched was when he referred to the famous temple-city of Sri Rangam . . . Verily, the Professor said, Sri Rangam comes up to the Hebrew Ideal, the ideal residence of the gods."[16]

II. The display rejected: failure in Palestine

It had long been a dream of Geddes' to work in Palestine, wishing to renew Jerusalem as an ancient acropolis; his motivation was apparently strengthened when his "old rival from Dunfermline days," Thomas Mawson, was commissioned to work in Athens.[17] This inclination was accompanied by strong religious sentiments, as Geddes revealed his interests in a letter to Amelia Defries, a Jewish friend and disciple, in 1913:

> [T]he great example, the classic instance of city renewal, (beyond even those of Ancient Rome and Ancient Athens), is that of the rebuilding of Jerusalem, and my particular civic interests owe more to my boyish familiarity with the building of Solomon's Temple, and with the books of Ezra and Nehemiah, than with anything else in literature . . . I still feel these as the great examples for the town Planning Exhibition! I hope in fact to set our artist this winter to work up a big frieze procession of the Dedication of Solomon's Temple, and another of Nehemiah's rebuilding of the Wall.[18]

Working in Palestine, Geddes constantly expressed his admiration of the Zionist society, picturing its recent homecoming as the reinstatement of a biblical entity in the Holy Land and assigning it the ancient role of a regional leader amongst its neighbouring countries.[19] Thus, Jerusalem was already built into the exhibition without any special adaptations needed. The exhibition accompanied Geddes on his planning visits to Palestine. It nevertheless remained in boxes until his second visit in 1920 when it was finally displayed for two weeks at the (Jewish) Boys' School in Jerusalem.[20] The content and the aims of the Palestinian Exhibition were, as usual, to outline the ever-fitting main aspect of the great human heritage, that of civilization as well as the practical aim of re-awakening citizens.[21] The exhibition was opened by a range of local officials and received with a variety of remarks:

> Mr. Nashashibi, the Mayor of Jerusalem emphasized the importance of combining the cultures of East and West, and expressed the hope that the High Commissioner may be successful in achieving his high minded programme for the improvement of Palestine's cities . . . Mr. Ussishkin, who brought the greetings of the Zionist Organisation, said in part: 'It is the Zionist Organisation which is responsible for the presence of Prof. Geddes in Palestine.[22]

But the exhibition was not successful, as was reported in the special edition of *The Palestine Weekly* devoted to town planning.[23] When asked about the evident failure, Geddes replied:

> After these ten days of opening to visitors, my impression is only too clear. In the last ten years I have held fifteen Exhibitions in as many cities . . . and this Jerusalem exhibition is as yet the most unsuccessful in arousing the attention of the educated, and professional classes, or the general interest of the public – with one solitary exception, that of Belfast, the city of Europe as yet most submerged of all in material interests, in political strifes and in religious hatred . . . That Jerusalem has to be improved, all sections of the public agree; but that this improvement . . . can only be realised in the measure of their general and individual arousal to a renewed spirit of citizenship, such as has existed at each and every constructive period of the city's history – this they have not yet awakened to see.[24]

To one of his Zionist collaborators, he later wrote in disappointment, "between the historic idealism and the idealism of the future here was the concrete, the visual and practical building up. But only the mere handful, even of Zionists, realised this. Education and interests here are auditive, not visual, and thus cannot be easily moved from their vague and generalising idealism."[25] A Zionist reporter portrayed a different interpretation of the exhibition and its failure to attract, relating to a different sort of revival. Siegfried van Vriesland, also the treasurer of the Jewish Agency realized that Jews had no local tradition; thus "we have to erect houses and build towns . . . with no other foundation, than the knowledge of foreign cultures and our imagination."[26] This, he claimed, was the sole role of the exhibition, in service of locally defined, Jewish, goals:

> The Exhibition of Cities and Town Planning is initiated to bind together those lovers of beauty in daily life who are concerned about the future. It will enlarge this circle of friends by teaching the art of reading maps of old towns and maps of regional survey . . . [the exhibition] will reveal to you a beauty undreamt of . . . see how slums in other cities were turned into beautiful gardens . . . let us learn from it . . .; after a long struggle in the dark ages of the Diaspora we Jews have at last reached the political dawn of our national restoration in our own land."[27]

Chapter 10

Surveys and Surgeries
Narratives of Old and New

I. The Survey and conservative surgery: narrating cities

Geddes surveyed and reported upon some 50 towns in India and in Palestine. The actual surveys lasted between several days to several months, and at least one city had not been visited by him at all.[1] As a result, the reports vary in length as well as in depth and detail. In India, Geddes repeatedly noted the lack of time to cover all that was needed for a proper survey, often declaring upon having to suffice with partial surveys only.[2] Geddes highlighted the value of the village, which he found to stand out "as a main human unit to be understood for general purposes, and not simply as the unit for civic studies, for reconstruction too."[3] The built elements which he marked for conservation and improvement were mainly temples and water tanks, which were grasped as traditional as well as beneficial elements to the city, and which could easily be related to each other through a network of small interventions.[4] As opposed to the British, who tended to condemn these elements due to their unsanitary state, Geddes suggested their full revitalization and incorporation within local and urban park systems,[5] a system which, according to Ferraro, allowed Geddes to express respect to local elements and to the city's history in general by highlighting pieces of "the holy past" for people to celebrate.[6] The "urban evils" Geddes described were consistent as well as familiar, including congestion and high-density living and also low sanitation and hygiene levels.[7]

Often leaving out the historical part of the survey, Geddes' appreciation of the city and its historical components sometimes bought out a similar attitude toward the old and the new. For example, the Nagpur report introduced the survey and its aim to study the city "in terms of its geography and history, both general and special;" however, immediately regretting for "again not having been able to overtake this Historic survey," Geddes identified the old town "as it was in the time of the first dynasty of Rajas," followed by the description of changes brought on by the railway age and by the blessed development and growth of the large civil stations and of its bazaars. "In conclusion, I have only to suggest the improvement of the better neighbourhoods above mentioned by tree planting etc., etc., and the stimulating of the more backward ones to desire such improvement also. It is plainly for this prosperous and pleasant Civil Station area to set the best of examples for the corresponding ones of the larger City."[8]

The conservative surgery in Barra Bazar: a critical improvement

Geddes' tools for conservative surgery, a practice shaped in India, were a particular interest of *Geddes in India* compiled in 1947. A long chapter quotes passages of Geddes' defence of existing streets and their piecemeal improvement, including recommendations for the extension of open spaces by clearing sites of fallen buildings and planting trees; linking the spaces by further small clearances, mainly at the expense of ruined and dilapidated buildings; and replanting gardens and trees.[9] Green lists the elements of Geddes' conservative surgery as "positive tools of planning"; nevertheless, he describes his actions as "selective clearance"[10] because a recurring principle of the practice was the removal of unwanted buildings and the rehabilitation of others, all defined as such by the planner-surveyor.

In 1919 Geddes was asked to comment upon a plan made by the Calcutta Improvement Trust for a dense business quarter. He was highly critical of the Trust's main recommendation concerning new roads to be cut through the quarter, as they exemplified "conventional aesthetics of the rigorously straight line of the older Paris-Berlin-American school."[11] Geddes suggested alternative routes which still necessitated destruction, albeit minimal, and which would be conducted upon a different set of selective guidelines: "clearing away of some of the most insanitary and dilapidated property."[12] Additionally, Geddes was quite critical of the local building type:

> What of the present type of accommodation of big Business in Barra Bazar – that of the courtyard ground floor (or upstairs sometimes) and with the dwelling space above thus restricted, and over-crowded and unhealthy accordingly? Is this so perfect as likely to survive? If not, should it be planned for indefinite continuance in the future . . .? [T]hough people here have grown accustomed to it, is it really in any way efficient and economical? I submit that it is the very reverse; and have not discovered any arguments, beyond use and wont, and present necessity, for its continuance . . . Furthermore, these courtyards readily become dirty, like the streets . . . to which their notorious unhealthiness is greatly due.[13]

Geddes therefore proposed the demolition of some of the unsatisfactory interior houses and of others which were allegedly "ill-built or ill-ventilated, un-repaired and even dilapidated tenements" and commended their cleared sites as playgrounds, "as notable in the worst quarters of Old Edinburgh and Old Dublin, and in American cities."[14] Therefore, "though defence may be made of the ordinary courtyard house, I here also defend the present transformation of it, as on the whole preferable for such new dwellings."[15]

Geddes was similarly critical of the working practices in Barra Bazar, believing them to be lagging behind the times and in need of radical overhaul; "what in Calcutta is done by a hundred coolies and bullock drivers, with costly superintendence, endless toils, delays and confusions, and corresponding expense can often be seen done in America by one or two skilled men." He called for more efficient business organization, justification being that business had to be "replanned and concentrated, with every modern appliance – that is now needed here, to bring Calcutta business more fully abreast of the times."[16] Eventually Geddes suggested a new building type as a solution for the relationship between dwelling and business,[17] combining concepts from both European and Indian cultures.[18]

Geddes' report for Barra Bazar, according to Martin Beattie, was accepted with ambivalence and criticized by the British colonial establishment as well as by the Indian businessmen. The Calcutta Corporation was not satisfied with Geddes' suggested improvements;[19] it dismissed Geddes' ideas about small local playgrounds, "as it was considered that these small patches of ground surrounded by high buildings with access through narrow lanes would not serve any useful purpose and would be used for dumping refuse."[20] However, Geddes' approach was apparently out of step also with the pace of modernization in certain sections of the community, which actually demanded a road-widening programme.[21]

II. Rebuilding Jerusalem as an ancient biblical city

When Geddes arrived in Jerusalem, the first plan for the city, commissioned by the British, had already been submitted. Prepared by the engineer William McLean, it suggested full conservation of the Old City, and a detached, grid-based, extension plan.[22] The plan was critically reviewed back in London. A fierce criticism written by H. V. Lanchester, who had worked with Geddes on the Madras Presidency plans, condemned the plan of using an inappropriate grid "more suitable for Washington or Michigan" and displaying a misfortunate disregard to the city's topography and to the cultural demands of the local inhabitants.[23] The plan was also followed by a fierce debate amongst the Jewish population, regarding its status in the city.[24] As Geddes soon associated with Charles Robert Ashbee, another former colleague and also the civic advisor to Governor Ronald Storrs, it was suggested to employ him in the preparation of a report to the Zionist Organization in London: 'Prof. Geddes knows how to maintain what is traditional and beautiful of the past whilst combining it with all the necessary requirements in the way of sanitation, hygiene and modern requirements."[25] Upon his arrival in Palestine in 1919, Geddes received a list of eight additional projects for the Zionist Commission, consisting mainly of the planning of new neighborhoods and agricultural colonies.[26]

Jerusalem of 1918 was a predominantly oriental, traditional city, whose character was being challenged by modernization and exposure to Western technology and culture. Competition for an imperial foothold in Palestine resulted in monumental edifices and large compounds of European religious and philanthropic institutions, mainly outside the old city. Zionist modernizing forces encouraged Jews to leave the crowded Jewish quarter, resulting in the construction of many Jewish housing estates around the city; a modern Jerusalem was slowly emerging. Upon the British occupation in December 1917 and the acquisition of a League of Nations mandate in 1922, Jerusalem, still recovering from the war, was emerging as an important political and cultural entity.[27]

Geddes' account of the city was altogether different, as reflected in his report, *Jerusalem: Actual and Possible*. It opened with a description of the survey and its goals:

> The method adopted for the preparation of the present sketch-plan is
> that which I am accustomed to employ in every city: – that of thorough
> and repeated perambulation day after day, in all directions, and practi-
> cally without use of any plans at all, until considerable familiarity with
> the whole city, old and new, has been obtained . . . in this way one
> gradually comes to see the qualities, the defects and possibilities of the
> areas . . . the needs . . . material and cultural . . . habitations and com-
> munications . . . religion, education . . . communications and buildings
> . . . central and suburban areas, old and new . . . domestic, general and
> public requirements.[28]

The Jerusalem which rises from Geddes' report creates a vivid image of an ancient
city, the result of carefully selected biblical elements chosen mainly for their oriental
imagery. Already in his first stop in Jerusalem, just after alighting from the train and
taking the views, Geddes noticed "the noble City Wall leading on to the ancient
Castle and Gate, but also the many modern disfigurements . . . on the one hand the
mean modern buildings in the valley [. . .] and on the other the exaggerated scale
and ill-designed detail of various modern religious buildings."[29] He praised Ashbee's
intention to rehabilitate the ancient citadel and the surrounding walls. Other features
which he marks out for rehabilitation and preservation were generally remnants of
Israel of old, such as pools and agricultural terraces, being "the only monuments of
biblical times which it is possible to restore to their pristine condition and beauty."[30]
He also listed cemeteries and major tombs, schools and welfare institutes, monas-
teries and convents, all reflecting the city's character.

The elements which he condemned were those which obstructed his
chosen image of the city, whether they hindered its unique built traits, were foreign
to its biblical landscape, or simply ugly. In this spirit, he mocked, amongst others,
the many monumental institutes built by foreign empires, demanding to pull down
the Turkish clock tower erected adjacent to the city walls[31] or foreign European buildings, to which he pointed as vulgar modern decoration. The recently built Jewish
quarters reminded Geddes of European ghettos and were generally destined for
removal.[32]

Conservative surgery in the Old City

In Geddes' plan for the Old City, which must be preserved in its entirety, no planning can be discerned; however, it was the site for the employment of conservative
surgery, which here too certainly involved demolition following selective criteria. In
Jerusalem, Geddes employed the technique for the rehabilitation of the ancient fosse
surrounding the old city wall, in which "the squalid buildings on the west side of the
road next the older dumping-ground along the valley, will naturally be removed to
make room for the necessary new markets and Khan."[33] The scheme also included
the replacement of a missing part of the city wall across the entrance roadway,
removed in 1898 to allow Kaiser Wilhelm and his entourage to enter the city, but
which Geddes considered desirable on both historical and artistic grounds.[34] In order
to further enhance the look of biblical Jerusalem, Geddes also commended the

demolition of Jewish buildings, including the Montefiore Houses en route from the train station to Jaffa Gate and newer neighborhoods along Jaffa Road:[35] "however admirable in their philanthropic intentions . . . much may still be done to ameliorate their aspect . . ."[36]

More complex treatment was suggested for the site of the sacred Jewish "Wailing Wall" and its vicinity, resulting in a plan which shows Geddes' problematic position in all its complexity. Geddes suggested the removal of the nearby Moslem "Mogrebbin village," which was boasting of vulgarly modern decoration and was generally, thus Geddes, unsuited to the locality. Moreover, "With a removal of a single row of houses, and with the acquirement of the small garden at the north end, the length of the Wailing Wall will be about doubled, and the space in front of it sufficiently increased."[37] The scheme was rejected. Nevertheless, following an Arab attack on Jewish worshippers at the Wall in August 1929, Geddes approached a few of his former collaborators, trying to convince them of the potential contribution of his scheme to alleviating the critical political situation. A letter to Storrs, by then the Governor of Cyprus, provides another account of Geddes' aim to provide safer access to the Wailing Wall instead of "that long lane of descent through unfriendly Arab quarter and especially through Moghrebbin [Geddes' spelling; NHR] houses, most unfriendly of all. My scheme however included the possible removal of their little quarter to a better vacant site, nearer the 'Dung Gate'." On the vacated site, he details, "there would be room for some decent cottages (I hoped Jewish) or perhaps better for some neutral building – or policemen's cottages."[38] Storrs claimed to have no recollections of the plan.[39] Arthur Ruppin, to whom Geddes had written about "the Moghrebbin houses, which have always been a danger, since of lower class inhabitants"[40] wrote in reply:

> Your suggestion is, from the technical point of view, without any doubt the best possible solution. Unhappily however it must be recorded that under present circumstances it is impossible to get the consent of the Moslem Supreme Council to get a road constructed which will pass through their land to the Wailing Wall . . . There is another plan similar to yours . . . this road would be parallel to the one devised by you, but it could pass through Jewish owned land.[41]

III. Building the New Jerusalem

Geddes' plan for Jerusalem was in fact a compilation of both McLean's existing plan for the city and of Ashbee's suggestions.[42] Geddes partially adopted the zoning system suggested by McLean which designated the Old City and its closest vicinity as an urban asset of great esthetic value and of unique archaeological importance. To the east, construction was totally forbidden so as to preserve the topographically dramatic and highly archeologically valuable area, including the formidable view of the Mount of Olives;[43] "the oliveyard below Scopas [i.e. Scopus] is at present the only spot which gives an idea of the ancient aspect of this valley and of what should thus become its future aspect as well."[44] To the west, Geddes suggested surrounding the Old City with a protective green belt incorporating those old artifacts to

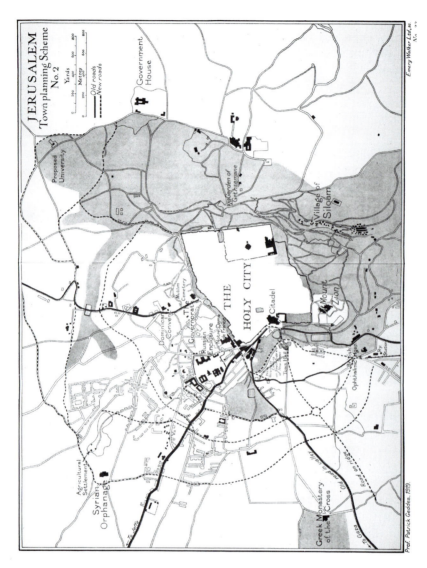

10.1
Jerusalem
Town Planning
Scheme, 1919.
*C. R. Ashbee
(ed.),* Jerusalem
1918–1920, Being
the Records of the
Pro-Jerusalem
Council during
the Period of the
British Military
Administration,
*London: John
Murray, 1921,
The Jewish
National &
University Library,
David and Fela
Shapell Family
Digitization
Project, Eran Laor
Cartographic
Collection,
the Hebrew
University of
Jerusalem.*

which he pointed in his survey and "The great Sacred Park of Jerusalem" to create "an almost complete Park Ring all around or through Jerusalem"[45] thus completely isolating the Old City.

The development of the new town was commended as a continuation of the Old City, as "here in Jerusalem, of all cities in the world, the new town owes its origin, its meaning, and even its future permanent existence, to the ancient city."[46] The suggested road pattern was accordingly developed along existing roads, adding on a new road northwards planned to lead directly to the site of the planned, already marked, Hebrew University. The architecture of the new city, according to the report, "should be as far as possible in the traditional style, i.e. with flat roofs or small domes, and not sloped roofs with red tiles."[47]

New additions to the city were planned according to the popular lines of the garden city, including some very near Herod's gate[48] and the new Jewish garden suburb, Talpioth, which included a school, place of worship, tennis courts, and playing fields, all within close walking distances.[49]

Chapter 11

The Regional Analysis
Rehabilitating the Mediterranean Basin

Geddes' early work in Cyprus dealt mainly with its physical reconstruction, analyzing the country as a representative valley section, a microcosm to the region of
the Mediterranean Basin. He treated problems of ruin brought about by centuries
of deforesting; his solutions included improved irrigation, tree planting, and skilled
farming.[1] Preaching in later years for regional reconstruction, Geddes mentioned
problems and solutions which he devised throughout the Empire regarding loss of
runoff water and the drying up of the water tanks in India,[2] and various examples
of planting of wasted areas for reforestation from the Mediterranean to Asia.[3]
However, Geddes claimed that the social and economic impact of his actions has
not been grasped, "both by our utmost imperialists and their severest Indian critics
. . . Witness even Mr Gandhi, with so much of spinning-wheel, but as yet nothing
of spade."[4]

I. Palestine in renewal

In an almost propagandist piece for the Jewish renewal of the land of Palestine,
Geddes described his local work as "travelling and planning, and this with an eye
to regional development."[5] Geddes' analysis of Palestine as an inherent part of the
Mediterranean Basin reflected his perspective of the local evolution, wishing to
renew the land as the cradle of Hebrew culture and, moreover, a regional leader.
"That would be a regenerated Holy Land; for in this 'building up the old waste places'
lies the concrete future of Zionism."[6] Agriculture being a major theme,[7] Geddes'
actions included contour farming, terracing, and tree planting for combating the
denudation which was rife in the Middle East.[8] The development of the primary rural
base of activity, Green proclaims, ultimately affected also "the promotion of hierarchical functions in urban settlement and the modification of existing morphological
patterns in the urban structure."[9]

The Jordan Valley in particular was envisaged by Geddes as a classic
valley section, viewed as a future clustering of colonial settlements for the purpose
of rural reclamation and development. The lower Jordan he saw as a potential area
for "experimental tropical agriculture" where he proposed to establish agricultural
colonies which may in winter form health resorts and tourist centers.[10] Geddes also
examined the possibilities for electrical development for irrigation, joining forces
with the Jewish engineer, Pinhas Rutenberg.[11] According to Green, Geddes clearly

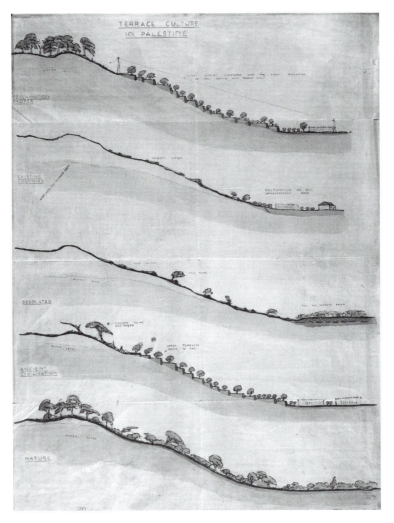

11.1
Geddes and Mears,
"Terrace Culture in
Palestine," 1919.
*From the maps
collection of the
Central Zionist
Archives, Jerusalem.*

envisaged the colonies largely populated by Jewish immigrants, for he isolated the capacity of the Jewish people to promote intensive agriculture.[12]

      The regional development was expected to have a direct impact upon the function of existing settlements. Jerusalem, which was perceived as part of the Jordan Valley, would become the regional focus for development on top of its already established role as a religious center.[13] Geddes' guidelines for the development of Tel Aviv, Jaffa, and Haifa as coastal settlements rested upon their role in the future economic development within Palestine and in the larger region, the eastern basin of the Mediterranean.[14]

II. The regional role of Tel Aviv: a new Mediterranean link

Geddes' appreciation of Palestine, claims Welter, was influenced by his understanding that the Zionist projects were most likely his last opportunity to realize in full an example of contemporary planning.[15] Accordingly, he explains, the 1925 master plan for Tel Aviv was a continuation of a mosaic of planning initiatives that contributed toward reviving the ancient region of Palestine: "Zionism stands for regional reconstruction, for better combination of town and country accordingly; so hence the opportunity of Tel-Aviv."[16]

The city of Tel Aviv, established in 1909, started out as an offshoot of the adjacent Arab city, Jaffa. It was the first Jewish neighborhood built outside Jaffa to hold urban aspirations and a clear self-identity.[17] In 1925, Meir Dizengoff, the mayor of Tel Aviv, asked Geddes to plan an extension for the city, which since its inception, and more so since it had been declared an independent township in 1921, was growing rapidly and with no official plan. The Zionist commission for Tel Aviv was followed by a similar commission from the British governor of Jaffa, wishing to ensure the co-ordination of the development of the two cities and for sharing the costs of the plan.[18] Geddes was hence to work on a joint plan for two months, out of which a quarter of his time – as well as a quarter of his fee – would be devoted to the planning of Jaffa. Geddes was aided by two local professionals: a Jewish architect, who had according to Geddes assisted him faithfully, and the Arab municipal engineer of Jaffa, who greatly disappointed him by being uncooperative.[19]

11.2
[Part] Plan of
Jaffa, 1918.
*Granted by
Jewish National
and University
Library.*

Geddes named his official report "*Town-Planning Report – Jaffa and Tel-Aviv*" and related to his joint planning commission as "Greater Jaffa." The report opens by a statement regarding the shared origin of both cities and the geographical logic for their joint planning.[20] However, Geddes never treated the two cities as one, revealing his overall regional perspective, as well as the relationship which he envisioned, and eventually fixed, between the two cities. The bulk of the report describes the development of Tel Aviv, the first Jewish city established in modern Palestine, as a leader in the Mediterranean Basin, a role model for new cities everywhere, resting upon Geddes' vision for the new city and society. Geddes' wish to renew the role of the ancient Hebrew culture as a regional leader amongst its neighboring countries, here through the functional role of the coastal city, was well expressed in his report: "Clearly realized then, is not once more the high function of a renewing Zionism, to repeat her ancient message upon our modern spiral . . . and to recall the ancient conception of Unity throughout the whole Universe?"[21]

The first chapter of the report is devoted to improvements to Jaffa's port and the development of a joint industrial area for both cities. Indeed, the regional function of Tel Aviv as a port city made the discussion of Jaffa's port a crucial planning matter. At that time, a "Jaffa port commission" was examining the present conditions of the port and suggesting its overall improvement. Geddes in fact claimed that Jaffa port is sufficient, using historical maps of the area to show flourishing ports within moderate distances from each other.[22] But Geddes did not take part in the commission's meetings and is not even mentioned by it. His suggestions regarding the port were in fact miniscule.[23] Rather, most of the discussion in the opening chapters relates not to the port but to its practical connections with Tel Aviv. Under the title "Further developments for Jaffa & Tel Aviv of Common Interest" several connections are suggested between the two, such as a new goods train station, new slaughter houses and associated cattle market, and a joint industry quarter to be erected in the neutral zone between them.[24] The rest of the report focuses on the development of Tel Aviv as a garden city, a role model for modern urban development. The comprehensive civic center which Geddes recommends for the city and its many cultural institutes are destined to be placed further north from the historical origin of the new city, the alleged basis for their joint development. The Arab city of Jaffa is almost absent from the plan.[25]

Traditional development and personal enhancement

Additional aspects of the regional function of Tel Aviv as a coastal city are portrayed in Geddes' plan for a local park system intended to enhance the functioning of the city as a center for tourism and recreation. Moreover, "the Marino Quarter" designed along the coast was meant to become one of the leading health resorts in Palestine, as another function of Geddes' park system was the physical and moral improvement of the inhabitants. The park in Tel Aviv was also to include a sanatorium pulling visitors from the close vicinity as well as from Europe and from Egypt. By suggesting a far-reaching comparison to Epidaurus, "where the resources for treatment were both physical and mental," Geddes expresses his wish to erect an open air theater which would serve, for example, for the performance of local dramatic masques.[26]

He brings up as an example, the school of Rabindranath Tagore in Calcutta, in which he saw a precedent and an encouraging example for "a real sports club in the cultural sense" and in the building of which he had only recently aided.[27]

The advised health sports activities are nevertheless well grounded in the local tradition. Thus, when Geddes recommends the erection of a park for horse riding, he warns against recurring shows of local deterioration: "riding is the education of youth to the manly and the chivalrous; but racing is everywhere its deterioration . . . And it is surely not for a Sports Club of professed Zionists – and here in this new city for the potential ennoblement of Israel – yet also not without elements of potential degeneration, to Phoenician and Philistine levels – to land itself to the deterioration of its young MACCABEANS to the level of jockeys and betting men."[28]

Having earlier agreed that Tel Aviv should have its own jetty, deemed crucial in face of the city's quick development and the vast import of building materials, he nevertheless rejected the original location suggested in favor of reserving the central beaches of the city for purposes of bathing.[29] Nearby, Geddes recommended developing an aquarium, similar to those which he had earlier suggested to erect in the port cities Madras and Colombo. The aquarium, which will supply basic functions for local fishermen, will also perform as a regional marine research center.[30] From the Tel Aviv Marino, "the patient is sent away, not merely temporarily relieved of his immediate symptoms, but re-educated towards general health and throughout a thus prolonged life and activity."[31]

Chapter 12

The Garden in the City
Civic Revival in Indore and Tel Aviv

I. The Diwali at Indore: recruiting tradition

One of the widely celebrated highlights of Geddes' work, a colorful endeavor often described, took place during his long planning commission to Indore, in 1918. Geddes was invited by Maharaja of Indore, to plan an extension for the city, which he did, on Garden City lines (as he did elsewhere in India).[1] During his long stay of six months at Indore, Geddes took on the task of treating the malaria which plagued the city. For this chance of local improvement, both urban and moral, Geddes employed a traditional festival, the annual Diwali. Having already commended traditional cleaning habits and bestowing upon them similar goals as those of modern town planning, the festival was a unique opportunity for cleansing the city on several planes.[2] Receiving full support for his initiative, Geddes became "Maharaja for a Day" and conducted the annual Diwali as "a civic pageant, a town-planning procession."[3]

The aim of the Geddes' Indian masque was clear: urban cleansing. He thus changed the route of the traditional pageant, announcing that the procession would take the path along which most houses had been cleaned and repaired. And indeed, following the announcement, he wrote, "a wave of housecleaning, painting, and repairing swept through every quarter of Indore." Additionally, the elephant on which rode Lakshmi, the goddess of prosperity, was also whitewashed, to suit the legend of her dazzling white elephant. The roles of the procession's traditional heroes were also changed: the Giant of Rama's legend was presented as "the giant of Dirt," followed by "the Rat of Plague" and not forgetting "model mosquitoes for malaria" which were later burnt, as custom dictated, in a great bonfire.[4] Also included were floats which represented all local crafts and introduced future gardens.

Distinctly,

> [. . .] enthroned on a stately car, a new goddess evoked for the occasion: Indore city. Her banner bore on one side the city's name in illuminated letters and on the other the city-plan in large outline, with heavy red lines showing the proposed changes to be made. Following his goddess were big models of the public library, museum, theatre, and other buildings P. G. had projected; and a whole group of floats contained models of the private homes that were to replace slum dwellings.[5]

Geddes awarded a unique and a significant role to the social untouchable, the local sweepers, who were dressed in white and received new brooms, "flower-garlanded," for the occasion:

> Their chariots were all fresh-painted, red and blue, and their big beautiful white oxen were not only well-groomed and bright-harnessed . . . every sweeper too was wearing a new turban, and of the town's color – as were all the employees and higher officers of Indore, as well as the mayor and myself; this had been arranged with his warm approval as symbol of the democracy of civic service.[6]

As the sweepers began their march, Geddes warmly greeted their leader. Apparently, it was Geddes' prerogative as a foreigner to do so: "Well done; a good idea! cried the mayor to me. Why? What? Said I. Said he, Custom would not let me do that, as a Brahmin, to an Untouchable; but as a European you were free to . . . you have treated them as men, as equals."[7]

Geddes believed this practice could be adapted anywhere, being a good lesson of citizenship and of its persuasive arousal.[8] The results of the "dramatized lesson in civics" were quickly apparent, he claimed, noticing a new spirit of house-pride and self-confidence spread among the Indians, renewed zeal amongst the sweepers. Practically all of the thousand plots laid out in garden suburb were taken up in a short time. Most important of all, the plague came to an end, and this was "partly through cleaning up the city and partly because its season was over."[9]

II. Tel Aviv, the Modern Garden City

Geddes' urban extensions were all based on the model of the Garden City ideal, which he regarded as allowing the best arousal of civic action on both physical and spiritual lines. In Palestine, his main endeavors of planning anew consisted of similar suggestions.[10] The main garden city Geddes planned in Palestine was Tel Aviv, which happened also to be his swan song both for being his last plan as well as for being his most comprehensive and eventually, most applicable. The model city rested upon Geddes' vision for the new local society, being also a reflection of his Western notions of a civilized society on the eve of the twentieth century.

Presenting the best traits of the renewing city and serving as a global example for old-new development, the plan for Tel Aviv presented a local innovation. In Tel Aviv, Geddes suggested for the first time a new model of road layout, consisting of distinct levels of roads and showing a clear separation between commercial and residential areas.[11] "Home ways," surrounding the residential block, were to be as short and as narrow as possible, protecting homes from dust and from the noise of the main roads, removed from "main ways," connecting between the blocks.[12] The hierarchy of roads, other than holding the great advantage of saving road space, would also allow for spaces for gardening of all types, which in Tel Aviv had a special meaning. Under the subheading "Garden Idealism in practice throughout Tel Aviv as Garden City," Geddes concludes, "there is no other modern city, which so specially owes its origin to a great wave of social idealism and aspiration, and which so actively and increasingly continues this."[13] This, too, was a direct connection between ancient tradition and the future: "For to 'sit under one's vine and fig tree,' is one of the most definite images alike of the Ancient bible and of the mind of the modern Zionist settler."[14]

Gardening and education

The connection between gardening, education, and civic responsibility in Tel Aviv is apparent almost from the very beginning of the report, when Geddes discussed the rehabilitation of the surrounding rivers by conferring the role of cleansing and upkeep of the river and its banks on the community.[15] Geddes described various other environmental solutions which incorporated education for civic action regarding the rehabilitation of the immediate environment of the city[16] as well as more individual projects, such as urban allotments and raising silk as a home activity with great implications on house cleaning.[17] Geddes' criticism of his contemporary educational system is apparent also in his praise for the "practical union" of various gardening endeavors in Tel Aviv educational system and the encouragement of establishing new ones.[18] The municipal gardens should all be connected along the main boulevard, which would be planted with groups of trees of various types.[19]

Finally, Geddes suggested to utilize the civic spirit already apparent in Tel Aviv for the formation of a horticultural society, which would assist in gardening around the residential blocks, and more importantly, conduct a healthy competition between local groups of volunteers.[20] The mayor, Geddes claimed, had already promised to come and visit "(and how better than by introducing the simple and charming old Indian Custom, of honouring successful leaders or workers, by the award of a flower-garland)."[21] Whereas in India Geddes recommended the decoration of the brooms with white ribbons, here, he suggested, the sign of victory will be the fruit themselves, "in purple and gold."[22] Finally, Geddes suggested adapting the American tradition of the Arbor Day, "a Tree-Planting Holiday for the schools," overlooking the recently renewed Jewish tradition of the same purpose.[23]

Educating workers

According to Tel Aviv's envisioned uniqueness as a "Fruit Garden city" Geddes saw the future of the city as an educational center of horticultural Art. He thus included a School of Gardening and Fruit Growing, as well as training for rural immigrants, in his plans for the local civic center.[24] "The arguments for such a progressive city policy are abundant and convincing; and on all levels, from those of health and domestic economy, to the enhanced happiness of the household . . ."[25] The colleges which Geddes planned for Tel Aviv, described in the final chapter of the report, were devoted to the education of working men and women. They supply a glimpse into his unique view of modern society and its local revival as a unique contribution of Tel Aviv to the renewing society everywhere. For, "Where in the wide world shall we find a more favourable situation for such a much needed Workers' College . . . than here in Tel Aviv?"[26] Finally, Geddes finds Tel Aviv the best place to rethink women's role in society as garden tenders, or in other words: child educationalists, and this through the proposed Women's College:

12.1
Tel Aviv General
Plan, 1926.
Tel-Aviv–Yaffo
Municipal Historical
Archives.

Though the vast majority of women find their life-course and their educational career in the home, there is perhaps no social invention and advance more definite in the West than their increasing development of educational facilities, preceding their life-settlement in homes of their own . . . it is time to be realizing that it is the sex especially occupied with conducting this . . . it is full time for future mothers to be prepared anew towards understanding, protecting and guiding this, far more understandingly than hitherto.[27]

Chapter 13

Civic Centers and Cultural Institutes

Enhancing Local Traditions

I. Enhancing religion in India

The cultural acropolis in Indian cities was generally arranged around local temples "of the old idealized order,"[1] also incorporating additional municipal and cultural institutes. Thus, the civic center of Indore, which was appropriately based beside existing temples and ghat, was enhanced by a central library, various museums, a theatre, and a music hall. Its proposed location was also the highest and the most striking site the entire city afforded.[2]

Similarly, the location chosen for the civic center in Baroda and its institutes was nearby the "largest and best situated of the city's tanks."[3] Here, however, Geddes suggested to replace the already existing temple, which he described as beautiful but small, with a "Central Temple for Baroda." Wishing to create "a place for education, municipality, law and religious edifices," the plan provided a monumental grouping of temples and bathing ghats on one side, and a government center on another, composed of "three towers of sovereignty, administration and religion thus furnish central perspectives."[4] Geddes concluded, "thus might be evoked new examples of that personal munificence towards public and religious ends which has for many ages been forthcoming . . . at once, happiness and health."[5]

II. Redefining heritage in Jerusalem: the Palestinian regional museum

In Jerusalem, a secondary civic center was proposed on a central site, including mainly educational institutes: district schools, a night school for boys and also one for girls, with the required "places of worship," a public garden, a school of music as nucleus of future conservatorium, hall for concerts and an open air theatre.[6] The proposed site was also considered by Geddes to be the best remaining site in all Jerusalem, "commanding both the Old and New city, and overlooking their main entrance, easily reaching all parts, and convenient for citizens,"[7] for fine public buildings, meaning municipal offices, and a town hall.

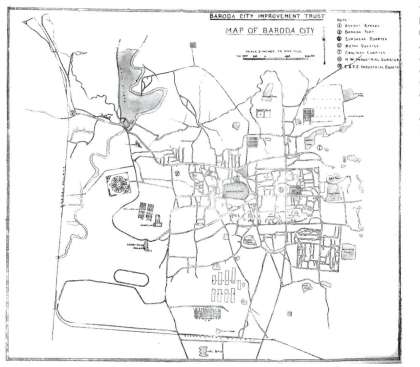

13.1
Map of Baroda City.
A Report on the Development and Expansion of the City of Baroda. Printed at the "Lakshmi Vilas" Press, Baroda, 1916.

In Jerusalem, however, it was the museum which provided a direct manifestation of Geddes' view regarding local tradition and its possible evolution. The suggested museum was described as "a Palestinian museum, a Jerusalem museum, or whatever it may be called on lines at once comprehensively regional and civic."[8] Following Geddes' general scheme, the outline of the museum imitated the "scenic presentments" of the Masques of Ancient and Modern Learning, recounting the local succession of historic cultures which have surrounded and affected both Hebrews and Palestine.[9]

> In fact, the long history of Israel, from the Patriarchs to the present . . . how attractive will be a series of good Relief Models of Jerusalem, illustrating . . . the extent and character of the city from its earliest Jebusite days, to its glories under David, its greatness under Solomon, and so on throughout its chequered history. In the sketch it will be noted that those Galleries, namely: (1) those of Geography (2) general history and (3) of Hebrew and Jerusalem history, all lead into a final Gallery, for the renewing Palestine with its developing Cities and Capital.[10]

The apparent mismatch between its description as "truly Palestinian" and its contents was nevertheless recognized and criticized by a British official:

13.2
Baroda
Municipal
Center.
A Report on the
Development and
Expansion of the
City of Baroda.
Printed at the
"Lakshmi Vilas"
Press, Baroda,
1916.

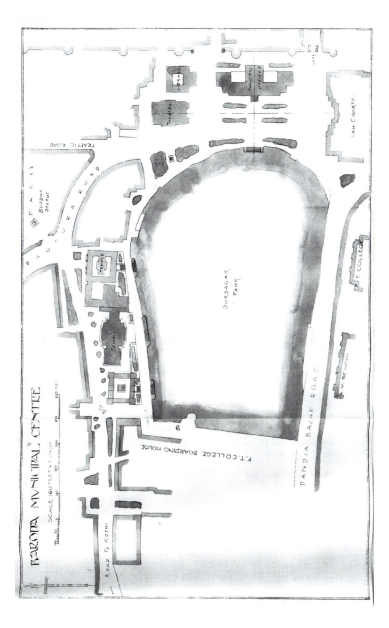

The museum should be Palestinian in the fullest sense of the term. It should be an institution in which the Christian and Moslem as well as the Jew should figure prominently . . . the plan as proposed by Mr. Geddes is not made from this point of view and contains many features which should be criticised. In the first place history and excavations inform us that the country was only partially occupied by the Jews . . . to show a parallel range and a distinct development of Jewish antiquities culminating in Zionism, without doing the same for other peoples would not only be scientifically a serious mistake, but it would be wholly unacceptable.[11]

III. Inventing modern Jewish culture in Tel Aviv

The civic center for the new city of Tel Aviv was designed to be built and placed on "the northerly plateau (the highest spot in Tel Aviv) in due acropolis fashion."[12] It was to include a few institutes which attested to the future identity Geddes envisioned for the city and for the Zionist society at large. Recounting a line of world-renowned Jewish musicians, Geddes assigns Tel Aviv with the role "to continue one of the most ancient traditions of Israel, and also that longest and most widely honoured and followed throughout the whole Christian world as well." Thus, Geddes wishes the city to take foremost lead as "the dramatic and musical centre for Palestine."[13] He recommended the building of an opera house, a conservatorium and a college for dramatic and musical college providing also training in Eurythmics and dancing.[14] Nurturing the Jewish musical genius, Geddes believed, would provide a local solution for world peace, or at least for abating Anti-Semitism.[15]

However, regarding more constructive arts, Geddes claimed that the Jewish culture is lacking, nevertheless recognizing a great opportunity to establish new Jewish art and create a new local identity.[16] The artistic style which Geddes deemed suitable for Tel Aviv (and Palestine at large) attested to the local characteristics that he wished to bestow upon the renewing society, as he turned mainly to traditional Arab arts and crafts. Geddes thus celebrated "the recent revival of Tile making at Jerusalem, of Pottery, and of glass making also," referring to the successful endeavors of Charles Robert Ashbee amongst the local population:[17]

> Given artistic leadership as well as business ability, is there not a future for the magnificent old oriental industry of Carpet Weaving? The abundance of camels in this whole region also invites the question of how far their very valuable contribution to textile industry may be better obtained and utilized.[18]

Regarding architecture, again, Geddes claimed that local Arabic style should be preferred. However, he agrees, this is a cultural matter, and so he suggests local adaptation of the Jews to their old-new home land:

> The present magnificent recovery of classical Hebrew as the spoken language of the Jews in Palestine is of course a first step or re-Orientalisation; but others are needed. Without recommending any more adoption of Arab Architecture, either in its simplest form in the hillside village . . . or still less desiring the ever elaborate magnificence of later developments of the Arabian style as in Cairo, it is important to realize that this [Arabic – NHR] architecture and decorative art, at her best, are second to none in the world.[19]

Chapter 14

Incipient Universities in Indore and Jerusalem

Cloisters between East and West

I. The proposed university for Central India, at Indore: a Western ideal

Geddes' ideal of a modern Indian university was clearly a Western one. Describing the requirements of the university and a regional research center "to an Indian friend" in 1903, Geddes claimed: "This whole construction expresses both these aspects of the Western mind, which are becoming interesting and suggestive to the Eastern one."[1] He believed that the new Indian university should be based upon his global suggestions for educational reconstruction, advocating similar methods in the name of modernization and Europeanization.[2] Courses which Geddes presented in Bombay, before he became Chair of Civics and Sociology as well as after, presented identical ideas, repeating his theory from base to top.[3]

Geddes' greatest report in India is considered to be the one he prepared for the Maharaja of Indore, which included the embodiment of his dream university. In fact, the report can be read as complimentary to his relatively technical *Cities in Evolution*, as it encompasses the whole of Geddes' ideas for the needed institutes in the city and their roles, elaborating once more on his overall theory. The second part of the Indore Report, *A Proposed University for Central India* opens with a history of "*universities in India and in Europe*," presenting the same critical reading of the above and the changes which Geddes had already suggested earlier. Various chapters describe associated institutes including a central library and a museum, a theater, an outlook tower, exhibition rooms, school of music, and a hostel system.[4]

The Indian outlook tower: an imperial descent

The most prominent element of the Indore university was the suggested outlook tower, which is also one of the few places that adheres, yet only partially, to the location of the pretentious endeavor. The top floor of the tower was to be devoted to the local city, holding maps and a complete town plan as the essential document of the present report. The next floor would be devoted to the Indore State, celebrating the inevitable Holkar dynasty "throughout its tradition and up to the present." However, from the next floor, devoted to India, one descends to "the Hall of Empire, and of English-speaking civilization," the geographical context widening into the political context of the British Empire. In this floor,

> since of widest indebtedness to the Whole Western Civilization, of which the English-speaking is but a branch, albeit in some ways the greatest, we may illustrate the essentials of European geography and anthropology, history and civilisation as a whole; and so not only of France, Italy, and other lands of alternating leadership, but all the Allies, the neutrals too, and even our present enemies.[5]

The recommended museum for Indore is also described as a type-museum, similarly utilizing the best examples of the best worldly museums;[6] the theater for Indore would be "as it began, alike in ancient Greece or India, or as it renewed itself at each great period of European and Indian culture."[7] It is left for the Lending Library to introduce "the civilizations of the Orient," describing China, Japan and the great Arabian and Persian cultures, "which have so specially influenced India."[8]

The report for Indore describes also the inherent relationship of the university and the city and the role of the first in the reconstruction of the second. This bond was also manifested in the "Memorandum giving an idea of what the university can do" which Geddes prepared at the request of the Committee on Collaboration Between the Bombay University and the Bombay City[9] as well as in his suggestions for the planning of a university in Benares, a commission which, to his great dismay, he never received.[10]

II. The Hebrew University in Jerusalem: educational leadership

The plan for Indore was the initial cause for Geddes' invitation to plan the Hebrew University in Jerusalem. Very proud of the result, he sent a copy of the accompanying report to David Eder, a British psychoanalyst, an elected representative of the Zionist Executive in Palestine, and also a friend of Geddes' since 1908, when they shared "renewed interest in religiosity and rising fascination with spirituality."[11] Eder indeed found "certain similarities between our needs in Jerusalem and the great Indore city" and asked Geddes to come. In fact, shortly after the British occupation of Jerusalem, Geddes had suggested to plan the city; at the time he approached Eder through Israel Zangwill, Eder's nephew and also an old acquaintance of Geddes since their joint work at the poor East End of London.[12] Back then, Eder had to decline: "I need scarcely tell you how I would rejoice to see you here, engaged in reconstructing . . . I cannot offer you an official invitation as the Zionist Commission is unfortunately not the reigning government."[13] However, by then the planning of the Hebrew University was on the agenda. Eder wrote to Chaim Weizmann, the head of the Zionist Commission to Palestine, and Geddes' appointment was soon under way.

For Geddes it was a dream come true. He had high hopes for the Hebrew University, believing it would be the first of the new and post-war order, a model institute.[14] As an early forecast for the reconstruction to come, Geddes proclaimed his trust in the promising location: "Nor can Israel, as the people who have most distinctively combined Oriental with Occidental ideals, ignore such suggestiveness as there may be in the developments of education among other Eastern peoples, each with its own culture, its corresponding share of light."[15] The central Great Hall of the university, substituting for a Tower (which was found unsuitable to the local topography and architecture and thus covered with a local dome) embodied many of these ideas. It was appropriately based on the ultimate symbol of synthesis:

> Israel has her distinctive plan, though not yet so far as I know thus uti-
> lised that of the Hexagon, which is central to the Magen David upon her
> banners. This plan too I had also reached independently, and alike on
> architectural grounds of sound construction, (as old as the bees), and on
> symbolic grounds as well, since a six-sided figure alone lends itself to the
> full notation of Life – life organic, life social and moral also.[16]

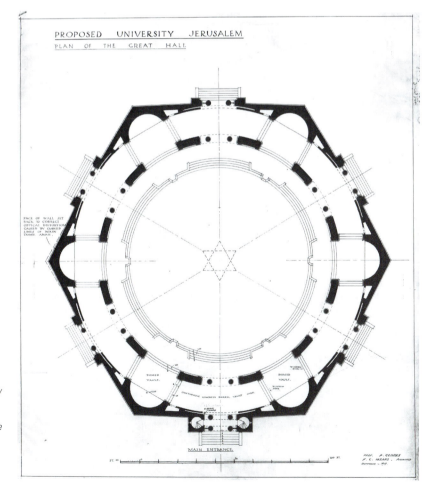

14.1
The Hebrew
University,
proposed plan
of the Great
Hall.
*Prof. P. Geddes,
and F. C. Mears,
"Proposed
University
Jerusalem, Plan
of the Great
Hall," December
1919. © Courtesy
of RCAHMS.
Licensor www.
rcahms.gov.uk file
no. SC 1093170
by permission
of Roger Mears,
Edinburgh.*

The Great Hall also had the role of hosting communal gatherings, a role fit for an urban cloister. As such, it would be used not only for graduation ceremonies and collective meetings, but also for "gatherings of the Jewish population on suitable occasions; and, above all, as a centre provided by the Zionist movement and the Hebrew University, for the coming of the Palestinian people at the various great occasions of the year."[17] Geddes' Hebrew University, however, was to be also a Palestinian university, manifesting an ancient, joint, regional goal:

> [T]he renewal . . . of the undying aspiration of the renewal of Palestine, and of its old and Sacred city; and these not only in and for themselves, but as the general and cultural centre in the fullest sense – of the whole Jewish people . . . bringing more and more clearly into view the yet wider claims of Israel throughout the ages, and of standing for these anew, and now more clearly than ever.[18]

Thus, more than just regional revival, the Hebrew University would also manifest the revival of the sought after, long-gone civilization, its purpose to "keep before itself the renewal of the high tradition of Israel among the peoples, and work with and towards the realization of those old and high ideals."[19] Great emphasis was put on the connection of the university to the city, both in the plan for the university and in the overall city plan. Physically, the university faced the Old City, mirroring it also in architecture and style. As a "nucleus to an educational centre" the planned university included housing of staff, including servants, students' hostels, and further educational institutes – teachers' college, training college, boys' and girls' high schools, students' societies with reading rooms and gymnasium and swimming baths; "a veritable Garden Suburb of the University must necessarily arise."[20]

In spite of the high regard for Geddes' work and the theoretical embracement of his plans, both for the University and the city of Indore, they never had the prerogative of building, and Geddes' overall contribution to the city, albeit its magnitude is considered more than ambivalent.[21] Neither was the Hebrew University, the cause for Geddes' commission in Jerusalem, built according to his plans. Most of the proposals were not accepted and he, refusing to give up, continued to try and convince of their appropriateness; Frank Mears revised his architectural drawings accordingly. A frustrated correspondence carried on between Geddes and the

14.2
The Hebrew University: plan for the Mathematics and Administration Buildings, P. Geddes and F. Mears, 1925. *Strathclyde University Archives and Special Collections, by permission of Roger Mears, London.*

university heads until the laying of its cornerstone in 1925 and beyond.[22] The integral planning of the university and the city was also criticized, as the direct relationship between them was apparently mainly Geddes' own idea.[23]

Part IV

Postcolonial Scrutiny

Chapter 15

Patrick Geddes and Colonial Town Planning

Geddes has often been claimed "a planner without politics" due to his declared detachments from power relations and imperial implications. Geddes was indeed never blunt in his support of the imperial situation, but the British Empire was nevertheless a part of him. The Empire for Geddes was first and foremost a geographical definition. He regarded it as a legitimate entity, purely a matter of geographical scale, and sometimes replaced it by similar categories such as "the English-speaking nations." It was an obvious step on the ladder of citizenship and he encouraged civic responsibility as an imperial identity.[1] Similarly, *Imperialism* was incorporated into Geddes' evolutionary scheme, forming a legitimate, albeit problematic stage in contemporary history;[2] it had a negative connotation when used as an economic term[3] or when used to describe regional metropolitanism.[4] However, the bulk of Geddes' work was carried out in the colonies, affecting imperial spaces and shaping colonial cities: matters of great concern for the sub-discipline of postcolonial studies, in which theoretical advances are well reflected in the changing study of colonial cities, their planning and their planners. It is impossible to study Geddes and his colonial endeavors outside of this framework.

I. Studying colonial cities

The colonial city was initially examined as a mere physical representation of the colonial power and its conceptions. Various characteristics of the city were discussed as means for the mediation of imperial notions through effective spatial technologies of town planning.[5] It was later discussed as a multifaceted "contact zone" of conflicting sets of economic as well as cultural systems and conventions, visualizing various relationships between the dominator and the dominated as well as the political agenda and the motivations behind it.[6] Finally the focus had shifted to study hosting cities on their own terms, mirroring the rise of subaltern studies and relocating Western narratives of progress in their wider colonial histories as part of the project of *Provincializing Europe*.[7] Contemporary approaches treat the colonial city as a complex product of conflicting sets of values, emphasizing hybridity and contestation rather than a simplistic, dualistic creation.[8] These examine different perceptions and utilizations of the built environment by various communities, treating the cities as "contested spaces" and searching for the undermining of imperial orders through negotiations over identity and place[9] also acknowledging the fact that colonial urban spaces are usually the location of "the crucibles of nationhood and the sites of postcolonial politics."[10]

II. Colonial town planning

Town planning in the colonies was initially described as an enlightening practice, a natural extension of European planning concepts.[11] The research later came to emphasize the formative attribute of town planning as an enforced practice, serving as efficient means to the extension of the concurring social, political, and economic relations onto the design of the cities, thus imposing foreign, modern techniques on local settings.[12] Such readings link the knowledge of a place and its inhabitants with planned subordination and control.[13] Colonial town planning was thus studied as an exported practice, manifesting a discourse shaped by Western experts and government agents in the service of a foreign power.[14] It was described as a mechanism through which cleanliness, civilization, and modernity were materialized upon the landscape, all in the name of a universal ideal city.[15] Western planning was inevitably considered to have depressed and pushed aside the local, subordinate society and its urban heritage.[16] The changes that took place upon the landscape were described as drastic and related to the imperatives of colonial projects, leaving the indigenous fractured and contested without being assimilated[17] and causing inevitable alienation from the city by the local population, often emphasizing the dichotomy between two separate cities.[18]

Eventually the planning of colonial cities became too a study of hybridity. Suggesting to "shift the spotlight to the importers of ideas and their local realities, incorporating their interactions with the exporters," Nasr and Volait focused on local activities and actors that have shaped the built environment and their relation to foreign planners, planning principles, and processes of city building. By examining how a local indigenous population responds to, modifies, controls or domesticates urban development strategies of an external authority or power, new researches view the lack of planning or the thwarting of the implementation of plans as representing as much a local choice as the successful introduction of foreign precepts.[19] New examinations by local narrators highlight the historical input of the local community,[20] also exposing later alternative plannings suggested by the local community[21] as well as local power conflicts which in their rivalry over shaping space, have overruled foreign imperial imperatives.[22] Finally, research confronts the shaping of postcolonial spaces, or rather the postcolonial shaping of spaces as a process of direct indigenization, inevitably engaging in a dialogue with the colonial past.[23]

III. The shifting historiography of colonial planners

The examination of the role of individual planners working in the colonies has changed accordingly. Initially, colonial planners were viewed solely as representatives of hegemonic power, being carriers and appliers of "expert" knowledge, codes and standards and imposing their vision as a product of the dominant socioeconomic culture.[24] Later, they came to be examined as having been influenced by, if not directly responding to, the priorities and the expectations of actors from host periphery cities as well. Consequently, assuming that individual planning conceptions have evolved to reflect local experiences, the definition of planners as foreign is not deemed suitable anymore; they are better described as "go-between"s.[25] Planners' personal histories thus enable a comparative assessment of the importance of local differences, as well as similarities, between colonies."[26]

Furthermore, moving beyond dualisms of center and periphery had also encouraged the examining of the work of professionals through a network conception of imperial interconnectedness.[27] David Lambert and Alan Lester claim that tracing the "life geographies"[28] of those who traveled and dwelt across trans-imperial spaces provides insight into "the dynamic trajectories and networks of knowledge, power, commodities, emotion and culture that connected the multiple sites of the empire to each other, to the imperial metropole and to extra-imperial spaces beyond."[29] Studying the work of imperial planners can therefore provide a more objective view of colonial relations and show how ideas, practices, and identities have developed *trans-imperially* as they moved from one imperial site to another, and as manifested through planning.

IV. Patrick Geddes, town planner in the colonies

Relying on contemporary writing regarding colonial cities and colonial town planning, Geddes' personal history can be examined as the life of an *in-between* professional whose work was carried out as part of a complex network of imperial connections and determined by a multiplicity of actors and local realities. Geddes' work as a planner in India and in Palestine was both exported by the British (including himself) as well as imported by local agents, and his work throughout the Empire should be considered as one town planner of many working throughout the colonies, forming a substantial professional network sharing various traits in spite of their varying personal aspirations or planning inclinations. Tracing Geddes' professional contacts in Britain, in India, and in Palestine allows discerning notions which have affected his work and influenced it, either encouraging him to suggest contradicting plans (such as the case in Calcutta) or otherwise embrace his colleagues' suggestions (as with Ashbee in Jerusalem).

Geddes was initially invited to Palestine by David Eder, following earlier collegial contacts. This includes his long-lasting relationships with the British Zionists, with many of whom Geddes had personal and professional relationships including Israel Zangwill and Amelia Defries; similarly, Geddes' relationships with local Indians can be discussed as part of a local academic elite with whom he had been closely associated, represented, for example, by his work alongside Rabindranath Tagore. Nevertheless, to India, Geddes arrived upon the invitation of Lord Pentland, an old acquaintance and native Scot.

Analyzing Geddes' work in India and in Palestine through the "Scottish Empire," Michael Fry highlights cultural differences and similarities between the two.[30] Both in India and in Palestine, claims Fry, Geddes' local notions can be described as natural Scottish tendencies, which emphasized morality and the understanding of environment.[31] The Scots' relation to the East was also an intellectual one, incorporating empirical observations in India within intellectual research, also emphasizing education as means for redemption.[32] Moreover, the Scots' natural closeness to both India and Palestine was brought upon by a colonial bond; "enjoying a recognised status in their own hierarchical society, they felt inclined to seek and admire in others a caste like themselves."[33] As a result, the Scots held Indian languages and monuments in high regard and developed a deep appreciation of the Indian civilization. Geddes' invitation by Lord Pentland, an old collaborator and countryman, continued a long line of local Scottish history.[34]

Geddes' passionate, religious interest in the Zionist homecoming, according to Fry, was also shared by his countrymen as a colonial affinity, fostering the spiritual and intellectual qualities of a small nation forging an independent identity.[35] However, the Scottish response to Palestine also moved between evangelist to Orientalist as their particular sympathy for the Jews emanated from their shared regard to the holy scriptures. The Scottish wished to restore "the civilised country" and encourage the repossession of the Jews of their native land; following their God, claims Fry, the Scottish chose the Jews.[36]

Thus, examining Geddes' urban plan as an imperial, urban microcosm, expressing imperial sentiments and portraying hybrid and contested endeavors, can provide a closer look at multifaceted imperial connections and trace reasons for various planning commissions, highlighting the local rather than the imperial role played by the colonial town planner. The story of Geddes as a colonial town planner highlights the complexity of the colonial situation and the particular uniqueness of India and of Palestine, as the comparison between two colonial settings, even on grounds of their modern planning, is not so straightforward as might seem on first glance. Discussing Geddes' work on British, Indian and Zionist commissions, thereby shifting the spotlight "to the importers of ideas and their local realities, incorporating their interactions with the exporters"[37] also brings out, as Judith Kenny has pointed out, varieties of the "compliance of the colonized with colonial practices and the hegemony of colonial culture."[38] However, before analyzing the different responses to Geddes' urban theory, the various uses of his work by local hegemonies in their competition over shaping society and space and the resultant differences between the two colonial sites, another critical layer will be suggested: By combining, for the first time, Geddes' geographical, imperial notions with his professional endeavor of modern town planning, Geddes' urban theory and plan will be presented as an enterprise of inherent colonial concept.

V. Patrick Geddes at the Intersection of Geography, Postcolonialism and Town Planning

Geography is currently considered to be part of the dominant discourse of imperial Europe that postcolonial critiques seek to destabilize, being urged to cope critically with the theoretical and actual sites of postcolonialism.[39] Both geography and postcolonialism have been criticized along similar lines for being preoccupied with immaterial cultural processes, and neglecting the material consequences of colonialism.[40] More particularly, the examination of the shaping of space, its conceptions and its tools is called for, allowing the use of empirical substance of archives and fieldwork in light of the tendency of the theories to abstract or to neglect altogether material processes and daily practices.[41] Thus, the intersections of postcolonial theories and geography seem to provide challenging opportunities to explore the spatiality of colonial discourse, the spatial politics of representation, and the material effects of colonialism.[42] Further yet, it is claimed, such issues should be examined within specific and defined contexts, such as the city.[43] The urban employment of geographical and imperial tools, together with concrete spatiality and regular documentation, make the city a good place to scrutinize colonialism. Urban geography, accused of being relatively late in embracing the cultural turn, is nevertheless "located at the cutting edge of geographical research that seeks to link the material and the immaterial."[44]

The infiltration of geographical tools and conceptions into the new science of urban planning was illustrated in Part II, particularly the survey which gave planners access to powerful knowledge of place and people, and similarly yielded professional products such as maps and plans.[45] The same tools also strengthened the educational role of the planner in his promotion of the city's social and environmental regulation, all in the sake of improvement. Geddes' urban plan, as discussed here, can be regarded as a direct extension of his more social and educational imperatives, manifesting them in a simplistic visual construct, thus serving as a comprehensive geographical, imperial tool. Geddes' planning tools were based on the belief in the visual power of both the planner and the recipient, as he put full trust in his own abilities to comprehend and to interpret the specific locality which he was examining and planning, offering equal credit to those for whom he was planning to share his vision. However, Geddes used his tools to visualize and to present the world by creating an image which served him in his ambition to know it as an imperial creation; one which could be moulded and shaped accordingly. The narratives which Geddes himself produced, and presented as natural local evolution, were eventually responsible for the critically selected social and physical elements.

Through Geddes' planning, the city was to be explored and mapped, and eventually regulated, according to moral standards of citizenship. His tools served to know the landscape by means of visualization, ordering, comparison, and display; practicing such notions in planning by means of selection, schematization, and synthesis.[46] Using his professional stand as a planner, Geddes composed a system of urban regulations which created local otherness through an agreed scale of citizenship, fostering the transformation of city and society alike. Through geography, Geddes linked places sentimentally, creating a common citizens' responsibility and planning in the name of imperial citizenship. Geddes' power as a planner can thus be likened to the already scrutinized power of the surveyor, the conqueror, and finally the ruler, administering and shaping the environment according to imperial needs or at least, limited imperial understanding.

Geddes employed his quasi-scientific methods for studying and analyzing the built heritage of the city which he was studying. His educational activities, deeply rooted in the geographical tradition, were used as regulatory means for the transformation of the society according to the predefined ideal. Finally, the resultant plan was a professional document of immense magnitude, as a practical vision of the city, a graphic manifestation of the planner's most inherent intentions and ideals. Geddes' planning, then, can be claimed to be a powerful professional mechanism for the enforcement of his geographical notions upon the city and its society.

Chapter 16

The Colonial Planning Gambit

In the Service of Imperial Societies?

Working throughout the British Empire, Geddes served various colonial societies, from the ruling British, through Indian princes to a rivalling Zionist hegemony. It can be claimed that Geddes' initial practice both in India and in Palestine was used to enhance the British planning practice, being imported by British governors and obviously mirroring imperial sentiments; however, it seems that each of these different societies employed Geddes wishing to achieve differing goals, which either fitted in with the interests of other groups in their colonial setting, or rather competed against them. Geddes' town planning scheme, devised to awaken a mutual transformation of environment and society, had been employed by British, by Indians, and by the Zionists to do just that, each for their own purposes.

However, the aims of Geddes' urban theory, a close-ended system, were pre-defined and thus unable to sustain any necessary variations or local considerations. The interaction with local population, brought upon by the planning process, was mainly one-sided and dictated only by him. The result represented mostly the preconceptions and the needs of the appointed planner, whether serving the colonial government or any other local powerful group which used the process of planning for its purposes. Geddes' aspiration to represent local population was therefore doomed for failure, not only because of the colonial traits of his urban paradigm, but also for its foreignness: the planner, as much as he might have wished to see himself otherwise, was a foreign figure of authority. Geddes' geographical planning tools, as discussed above, further alienated him from the local community.

I. Directing Indian evolution: between modernity and tradition

Local Indian rulers adhered to Geddes' modernist objectives, which seemed to have been combined with local features, constituting a sensitive alternative to the general British attitude toward Indian culture and cities. It can further be claimed that while using Geddes' planning to distinguish themselves from the British government, the local elite adopted the imperial paradigm also in order to distinguish themselves from the rest of the indigenous population, striving to create a localized enlightened environment and society alongside and yet in spite of the British colonial rule. Along these lines, Geddes' educational basis for planning, being first and foremost his traveling exhibition and accompanying lectures, were embraced in accordance with the patronizing wish to bestow local enlightenment. Notwithstanding, Geddes' Indian plans, mainly those for garden suburbs, seemed to be perpetuating the local social division, thereby strengthening the layered politics within. Geddes' own honest attempts for reconciling between the castes, manifesting again his inability to fully decipher the intricate social relationships (such as during the Indore Diwali) feel foreign and forced.

Homogeneous surveys and hybrid plans

Helen Meller describes India's appeal to Geddes as a country which constituted the perfect combination between old and new traditions.[1] Moreover, Meller claims, Geddes had been fascinated by the east, longing to India – as many of his contemporaries did – "for spiritual enlightenment in their distress at the results of Western industrialisation."[2] For Geddes, agrees Ferraro, India always remained a mass of anonymous tradition.[3] Thus, Geddes' account of Indian history, as can be traced through the surveys, seems to be that of a well-educated visitor, pointing mainly to widely acknowledged highlights of the local cultures and resulting in a superficial and rather homogeneous reading. Local culture was not very well interpreted or represented, and was often dismissed as incomprehensible. The primacy given to religion could most easily be detected in regard to elements discerned for conservation, whereas the temple and the water tank, being easily conceived urban elements, were incorporated in the sacred parks, providing Indian cities with a direct reinstatement of their essence. Goodfriend attributed Geddes' conservation to *traditionalization*, condemning him of renewing and adapting traditional elements of a cultural order to modern circumstance, and giving buildings, landmarks and amenities an overall significance according to his own interpretation.[4]

Revealing a restricted understanding of the local environment, Geddes' Indian reports hence dwell on familiar urban evils including overcrowding due to housing shortage, public health problems, and the loss of civic responsibility. The dogmatic nature of Geddes' global scheme provides explanations for the repetitive nature of his urban solutions.[5] Furthermore, Geddes treated the historical era of the British Empire as legitimate as those preceding it, and one of great promise, too.[6] This was well illustrated in his plan for a local museum, its contents being familiar and expected, manifesting, once again, Geddes' occidental worldview. The scheme for the Outlook Tower in Indore too was a local adaptation of Geddes' Edinburgh institute, as he easily incorporated the local dynasty within the imperial hierarchy. The University for Indore was a direct manifestation of Geddes' ideal with very little local input. Geddes' local corollaries for civic institutes in the Indian urban landscape relate almost completely to buildings of spiritual significance; similarly, the bastardized Indore Diwali could be read as a local hybrid of modernized tradition.

On these lines, Geddes did not condemn British additions to the landscape, finding them a natural contribution to and sometimes even good examples for further development. In fact, very often Geddes condemned local industry and housing, suggesting more worthy foreign alternatives on the bases of being more efficient and more hygienic. Planning for Barra Bazar in Calcutta, Meller claims, Geddes had become a victim of his own propaganda, being totally unresponsive to any other viewpoint than his own;[7] the result, adds Martin Beattie, manifested in "hybrid visions of health and hygiene" as Geddes combined concepts from both European and Indian cultures to form new notions of city space in a colonial world.[8]

Indeed, it is hard to say what Geddes actually took from India, if at all. This notion can be illustrated by a short correspondence Geddes conducted with Mohandas Gandhi in 1918. In a letter to Gandhi, Geddes condemned the copying of "the customary and orderly ritual of every British congress" at the Hindi conference (held in Indore in 1918). Instead, he recommended using an open-air theater and amphitheater, "the supreme material achievement of the Hellenic culture."[9] Gandhi replied that he would have preferred an Indian-style early-morning maidan.[10] In a following and final letter, Geddes commented critically about the building types used in India; Gandhi's response was a similar polite dismissal.[11] Thus, although Geddes was generally warmly received by local elites, his plans were not similarly embraced. Geddes' suggestions, although sometimes cheaper than those of the improvement trusts, were often too large and too vast and generally not adequately adapted to Indian landscape and society. In Indore, in spite of the locals' honest intentions of applying the plans, they found them too vague, eventually restricting the city's development until finally discarding of them.[12]

II. Palestine: a dismissed biblical regionalism

Geddes' target, to plan a renewing homeland by shaping Palestine as well as its inhabitants following his Jewish sentiments, was probably well adhered by the Zionists in their obvious intention of a local evolution.[13] In Jerusalem, the Zionists were arguably attracted to Geddes' outstanding definition of the university as a modern cloister, housing local intellectuals and directing future urban and social development. Moreover, planning new cities and renewing old ones according to modern sciences, and as represented by the popular garden city paradigm, was probably much appreciated by the Jewish pioneers in Palestine. This can be seen, for example, in the embracement of Geddes' plan for Tel Aviv, embodying the Zionist narrative as a leading new creation which was soon associated with the prevailing notions. Geddes, who was the first planner to supply the city with a comprehensive planning concept, introduced a new spatial system which would eventually comprise an overall civic revolution, his plan signifying the idea that shaping space orderly was a crucial aspect of the modern city. Disregarding and even defying British colonial rule, Geddes' Jewish employers, who formed only a small part of the local population at the time, also ignored the majority of the indigenous Palestinian population, even restraining it in the process of planning.[14]

Defining Palestinianity

The history of the land of Israel, the home of a constituting civilization which had already been examined extensively by Geddes, was easily narrated. Geddes aimed to revive a regional Palestinian and a Hebrew identity, rehabilitating and planning anew cities accordingly, wishing to "re-Hebraize the Jews" in the process, according to

Fuchs and Herbert.[15] Geddes' systematic ignoring/disregard/neglect of other populations residing in Palestine can be illustrated in his plans for the Jordan Valley as well as in his partial plan for Jaffa and Tel Aviv, which ultimately left out the geography of the region, its history, and most of its inhabitants.[16] The survey in Jerusalem, in which the old city was searched for, was meaningless when faced with the real city. The sanctified elements were those of the biblical past; park systems were correspondingly planned around ancient graveyards and water tanks, which Geddes had come to know and appreciate in India. The plan for the Wailing Wall, which similarly ignored all but the old-new vision, bluntly overlooking the delicate political situation, was rejected. The suggested museum for Jerusalem, describing the history of the Zionist revival as the leading force of the region, was equally objected on political grounds.

The failure of Geddes' plans for the Hebrew University was apparently inevitable, as Geddes, who was so concentrated in his own worldview, ignored Jewish thought and discussion and produced a plan which was totally impractical.[17] Describing Geddes' work in Palestine as part of the overall British project of defining *Palestinianity*, "a local version of Colonial regionalism," Ron Fuchs and Gilbert Herbert illustrate Geddes' celebration of the indigenous, the traditional, and the Oriental[18] which resulted in a "sublimated, universalized Zionism."[19] Geddes, they claim, who had been "strangely enough" chosen by the Zionists to design the Hebrew University, used the plan in aid of reconciling Zionism to Palestine through the use of local architectural features.[20]

The Jewish resurrection in the Holy Land, however, needed no evolutionary assistance from the outside: it had its own narrative. Furthermore, Geddes' personal aims collided with those of his Zionist employers. In his wish to see the Zionists assume an ancient role of past cultures, Geddes avoided seeing Zionism as it truly was – Western and modern – and forfeited the cooperation of his local colleagues. Geddes' educational endeavors, which were the most direct manifestation of the collision, were a mutual disappointment. The Exhibition was neglected by all but the Arab leadership, possibly hoping for more; Van Vriesland's emphasis of its professional, practical aid only, seems to be an accurate explanation for its dismissal by the Zionists. The proposals for education in Tel Aviv had a similar fate.

The plans for Jerusalem and Tel Aviv: a local success?

Geddes' plans for various places in Palestine had a different fate: they were mostly implemented. The suggested plan for Jerusalem of 1919 formed the basis of Ashbee's plan of 1921, which was approved by the British authorities and eventually became the first statutory plan for the city.[21] Introducing no conceptual ingenuities, it was almost the same plan which demonstrated Geddes' desire to bring the city back to some imaginary past and freeze it there. Thus, to this day, Geddes' Jerusalem plan of 1919 dictates the development – and mostly the preservation – of Jerusalem on many planes. The conservation of the Old City of Jerusalem was a great success, its wall eventually cleared of most of its encroachments and surrounded by a green belt; it could in fact be said that Geddes managed to create a local Acropolis, at least in the physical sense of the word. Additionally, although the new city was in reality separated from the Old City by the protective green belt, its development is still dictated

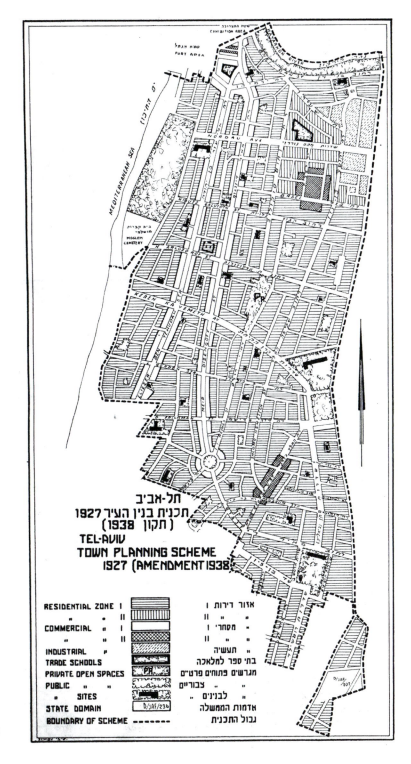

17.1
Tel Aviv Town
Planning Scheme
1927 (1938
Amendment)
*Tel-Aviv–Yaffo
Municipal Historical
Archives.*

upon the original directions which Geddes had set in his plan. Thus, while Geddes' educational endeavors and his own ideal of biblical Jerusalem were abandoned, his ideas are forever recorded in the everyday life of the city and its inhabitants.

In Tel Aviv, on the other hand, by the time Geddes' plan was approved, planning had to catch up with the fast development of the city. Private market activity led to growing gaps between land supply and demand, resulting in ascending land prices. Additionally, as the execution of the new town plan coincided with the arrival of new architectural ideas of the Modern Movement, the plan was considered restraining by architects who criticized the individual building plots and the alignment of the buildings. Thus, although Geddes' suggestions regarding the roads were generally carried out, many of his other local urban concepts were soon discarded,[22] and the Garden City he envisaged was transformed into a different city altogether.[23] The actual development patterns of housing in Tel Aviv, claims Kallus, ridiculed the spirit of the scheme and the changes in plot and building size constituted a crude violation of the spirit of the Geddes' report, leaving "only the street layout in Tel Aviv as a witness to the ideals of the time and of the man presenting them."[24] In any case, Geddes' Tel Aviv, which evidently never allowed the more educational and cultural aspects embedded in the report to manifest, nevertheless enabled its quick growth and development as a successful modern Jewish city. The plan was amended significantly in 1938 and has remained the only official plan for the city since.

Conclusion

The Historiography of Town Planning, a Postcolonial Reading

Tracing Geddes' urban plan for over 30 years has shown that it remained constant throughout the years, reflecting mainly his fixed worldview and inflexible practice.[1] Arriving in India and in Palestine with a preconceived, embracing and meticulous scheme, Geddes' notions could hardly change to accommodate reality, a failure which is all the more apparent in light of his honest intentions of being loyal to his clients. As a result, he also failed to relate successfully to planning challenges which were set before him.[2] Going back to look for the ideals beyond long-forgotten traditions, Geddes chose those which suited his purposes, sometimes distorting them in the process.[3] Many elements received concrete shape only following practical use, accumulating diverse meanings in the process. For example, Geddes' use of urban parks revealed the uniformity of his theory, reflecting in the process differences of appreciation and utilization of the landscape by the British, Indians, Arabs, and Jews.

Geddes' fixed notion of shaping the city and the society according to his worldview can be traced through his geographical planning tools. Their success was limited, and depended mainly on their acceptance by the local society which employed him. Nevertheless, analyzing Geddes' more successful plans allows us to trace the direct impact of his geographical notions upon the landscape. As a graphic application of his more social and educational intentions, the seemingly technical plans cast in stone Geddes' analysis of the planned city, its supposed evolution, and its envisioned future. The implementation of the plans immediately gave life to Geddes' worldview, which was occidental, imperial, and mainly very biased: It was Geddes' position as a British planner which enabled him to select those physical and social elements which he deemed necessary for his future plan.[4] These, as described above, reflected mainly imperial sentiments, common to Geddes and to his British colleagues.[5] Thus, while most of Geddes' endeavors as a planner in the colonies rightfully award him with the title of "a magnificent failure," Geddes' more successful planning can be claimed as a powerful professional mechanism for the enforcement and eventually the perpetuation of his geographical, and unavoidably imperial, notions upon the landscape.

However, the actual definition of his "failure" or "success" depends, for the most part, on the expectations of his employers: the implementation of Geddes' plan in Jerusalem can be regarded a success mainly in the eyes of the British; the plan for Tel Aviv, in spite of its only partial implementation, was regarded a successful manifestation of the early Zionist intentions of the first Hebrew city; while the plans in India could not have been deemed successful for any of the locally competing groups. The question of a "successful" or a "failing" plan is a crucial issue in the historiography of planning, and the historiography of Patrick Geddes as a planner, his urban plan and his practical experience is here suggested as a case study for the history of town planning as a whole.

I. Geddes as a case study for the history of town planning

The discrepancy between the visionary aura that surrounds the historical Geddes reflected by so many of his commentators, and the image that emerged from a detailed quasi-archaeological scrutiny of his legacy stood at the heart of the present study. It seems as if the positive outlook upon Geddes as a planner of good intentions, and the generally positive approval of his plans and treatment of society have obstructed and reputed any critical or less positive treatment of his work. The perception of Geddes today is the product of his revival as a humanist planner, having been considered a unique representative of the affirmative action of planning altogether.[6] The rich discussion concerning him since his own days until the very present has eventually stagnated, and no further breakthroughs have been made. Since Geddes' place as a planner had been re-established, his interpretations are repeated, finding new projects to describe and further points of comparison but always arriving at familiar conclusions. Many publications have adopted a chronological narrative of events, being sometimes very detailed but also descriptive and selective.[7] The major books are biographical, rightfully described by Mercer as "ranging in tone from bare-faced worship to enthusiastic respect,"[8] celebrating his life and his achievements and heavily relying on previous writings as well as on personal correspondence. It seems that Geddes' work and legacy have been protected from scrutiny, his overall perception shielding him from any other type of interpretation and forbidding a more in-depth examination. The monolithic reading of Geddes' planning oeuvre belittles the criticism and highlights the accomplishments, sanctifying both his goals and his means. This had recently changed with the reading of Geddes' work from a more critical, geographical point of view, though one which did not yet infiltrate into the study of planning itself.

In spite of the accumulating criticism and the claim for Geddes' misplacement along the years, it is obvious that studying him as a representative of his era is a correct notion. As a planner in the colonies Geddes was not fundamentally different from his colleagues. His perceptions of India and of Palestine resemble those of his contemporaries, noting similar admirable features while condemning others. Overall, Geddes' planning solutions were not very different from those used by others. In spite of partial admiration of local ancient urbanism, Geddes' suggested urban model was based upon European standards. In many cases Geddes' suggestions were not so dissimilar to those of his colleagues. His defense of traditional local roads reflected that of Camillo Sitte at the time,[9] while the suggestions for alternative routes through conservative surgery were sometimes just as damaging as those they were supposed to replace; the main difference between him and his friends might be the fact that he was not in a position to implement his plans. Thus, although Geddes is considered a unique planner, he can be reflective of the movement as a whole. Many issues in Geddes' planning theory and general approach are based on common grounds as those of many of his contemporaries;[10] as a geographer, Geddes shared the professional notions and practical tools of his fellow geographers. Finding the solution for social problems in town planning, as shown above, was a path taken by many of his fellow urban workers.

Hasselgren claims that many read Geddes today looking for "signposts of sanity, finding inspiration in the echoes of the Geddesian approach which they discern in environmental education, in the movement for a less bureaucratically orientated approach to planning, in the concern for the biological integrity of our environment, and in the search for alternatives to industrial society and its undoubted ills."[11] Thus, Geddes has been accredited with all the good traits of planning as we know it today, his "catch phrases" used to justify and to magnify the role of planning and the authority of the planner. As a crowned pioneer, Geddes supplies planning with an innocent and an optimistic return to the basic, affirmative intentions of the discipline, his unique "humanist" approach to planning representing and assuring the best possible practice. The anachronistic attribution to Geddes of altruistic and sensitive intentions is cynically used to justify and to promote the power of planning. The selective and uncritical reading of Geddes' theory and colonial projects provides an historical support to these aims. The encouragement of the perception of Geddes' work as detached from the power of the planner and separated from the regulative discipline of planning allows a better understanding of his return to the bosom of the planning world and his total acceptance by planners everywhere. The ambiguity of Geddes' writing and the magnitude of his work, together with the ongoing stagnation of his positive research make it easy, simple, and safe for use.

In this book I have suggested a practical reading into Geddes' urban theory, putting together some of his critical readings along the years and exposing their overall magnitude. The result was a workable paradigm for the analysis of Geddes' colonial work, which was presented as a geographical, colonial, urban plan. It is here claimed that re-reading Geddes' story critically, analyzing his current appreciation as a planning hero while studying anew his constituting ideals, enables a better appreciation of planning, seeking values, underlying assumptions and discourses that have shaped – or failed to shape – twentieth-century planning practice and planning procedures in general.[12] Understanding why Geddes is periodically "rescued by his disciples," as depicted by Hebbert, would also assist in understanding the contemporary value of his renascent "practical vision."

II. Modern town planning: a postcolonial historiography

As could be expected from the current postmodern period, the discussion in Geddes has expanded greatly in recent years. Geddes' theory and various endeavors are dealt with by various approaches; their only common denominator might be a critical point of view. The postcolonial approach might be the most critical of all, maybe because its initial starting point is most critical and aggressive. In the present work, Geddes was examined for the first time as an accomplice of the British Administration rather than an individual opposing it, revealing mutual challenges and dilemmas and representing consequent results in planning. Geddes' plan was discussed as a reflection of the imperial situation as a whole, examining its preconceived notions and its fundamental worldly schemes which would not change in the face of constant local variations. Thus, although the postcolonialist theory might be only one prism through which to examine the history of planning, enabling new questions and making easier the answering of already existing ones, it is here regarded as the primary critical tool for the analysis of the evolution of town planning, suggesting to view and to analyze town planning as a project of colonial origins and traits from its earliest conception.

Following Sandercock's proposition to demythologize the heroic image of planning lead to a broader and a more inclusive view of planning.[13] New methodological approaches to the study of the colonial city, together with the deconstruction of canonic texts,[14] raised questions which relate to the historiography of planning as a whole, mainly regarding the variety of research materials, their producers and their accessibility.[15] Archival material, naturally emphasizing certain power relationships, was questioned,[16] as was the choice of the historical narrative and the present narrator.[17]

Studying Geddes at the intersection of geography, postcolonialism, and planning allowed a more in-depth scrutiny of his work and aspirations, personal and professional, latent and overt. Moreover, by accentuating the preconceived nature of Geddes' theoretical framework, it was also possible to suggest that his urban plan, which served the imperial system in various ways, also reflected it as a closed gambit. Geddes' aspiration to know and to control the city and its society, alongside his unavoidable failure to truly incorporate local voices, can be easily compared with similar imperial thinking. The analysis of Geddes' urban paradigm and its manifestations throughout the Empire illustrated the coloniality of Geddes' urban scheme. Studying Geddes' work along with the rest of town planning in the colonies, as well as a representative of town planning as a whole, it is easy to imply that Town Planning overall is a colonial, civilizing project.

The historiography of town planning: a new beginning

Modern town planning, developing mainly in Britain at the end of the nineteenth and the beginning of the twentieth centuries, correlated with the high era of the Empire, doubtless absorbing many of its aspirations. The constituting ideals and major implements of town planning drew on geography, already a much-disputed imperial discourse. The basic conceptions and acquired tools of the formulating practice are claimed here to be an accumulated produce of the long, ongoing dialogue between the Empire and its colonies, its mutual and long-lasting effects upon cities already discussed.[18] It is today believed that "urbanism and urbanisation in the metropole cannot be understood separately from development in the colonial periphery."[19] It is generally agreed that colonial mentalities and practices of categorization and governmentality often folded into the management of a new underclass of urban industrialization, and that the Empire produced new social and material arrangements in cities.[20] Throughout the Empire, spaces were being imagined, explored and reported according to a conceived ideal; a British, Western, imperial ideal. Notions of unfamiliar territories on various scales calling for exploration and regulation yielded meaningful dichotomies such as "dark and light" and "civil and savage," and gradually enriched the vocabulary of those concerned with urban squalor and urban poor, making it equally applicable for colonial territories as well as for untamed parts of the city.[21] Environments and societies were evaluated according to a civic standard, their mutual reflection believed to be signs of manifested citizenship or its lacking.

Geographical, and eventually planning, tools both educational and regulatory were being formulated/devised/concocted to perform a mutual transformation; the way in which these notions and mentalities translated into British town planning has not been examined yet. Planners practiced their new trade mainly in the Colonies, where it was easier to erect new cities and rebuild existing urban cores; but town planning in the colonies is just one manifestation of town planning in general. Town planning was eventually created as the newly institutionalized discipline for regulating and for civilizing both City and Society at home and abroad.

Appendix: Geddes' Urban Scheme

A Comprehensive Reading

I. The holistic evolution of the city and society

Geddes' notion of the totality of the relationship between the individual, the society and the environment is encapsulated in his basic nine-square diagram (Fig. A.1). The notation in its many variations describes the reciprocal relationship between its components.[1]

The reciprocal relationships amongst the diagram's components implied that the makeup of the environment determined the nature of the personal occupations, the mode of social organization and appropriate institutions within it. Equally

PLACE	Place-WORK	Place-FOLK
Work-PLACE	**WORK**	Work-FOLK
Folk-PLACE	Folk-WORK	**FOLK**

A.1
The basic reciprocal relationship between society and environment.
After various sources, e.g. "Civics: As Concrete and Applied Sociology, Part II," Sociological Papers II, Published for the Sociological Society, London: Macmillan & Co., 1906, p. 72.

implied is that people and their traits are reflected in their environment, which is being continuously shaped by man's activities overall. The individuality of the city and the personality of its individuals and society thus develop together.[2] A complete and a satisfying relationship between the three components were the prerequisite for a healthy life.[3] Rebutting claims of determinism, Geddes emphasized the superiority of man over environment and the free will "to select among the factors afforded by a given set of circumstances."[4]

This complex relationship between man, society and environment is not stable, but rather perpetually developing in a recurring cycle, in which each of the components goes through a process of development, stagnation, and decay.[5] The process of change and transformation is caused by both active and passive aspects: either "man guiding his daily life and remaking place" or "man shaped by place and his work."[6] The success of the process determines whether it would result in evolution or in degeneration.[7] This is portrayed schematically through the perpetual individual process, starting with simple daily *Acts*, which are turned into permanent *Facts*, undergo a conscious process of *Thoughts* and eventually manifested in, hopefully improved, *Deeds* (Fig. A.2).[8]

In the collective process, individual *recollections* agglomerate into *tradition*, which is *idealized* with time and eventually *materialized* again as a new reality.[9] In this ongoing cycle of personal and collective evolution, often symbolized by a swastika, past survives into the present while also containing the future as potency or germ.[10]

Geddes identified the third part of the cycle – individual thoughts or collective idealization – as the most crucial one, upon which the success or failure of the evolution was determined. In this stage, the positive traits of the existing social heritage are uncovered and refined in order to be re-materialized again as a new and better reality.[11] The reciprocal action would be eliminating negative inheritance, what Geddes called Social Burden.[12] The result would be Eutopia, locally based and logically explained, as opposed to the traditional, idealized, non-place Utopia.[13]

Finally, the City in Geddes' thinking is the fullest and most developed expression of the evolutionary process. As physical inheritance is believed to be embodied in the built environment, examples and expressions are found in the architecture of every city; town plans too were systems of hieroglyphics in which man has written the history of civilization. A series of tours from Westminster to the City of London, examining remnants from various historical eras serving to study

A.2
Schematic evolution of the individual.
After various sources, e.g. A. Defries, The Interpreter Geddes: The Man and his Gospel, Foreword by Rabindranath Tagore, Introduction by Israel Zangwill. London: George Routledge & Sons, 1927, p. 82.

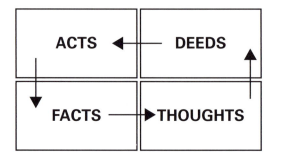

the history of London, provided one detailed example.[14] Other illustrations included the plough-furrow which determined the average size of the building block, and the radiating plan of the French architects which originated in forest rides laid out for the safety, and convenience of the hunt.[15]

II. Ideal types in geography and history

Geddes referred to evolutionary success in economical terms as "an average of wealth"[16] or in medical terms: "in order to know and to treat the abnormal we must know something of the normal course of evolution,"[17] implying the notion of an ideal standard and deviations from it. Frederic Le Play's geographical regionalism and August Comte's historical humanism provided Geddes with a transverse and a longitudinal analysis across space and time.[18] Geography was used to describe relationships prevalent in a given time, via the "call of family, neighbourhood and region," while history allowed to describe the appearance of the above relationship in various periods as a "widening appeal of nation and federation, of civilization and humanity,"[19] culminating in a comprehensive worldly scheme.

"We need a systematic correlation of each region with its people, of each people with its region; proceeding from simpler examples towards more complex, and awaiting full comparison before positively laying down geographical and social laws."[20] The *Valley Section*, defines a typical region, from a mountain top to an estuary, describing the types of people living in it, their occupations and natural habitats. Geddes used it as a global cross-section, an ideal geographical unit and a constructive formula[21] (see Chapter 6, Fig. 6.1). Geddes argued that the Valley Section is the characteristic unit for much of the familiar world and provided ample examples over time and space.[22]

Each of the components of the Section represents an ideal to be achieved: an occupational ideal, an ideal settlement, and finally, an ideal whole. Each element, in the perpetual process of evolution, is being pulled between potential extremes of good and evil.[23] In various stances in history, for example, the Hunter could be incarnated in a positive king or a destructive warrior; constructive Shepherds are often incarnated in spiritual leaders, thus determining the faith of their societies.[24]

The Valley Section also illustrated the relationship between the city and its region. While civic life was the crown and fulfillment of regional life, the

A.3
"The Valley in the Town."
From "Talks from My Outlook Tower," The Survey, 1925, Strythclyde University Archives.

MINER WOODMAN HUNTER SHEPHERD POOR PEASANT PEASANT FISHER
(METALWORK)(BUILDER) (SOLDIER) (RELIGIOUS WEAVER CARAVANEER) (BANKER) (LAWYER & POLITICIAN) (MERCHANT & NAVY.)

contribution of the region to the city was also of immense importance, including, for example, retaining the historic stages of civilization and the simple origins of urban institutions.[25] "It takes a region to make a city," Geddes proclaimed, meaning that the elements of the Valley Section are fully manifested in the city; he regarded urban occupations to be derivatives of the regional natural ones (Fig. A.3).[26] The city – under this interpretation, an accumulated expression of the natural occupations – can thus also be read as a historical chart of the evolution of human life.[27]

Finally, a good relationship amongst the Section's components implies the successful evolution of the valley as a whole. Proper development of individuals would lead to the evolvement of proper society and successful region, resulting in peace rather than war (Fig A.4).[28]

The Masque of Learning (1912) presented various phases of successful integrations of the components of the Valley Section, which result in a cultural summit, and presented their inherited "Heritage and Burden."[29] *The Tree of History* or the Arbor Saeculorum is a comprehensive symbolic representation of the evolution of the world's civilizations, presenting major historical eras and their main characteristics. The stem of the tree is wrapped in a spiral of smoke leading to a bud at the top, symbolizing the evolvement of human history and its future. The branches of the tree consist of groups of four leaves for each period, representing the four major groups of society, as described by August Comte, and embraced by Geddes, as *People, Chiefs ('temporals'), Intellectuals,* and *Emotionals ('spirituals').* The

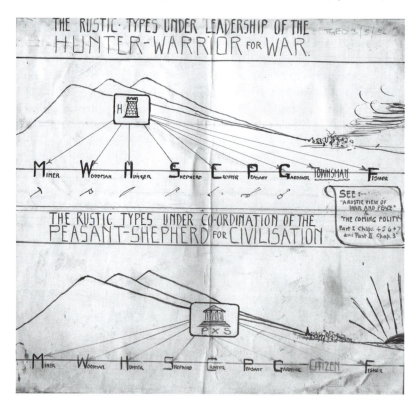

A.4
Success and failure of the "Valley Section" symbolizing rustic types under leadership of the Hunter Warrior for War and under co-ordination of the Peasant-Shepherd for Civilization. *Strathclyde University Archives and Special Collections.*

different stages in the Tree are, from the bottom to the top, the Hebrew Civilization; the Greek civilizations; the Roman Empire; the Middle Ages; the Renaissance; the French Revolution; and finally, the current Industrial Age. The butterflies at the top symbolize the future, Neotechnic, 'eutopian' age (see Chapter 6, Fig. 2).

India, representing several Eastern cultures, is described as an empire of "vast philosophies and comprehensive symbolisms."[30] India is also home of the castes, Sudra, Vaisya, Brahmin, Kshatrya which are easily paralleled to the typical Occidental ones: "These four great castes not only India but every other civilization has more or less developed . . . labourers and merchants, priests and warriors . . . from these four initial castes of India later castes have differentiated . . . has not the same happened once and again in the West . . .?"[31]

III. The Ideal City

"This tree of history, the observant traveller will find in every city he visits, every village, often hamlet even. Upon the changing town-plan, with its corresponding monuments, edifices, survivals of all kinds, he reconstructs the main aspect of its branchings, and this often in the strangest completeness of detail."[32] An ideal city is where the full representation of the four groups in the city occurs, boasting of a cultured society and bettered individuals;[33] thanks to its historic buildings, the city is also where Comte's schematic division of society could be most easily discerned.[34]

In the attempt to supply comprehensive analytic tools, Geddes devised various diagrammatic "thinking machines," affording a compilation of facts and dates and allowing their orderly arrangement and comparison. *The Charting of Life* presents a working scheme for the advised evolution of an individual, a society and a city (Fig. A.5). As a comprehensive table, it portrays all anticipated changes, as the overall quadruple progress represents the four evolutionary steps of rising conscious-ness and change a town has to go through on its way to becoming a proper City.[35]

The "Town" at the top left corner (Chapter 6, Fig. 3) is the outcome of the basic relationship between *Place*, *Work* and *Folk*, a spontaneous or planned nucleus of occupational, military, administrative, educational, or spiritual nature.[36] Its accumulated experience develops into local tradition, which is represented in the bottom left square by the "School" of thought. The *School*, however, is eventually condemned for stagnation, reflecting the communal decay.[37] The local tradition, represented by the local School, is examined and criticized, first by a small group and later by an institute signified here by "a medieval *Cloister*, University, Studia," represented in the lower right square, and back into the incipient, future, *City*. The Town, the School, the Cloister and the City, all archetypal types of contemporary institutes, represent the suggested process of progression, from "the individual's activities" to "highest deeds in City."[38]

IV. The Acropolis

As the actual site of the transforming function, the civic center was the place of interaction "of dream and deed, with religion and polity, with thought and action, art and drama," and physically manifested by "Acropolis, Temple, Academe and Theatre."[39] Geddes' index museums, outlook towers, and the universities, according

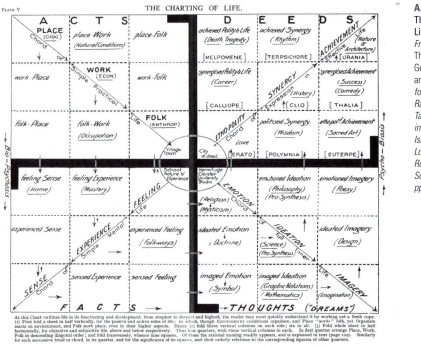

A.5
The Charting of Life.
*From A. Defries,
The Interpreter
Geddes: The Man
and his Gospel,
foreword by
Rabindranath
Tagore,
introduction by
Israel Zangwill.
London: George
Routledge &
Sons, 1927,
pp. 128–9.*

to Welter, can be grouped under the term *academe*. The *Theatre* was the place to perform masques and to celebrate the city with communal events. The *Temple* is a religious or quasi religious building or space, symbolizing the spiritual achievements of the City,[40] while the *Acropolis* itself refers to both to the final assemblage of the four, and to its physical location within the urban fabric.

Notes

Introduction

1 Latest works about Geddes include: V. M. Welter, J. Lawson (eds), *The City after Patrick Geddes*, Bern: Peter Lang, 2000, a result of an international symposium held at the University of Edinburgh in 1998; G. Ferraro, *Rieducazione alla Speranza: Patrick Geddes Planner in India, 1914–1924*, Milano: Jaca Books, 1998; V. M. Welter, *Biopolis: Patrick Geddes and the City of Life*, Cambridge, MA: The MIT Press, 2002; F. Fowle and B. Thomson (eds), *Patrick Geddes: The French Connection*, Oxford: White Cockade, 2004; W. Stephen (ed.), *Think Global, Act Local: The Life and Legacy of Patrick Geddes*, Edinburgh: Luath Press, 2004; last two were published following Geddes' 150 years centennial.

2 See elaboration and discussion in Part I.

3 H. Meller, *Patrick Geddes: Social Evolutionist and City Planner*, London: Routledge, 1990, p. 156; Ferraro, *Patrick Geddes Planner in India*, p. 28; I. B. Whyte, "The Spirit of the City," in Welter and Lawson, *The City after Patrick Geddes*, p. 30. See elaboration and discussion in Part I.

4 See Part I, Chapter 3.

5 P. Burgess, "Should Planning History Hit the Road? An Examination of the State of Planning History in the United States," *Planning Perspectives* 11, 1996, 201; A. Sutcliffe, "Why Planning History?" *Built Environment* 7(1), 1981, 65–7; G. E. Cherry, "Today's Issues in a 20th Century Perspective," *The Planner* 11, January 1991, 7–11; H. Meller, *Towns, Plans and Society in Modern Britain*, prepared for the Economic History Society, Cambridge: Cambridge University Press, 1997, pp. 1–7; P. Hall, "The Centenary of Modern Planning," in R. Freestone (ed.), *Urban Planning in a Changing World: The Twentieth Century Experience*, London: E. & F.N. Spon, 2000, pp. 20–39.

6 L. Sandercock, "Introduction: Framing Insurgent Historiographies for Planning," in L. Sandercock (ed.), *Making the Invisible Visible: A Multicultural Planning History*, Berkeley and London: University of California Press, 1998, p. 3.

7 Ibid., p. 2.

8 Ibid.

9 R. Freestone, "Learning from Planning's Histories," in R. Freestone, *Urban Planning in a Changing World*, p. 5. Peter Hall's book, a contemporary classic, is illustratively described as "an authoritative thematic-chronological overview of Western planning theory and practice from a late modern perspective, tidying up much of the received wisdom of planning history and updating it to the present-day through a grand paradigmatic evolution driven by the prescience and wisdom of a pantheon of visionaries," p. 6.

10 L. Sandercock, *Cosmopolis II: Mongrel Cities in the 21st Century*, London and New York: Continuum, 2003, pp. 39–40.

11 A. Sutcliffe, "Why Planning History?"; R. Freestone, "Introduction," in R. Freestone (ed.), *Urban Planning in a Changing World*, p. 1.

12 R. A. Beauregard, "Subversive Histories: Texts from South Africa," in L. Sandercock (ed.), *Making the Invisible Visible*, pp. 184–97; J. Muller, "Although God Cannot Alter the Past, Historians Can: Reflections on the Writing of Planning Histories," *Planning History* 21(2), 1999, 11–9; Sandercock, "Introduction," in *Making the Visible Visible*, pp. 2–5.

13 Beauregard, "Subversive Histories," p. 184.

14 I. Borden, J. Rendell and H. Thomas, "Knowing Different Cities: Reflections on Recent European Writings on Cities and Planning History," in Sandercock (ed.), *Making the Invisible Visible*, p. 135.

15 Sandercock, "Introduction," p. 1.

16 Ibid., pp. 6, 1, 20.

17 Muller, "Planning Histories," p. 15, quoting H. White, *The Content of the Form: Narrative Discourse and Historical Representation*, Baltimore, MD: Johns Hopkins University Press, 1987.

18 D. Krueckeberg, "Planning History's Mistakes," *Planning Perspectives* 12, 1997, 269–79; Sandercock, *Cosmopolis II*, p. 37.

19 O. Yiftachel, "Planning and Social Control: Exploring the Dark Side," *Journal of Planning Literature* 12(4), 1998, 403–4; see also M. C. Sies and C. Silver, "Introduction," in M. C. Sies and C. Silver (eds.), *Planning the 20th Century American City*, Baltimore, MD: Johns Hopkins University Press, 1996, p. 8.

20 I. Borden, J. Rendell and H. Thomas, "Knowing Different Cities: Reflections on Recent European Writings on Cities and Planning History," in Sandercock (ed.), *Making the Invisible Visible*, p. 137.

21 G. Cherry, "Biographies and Planning History," in *Pioneers in British Planning*, London: The Architectural Press, 1981, p. 4.

22 "The Great Man Theory of History," E. H. Carr, *What is History?* Harmondsworth: Penguin, 1965, p. 107, quoted in Muller, "Planning Histories," p. 14.

23 D. A. Krueckeberg, "Between Self and Culture or What are Biographies of Planners About?" *Journal of the American Planning Association* 59(2), Spring 1993, 217–21; Muller, "Planning Histories," pp. 11–13.

24 Krueckeberg, "Planning History's Mistakes."

25 Muller, "Planning Histories," p. 11, 13.

26 Sandercock, "Introduction," p. 14; see also M. C. Sies and C. Silver, "Introduction," in M. C. Sies and C. Silver, *Planning the 20th Century American City*, Baltimore, MD, and London: Johns Hopkins University Press, 1996, p. 24.

27 "Any consideration of the past must use some kind of mediating concept to negotiate between its specific substance and the present condition of the historian. Theory is the making explicit of this negotiation, setting out the interpretive agenda not as an implicit invisible subterfuge but as a necessarily implicated set of thought processes." Borden, Rendell and Thomas, "Knowing Different Cities," in Sandercock (ed.), *Making the Invisible Visible*, pp. 137–8; Muller, "Planning Histories," p. 16.

28 Krueckeberg, "Between Self and Culture."

29 J. J. Ferreira and S. S. Jha (eds), *The Outlook Tower: Essays on Urbanization in Memory of Patrick Geddes*, Department of Sociology, University of Bombay, Bombay: Popular Prakashan, 1976 [Upon the Golden Jubilee of the Department of Sociology 1969]; W. Stephen (ed.), *Think Global, Act Local: The Life and Legacy of Patrick Geddes*, Edinburgh: Luath Press, 2004.

30 J. A. Hasselgren, "What is Living and What is Dead in the Work of Patrick Geddes?" in *Patrick Geddes: A Symposium*, University of Dundee, Special Occasional Paper in Town and Regional Planning, (1 March 1982), an event organised by the Department of Town and Regional Planning to celebrate the centenary of the foundation of the university, pp. 43–4.

31 Ibid., pp. 31, 33–6.

32 M. Bell, R. Butlin and M. Heffernan (eds), *Geography and Imperialism 1820–1940*, Studies in Imperialism, New York: Manchester University Press, 1995, p. 4.

33 H. Meller, "Geddes and his Indian Reports," in *Patrick Geddes: A Symposium*, p. 5.

1 The Town Planner as a Miracle Worker: Patrick Geddes, 1854–1932

1 H. Carter, "The Garden of Geddes," *The Forum* 54, October 1915, 455–71; (November 1915) pp. 588–95; G. Gardiner, *Pillars of Society*, London: James Nisbet & Co., 1913, p. 183, 185; A.

Defries, *The Interpreter Geddes: The Man and his Gospel*, London: George Routledge & Sons, 1927, p. 104.

2   Various contributions to Defries' book illustrate this. Israel Zangwill admits to having "neglected him as grossly as the bulk of his contemporaries have done"; "The Apostle of Eutopia," in *The Interpreter Geddes*, p. 10. Lewis Mumford suggests a few answers to the polemic question, "Who is Patrick Geddes?" marveling at his various professional endeavors; "Who is Patrick Geddes?" (From *The Survey*, New York, 1925) in ibid., pp. 1–7. Sir Chimanlal Setalvad, vice-chancellor of the University of Bombay and Minister of Public Works wonders at the little recognition Geddes received in Britain, being personally impressed by Geddes' "quixotical personality who dabbled in almost everything under the sun"; "Geddes in India," in ibid., pp. 327, 329.

3   "Geddes and Edinburgh," (from I. Zangwill's "Without Prejudice," first published in *Pall Mall Magazine* February 1895[6?]), in Defries, ibid., pp. 315–16; J. Mavor, in *My Windows on the Street of the World*, vol. 1, London: J. M. Dent & Sons; New York: E. P. Dutton & Co., 1923, pp. 213–16.

4   Carter, "The Garden of Geddes," pp. 592–3; see also Gardiner, *Pillars of Society*, p. 183.

5   Mavor, *My Windows on the Street of the World*, p. 216; C. Zueblin, "The World's First Sociological Laboratory," *American Journal of Sociology* 4(5), March 1899, 577–92; Carter, "The Garden of Geddes," p. 471.

6   W. I. Stevenson, "Patrick Geddes and Geography: Biobibliographical Study," *Occasional Papers* 27, 1975, Department of Geography, University College London, p. 9.

7   Defries, *The Interpreter Geddes*, p. 104.

8   After H. E. Meller, "Patrick Geddes: An Analysis of his Theory of Civics, 1880–1914," *Victorian Studies* 16(3), 1973, 293.

9   E. Aves, "*City Development: A study of Parks, Gardens, and Culture-Institutes, A Report to the Carnegie Dunfermline Trust*, by Patrick Geddes [book review]," *The Economic Journal* 16(62), 1906, 243–6; P. Geddes, "Civics: As Applied Sociology," Discussion, *Sociological Papers* I, edited by the Editorial Committee, Sociological Society, London: Macmillan, 1905, pp. 141–3.

10 "Only the *Morning Leader* managed the perspicacious remark of calling Geddes 'a revolutionary conservative,'" NLS MS/10612/165, quoted in H. Meller, *Patrick Geddes: Social Evolutionist and City Planner*, London: Routledge, 1990, p. 168.

11 October 1904, NLS MS/10536 in Meller, ibid.

12 2 August 1904, NLS MS 10536 in Meller, ibid.

13 C. Booth, "Civics: As Applied Sociology," Discussion, pp. 127–9; W. Crane, ibid., p. 131.

14 T. Barclay, ibid., pp. 124–5.

15 P. Abercrombie, "Geddes as Town Planner," in A. Defries, *The Interpreter Geddes*, p. 323.

16 "Town Planning Conference of the Royal Institute of British Architects," *Town Planning Review* 1(3), 1910, 180, 182.

17 P. Boardman, *Patrick Geddes: Maker of the Future*, Chapel Hill: University of North Carolina Press, 1944, p. 251.

18 Abercrombie, "Geddes as Town Planner," p. 323.

19 Meller explains that Geddes was never invited to exhibit in Birmingham and in Manchester due to his failure in gaining the support of T. C. Horsfall, who worked in the slums of Manchester since the 1880s, and J. S. Nettlefold, a housing pioneer and industrialist from Birmingham. Meller, *Patrick Geddes*, pp. 160, 179. See also P. Chabard, "Competing Scales in Transnational Networks: The Impossible Travel of Patrick Geddes' Cities Exhibition to America 1911–1913," *Urban History* 36(2), 2009, 202–22 and for an analysis of the failure of Geddes' exhibition to display both in Britain and in the United States and a visual image of Geddes' failed targets for displaying the exhibition, p. 204.

20 "A Town Plan for Dublin," *Town Planning Review* 5(1), 1914, 68; "Dublin Competition and Exhibition," ibid., 5(2), 1914, 172–3; "Civic Exhibition, Dublin," ibid., 5(3), 1914, 249.

21 Meller, *Patrick Geddes*, p. 189.

22 Defries, *The Interpreter Geddes*, p. 87.

23   "Editorial Notes," *The Advocate*, 2 March 1916.

24   "Professor Geddes on Town-Planning in India, an Interview," *The Advocate*, 1–2 March 1916, 2 March 1916. "Professor Geddes, we are delighted to hear, has decided to devote a series of lectures to the problems of planning an ideal Calcutta and it is obvious that he is going to have much of interest to say . . ." "Town Planning, Speech by Lord Carmichael: Professor Geddes at the Town Hall," *The Statesman*, 21 November 1915; a series of articles reporting on Geddes' exhibition and lectures in Calcutta, *The Statesman*, November 1915; "Town Planning: Professor Geddes' Fifth Lecture," *The Statesman*, 26 November 1915; "Town Planning," *Bengalee*, 25 November 1915; "The Town-Planning Exhibition," *The Empire*, 27 November 1915; "Town Planning Exhibition, Nagpur," *Nagpur & Berar Times*, 22 January 1916; "those interested in the future development of Lucknow . . . will now have an opportunity of studying the subject under exceptionally advantageous conditions," "The Civic Exhibition of Cities and Town Planning," *The Indian Daily Telegraph*, 24 February 1916; "Taking advantage of his visit to the Exhibition of Cities and Town-planning which is being held at Kaiserbagh Baradari, Lucknow, our special representative called on Professor Patrick Geddes to ascertain his views on the town-planning movement that is spreading in this country"; "Civic Exhibition," *The Indian Daily Telegraph*, 15 March 1916; followed by a series of articles on 22 March 1916, 23 March 1916, 26 March 1916, and more.

25   It should be noted also that neither H. V. Lanchester's nor Linton Bogle's much-appreciated works about town planning in India, written at the time, mention Geddes in any way.

26   A "Special Town Planning Number" of *The Palestine Weekly* 1(39), 1920, was devoted to discussing Geddes' Town Planning Exhibition and to support his contributions.

27   S. B. "The New Jerusalem" [n.d.] T-GED 1/7/25.

28   For example: "Prof. Patrick Geddes' Report on the Possibility of Improvement of Jerusalem, submitted to the Chief Administrator of Palestine," *Town Planning Review* 11(8), 1921, 190.

29   Boardman, *Patrick Geddes, Maker of the Future*, p. 355.

30   "[T]he longing to return to simpler and healthier conditions has engendered the wish on the part of the colonists to acquire even in their towns some of the beauty and closeness to nature that is to be found in the country . . . the practical outcome of their kinship to this movement is exemplified in most of the new Jewish colonies." "Jewish Settlements in Palestine," *Garden Cities and Town Planning* 11(8), 1921, 190–1; D. Trietsch, "Garden Cities for Palestine," *Garden Cities and Town Planning* 13(1), 1923, 11–12; "Town-Planning in Palestine," *Garden Cities and Town Planning* 15(11), 1925, 267–8. About the work of the Jewish Architect Richard Kauffmann; "R. Kauffman, Planning of Jewish Settlements in Palestine," *The Town Planning Review* 22(2), 1926, 93–116; and P. Geddes, "The City of Jerusalem," *Garden Cities and Town Planning* 11, 1921, 251–4.

31   "Haifa's Future, Vision of the Town Beautiful: Interview with Prof. Geddes," *The Egyptian Gazette* (15 September 19?) CZM L18/80-11.

32   C. Zueblin to Geddes, 17 April 1920, NLS MS10546/135-7; T. Adams to Geddes, 5 September 1921, NLS MS10547/43: "I enclose a leading article from the *Citizen* of Ottawa, on 'Town Planning new Jerusalem.' I see from this and from another clipping containing your photograph that you are placed in the rank of the knights and I presume this is only slightly premature. I should be grateful to hear a little more of your contemplated work at Jerusalem, so that we can give some accurate facts regarding it in our publication."

33   "Proposed Hebrew University," *The Architect*, 6 November 1920; "If and when completed, the Hebrew University will undoubtedly be the greatest and noblest structure of its kind, and would be the most inspiring house of learning ever conceived, as well a the grandest and most eloquent symbol of the renaissance of Judaism and the restoration of the Jewish people." S. D., "The Hebrew University in Jerusalem," *The Jewish Chronicle*, 30 April 1920, T-GED 12/2/335; S. B. [Sybella Branford?], "The Hebrew University in Jerusalem," *Nature* 115(2897), 9 May 1925, 681–2. See also "The New University at Jerusalem," *The Graphic* 16(2884), 1925 [London]; "Lord Balfour leaves England this month on a visit to the Holy Land, during which he will open the new University of Jerusalem." "The New University at Jerusalem," *The Observer*, 1 March

1925; "Industries of the University: Further Talk with Professor Geddes," *The Palestine Weekly*, 10 April 1925; P. Geddes, "The Hebrew University of Jerusalem," *Sunday School Chronicle and Times*, 21 May 1925; "Professor Patrick Geddes on the Site and Design," *The Scotsman*, May 1925. Geddes attended the ceremony also on behalf of the President of the Sociological Society, Sir Francis Younghusband, as reported in *The Sociological Review* next to a letter by Geddes' written as a member of Council. The Zionist University, *The Sociological Review* 17, 1925, 223–4. See also H. Sacher, "The Hebrew University at Jerusalem, to be Opened on April 1: Working out a Great Idea," *Manchester Guardian*, 16 March 1925.

34   Defries, *The Interpreter Geddes*, p. 271.

35   J. Bryce, "Proposed National Institute of Geography," *The Scottish Geographical Magazine* 18, 1902, 217; A. Geikie, ibid., 219; C. R. Markham, ibid., 218.

36   Meller, *Patrick Geddes*, p. 143. Geddes' papers dealing with planning directly or indirectly were published mainly by *The Sociological Review*. Geddes also published in various planning journals, complaining of "geographic small-mindedness and bickering tedious." According to Stevenson, "the only geographical journal he held in any regard" was *The Scottish Geographical Magazine*, where he chose to publish the Edinburgh Report (1902), Occasional Papers, p. 8.

37   Meller, *Patrick Geddes*, p. 143; E. Howard, "Civics: As Applied Sociology," pp. 119–22.

38   J. M. Robertson, ibid., pp. 122–4; T. Barclay, ibid., pp. 124–5; "It is very interesting to 'survey' history in the course of a summer ramble to the ruins of some old monastery, but unless the monks had kept records of what had been done there in bygone days, the mere outward survey will not carry us further than Patrick Geddes is carried in the very general map which he makes of the whole field of history. In other words, history, in any proper, sense, demands more than 'survey' in Patrick Geddes's sense of the word." J. H. Harley, ibid., pp. 131–3.

39   W. I. Thomas, ibid., pp. 135–6; Harley, ibid., pp. 131–3.

40   Robertson, ibid., pp. 122–4; see also Booth, ibid., pp. 127–9.

41   "It is extremely interesting to speculate that the Place de l'Etoile is an evolution from the plan of the game-forest, with its shooting avenues radiating from a centre, but it would be difficult to show that there is any historical connection. The thing is not proved." Robertson, ibid., pp. 122–4; "The value of the surroundings depends at least as much upon the capacity of the individual citizen, singly and collectively, to utilise what he or she is brought in contact with as upon the peculiarities of these surroundings themselves . . . and they vary form age to age and in place and place." J. L. Tayler, ibid., pp. 125–7.

42   Meller, *Patrick Geddes*, p. 144; C. Booth, "Civics: As Concrete and Applied Sociology, Part II, Discussion," *Sociological Papers* II, published for the Sociological Society, London: Macmillan & Co., 1906, pp. 112–13.

43   Swinny, in ibid., pp. 113–14; "Would Geddes Consider it the Duty of Any Londoner . . . to Map out London, and also the Surrounding Districts?" E. S. Weymouth, ibid., pp. 116–17.

44   "The Museum and the City: A Practical Proposal, Read at the Dundee Conference, 1907," Reprinted from *The Museums Journal*, 1908, 371–82, T-GED 5/3/26.

45   G. Ferraro, "Il gioco del piano. Patrick Geddes in India 1914–1924," *Urbanistica* 103, 1995, 152 ref. 19; P. Geddes, "Regional and City Surveys as Affording Policy and Theory for Town Planning and City Design," *Town Planning Institute Papers and Discussion* 3, 1920–1, 119–27; "Discussion," ibid., 128–31.

46   J. Tyrwhitt, introduction to *Cities in Evolution by Patrick Geddes*, edited by the Outlook Tower Association Edinburgh and the Association for Planning and Regional Reconstruction, London. New and revised edition, London: Williams & Norgate, 1949, p. xi.

47   G. G. C., "Cities in Evolution: An Introduction to the Town Planning Movement and to the Study of Civics (review)," *The Geographical Journal* 47(4), 1916, 309–11.

48   F. K. Teggart, "Science and Politics: The Coming Polity: A Study in Reconstruction (book review)," *Geographical Review* 9(4), 1920, 366.

49 Meller, *Patrick Geddes*, p. 317; "at that period the Outlook Tower was an all-but-deserted place . . . as if to jeer at Geddes' actual presence, everything had crumbled and fallen apart." L. Mumford, "The Disciple's Rebellion: A Memoir of Patrick Geddes," *Encounter* 27(3), 1966, 17.

50 P. Abercrombie, "Geddes as Town Planner," in A. Defries, *The Interpreter Geddes*, p. 324.

51 Meller, *Patrick Geddes*, pp. 155–7; 293–300. "Professor Geddes has published some most helpful and stimulating essays on this subject [the Survey]; and although it may not always be practicable to carry the survey to the extent suggested by him, there can be no doubt about its importance." R. Unwin, *Town Planning in Practice*, London: T. Fisher, 1994 (1909), p. 141; "Geddes was the first to direct attention to the need to classify and study the functions of the several components of these complex [regional] communities"; "In England we have specialized in regional surveys, rather than civic . . . so far there have been few intensive studies of single cities . . . Geddes' Edinburgh has not yet been reduced to workable dimensions"; Chapter 2, "A Theory of Civic Planning: Regional Studies" has no mention of Geddes. P. Abercrombie, *Town and Country Planning*, London: Thornton Butterworth, 1933, pp. 22, 130. See also M. Miller, "Raymond Unwin 1863–1940"; G. Dix, "Patrick Abercrombie 1879–1957"; G. Cherry, "George Pepler 1882–1959," in G. Cherry, *Pioneers in British Planning*, London: The Architectural Press, 1981, pp. 72–102, 103–30, 131–49 respectively.

52 For example, Dr. Marion Newbigen, who wrote about regional surveys in 1913, did not mention Geddes at all. Meller, *Patrick Geddes*, p. 136.

53 Ibid., pp. 303–4.

54 S. K. Ratcliffe, "A Light that Lighted other Minds," *The Sociological Review* 24, 1932, 366–7.

55 G. Slater, "Illuminations . . . as by Flashes of Lightning," ibid., 372–3; Sir A. Thomson, "Obituary: Sir Patrick Geddes," *The Times*, 19 April 1932; "One Who Loved his Fellow-men: Sir Patrick Geddes, A Long Life of Doing Good for Each and all," *Children's Newspaper*, 27 April 1932.

56 "ARTIFEX," "Sir Patrick Geddes: Town Planner, Scientist, and Social Reformer," *The Irish Builder and Engineer*, 7 May 1932; "One Who Loved his Fellow-men"; C. R. A., "Sir Patrick Geddes," *The Times*, 21 April 1932; K. Ratcliffe, "A Light that Lighted other Minds."

57 D. Price, "At Montpellier," *The Sociological Review* 24,1932, 379.

58 "Humanity and Town Planning," *The Birmingham Post* quoted in "Notes and News," *Garden Cities and Town Planning* 12(4), 1932, 113; also E. McGegan, "Geddes as a Man of Action," *The Sociological Review* 24,1932, 355–7; K. Ratcliffe, "A Light that Lighted other Minds."

59 "Notes and News"; C. R. A., "Sir Patrick Geddes."

60 "One Who Loved his Fellow-men"; "Obituary: Professor Sir Patrick Geddes," *Journal of Town Planning Institute* 18(7), 1932, 184; Ratcliffe, "A Light that Lighted other Minds"; "Death of Famous Scotsman, Sir Patrick Geddes; Distinguished Work in Many Spheres," *Glasgow Herald*, 18 April 1932; "Sir Patrick Geddes: Noted Scot's Death in France, Town Planning Pioneer," *The Scotsman*, 18 April 1932; McGegan, "Geddes as a Man of Action"; The Earl of Sandwich: Lord Lieutenant of Hunts, "The Saving of Crosby Hall," *The Sociological Review* 24, 362–4; R. Stevenson, "The Social Reformer," *The Sociological Review* 24, 1932, 353–4.

61 *The Scotsman.*

62 McGegan, "Geddes as a Man of Action."

63 See, for example, "Obituary: Professor Sir Patrick Geddes."

64 McGegan, "Geddes as a Man of Action."

65 C. R. A., "Sir Patrick Geddes."

66 Ibid.; "ARTIFEX," "Sir Patrick Geddes."

67 *Glasgow Herald*, 18 April 1932; *The Scotsman*; Sir Patrick Geddes, "Biology and Town Planning," *The Times*, 18 April 1932; McGegan, "Geddes as a Man of Action"; Thomson, "Obituary: Sir Patrick Geddes."

68 Thomson, "Obituary: Sir Patrick Geddes"; "One Who Loved his Fellow-men"; "ARTIFEX," "Sir Patrick Geddes"; "Notes and News."

69 C. R. A., "Sir Patrick Geddes"; "Sir Patrick Geddes"; H. V. Lanchester, "Town Planning in India," *The Sociological Review* 24, 1932, 370–1.

70 Thompson, "Obituary: Professor Sir Patrick Geddes."

71 "Staff and Board of Survey Associates, From New York," *The Sociological Review* 24,1932 380.

72 "Only by degrees there came a realisation that each one of his undertakings was related to a central idea . . . an overgrowing desire to find means of declaring the unity of science and art, of experience and expression, in an age of too many detached specialised activities . . . His great contribution towards the art of Town planning lies largely in his insistence on broad-based preliminary study, carried far beyond statistical and technical data, and directed towards better understanding of the peculiar and unique spirit of any given place . . . So he interpreted the temples, the cathedrals, and so he planned the university of Jerusalem . . . So too he planned his outlook towers, as centres of regional and local surveys." F. C. M., *Architectural Review* [MS10652/55].

73 McGegan, "Geddes as a Man of Action."

74 "ARTIFEX," "Sir Patrick Geddes."

75 M. Pentland, "An Ideal Rising from the Real," *The Sociological Review* 24,1932, 368–9.

76 "ARTIFEX," "Sir Patrick Geddes."

77 "Better Indian Cities: Sir P. Geddes Dead," *Times of India*, 19 April 1932.

78 R. Mukerjee, "In India," *The Sociological Review* 24, 1932, 374–5.

79 Slater, "Illuminations . . ." *The Sociological Review* 24, 1932, 372–3; "ARTIFEX," *The Irish Builder and Engineer*.

80 "The Late Sir Patrick Geddes: Report on Town Planning in Colombo," *Times of Ceylon*, 25 April 1932.

81 "The work of Patrick Geddes in India was of exceptional value owing to his sensitive perception of the historic continuity of Indian ideals and methods and to being able to visualise the fact that the right course was . . . to recapture the highly developed civilisation of the past. Geddes . . . could free himself from 'Western bias' and thus his general solutions were historically logical – evolutionary rather than destructive . . . The educated Indian as a rule takes a greater pleasure in mental exercises than in their practical application, and the demonstrations of principles of action was greatly appreciated even when the effort to put these into operation too often failed to produce results." Lanchester, "Town Planning in India."

82 Stevenson, "The Social Reformer"; "Death of Famous Scotsman."

83 C. R. A., "Sir Patrick Geddes"; "ARTIFEX," "Sir Patrick Geddes"; Slater, "Illuminations . . ."

84 Slater, "Illuminations . . . ."

85 "[T]hat this magnificent conception [the university] has not yet been realised is due, not to Geddes, nor to the architects who worked with him and under his directions [. . .] Suffice it to say that there are few who could rise to the lofty heights of Geddes's imagination or of his practical knowledge. Petty minds have endeavoured to bespoil what Geddes and his two assistants had conceived on noble and enduring lines. [. . .] I would not have it thought that Geddes's sojourn and work for Palestine were a failure." D. Eder, "In Palestine," *The Sociological Review* 24,1932, 376–8.

2 1940s–1960s: Geddes' Role in Reconstruction

1 A. Geddes, "Patrick Geddes as a Sociologist" [from a lecture given at the Outlook Tower to the Sociological Group in December 1933, edited by Mrs. J. Geddes from a single manuscript] in J. J. Ferreira and S. S. Jha (eds), *The Outlook Tower: Essays on Urbanization in Memory of Patrick Geddes*, Department of Sociology, University of Bombay [upon the Golden Jubilee of the Department of Sociology, 1969] Bombay: Popular Prakashan, 1976, pp. 14–19; E. McGegan, "The Life and Work of Professor Sir Patrick Geddes: Biographical," *Journal of the Town Planning Institute* 26, 1940, 189–91; A. Geddes, "The Life and Work of Professor Sir Patrick Geddes: His Indian Reports and their Influence," ibid., 191–4; F. Mears, "The Life and Work of Professor Sir Patrick Geddes: Geddes' Contribution to Planning in Evolution," ibid., 194–5.

2 P. Boardman, *Patrick Geddes: Maker of the Future*, Chapel Hill: University of North Carolina Press, 1944. It may also be noted that Boardman's account was based on imperial perception as Geddes's mission is described as the extension of the responsibility of the British government; in Ireland though is not British but Scottish; and in India he is not understood at all by the government officials. Boardman wrote an earlier monograph about Geddes, describing him as an educationalist: *Esquisse de l'Oeuver educatrice de Patrick Geddes*, Montpellier: Imprimerie de la Charite, 1936. Mumford claims that Geddes found Boardman too late, meaning that he might have been the collaborator whom he had been searching. "The Disciple's Rebellion: A Memoir of Patrick Geddes," *Encounter* 27(3), 1966, 18.

3 H. W. Odum, "Patrick Geddes' Heritage to 'The Making of the Future'," *Social Forces* 22(3), 1944, 275, 278. Meller describes Odum's own work as directly affected by Geddes. H. Meller, *Patrick Geddes: Social Evolutionist and City Planner*, London: Routledge, 1990, p. 322.

4 P. Boardman, "Not Housing But Home-Building: The Life-Centered Approach of Patrick Geddes," reprinted from *Teknisk Ukeblad* (no. 30), Kronprinsensgt 17, Oslo, Norway, 1948, p. 8 [ref. 1]; V. M. Welter, "Stages of an Exhibition: The Cities and Town Planning Exhibition of Patrick Geddes," *Planning History* 20(1), 1998, 25–35.

5 *Patrick Geddes in India*, edited by J. Tyrwhitt, with an Introduction by L. Mumford and a preface by H. V. Lanchaster, London: Lund Humphries, 1947.

6 J. Tyrwhitt, "Editor's Note," in *Patrick Geddes in India*, p. 6.

7 H. V. Lanchester, preface to *Patrick Geddes in India*, p. 14.

8 B. Lasker, "Patrick Geddes in India" (book review), *Pacific Affairs* 21(1), 1948, 74–5.

9 C. B. F., "Patrick Geddes in India," edited by J. Tyrwhitt, review, *The Geographical Journal* 115(1–3), 1947, 115–16; Boardman, *Not Housing But Home-Building*, pp. 1–15.

10 Lasker, "Patrick Geddes in India" (book review), pp. 74–5. In 1948, Arthur Geddes published "Geography, Sociology, and Psychology: A Plea for Coordination, with an Example from India," *Geographical Review* 38(4), 1948, 590–7, showing the importance of the regional survey for understanding the psychology of communities and calling for sociology to widen its surveys from locality to region.

11 *Cities in Evolution by Patrick Geddes*, edited by the Outlook Tower Association Edinburgh and the Association for Planning and Regional Reconstruction, London. New and revised edition, London: Williams & Norgate, 1949, p. ix. The book omits mainly chapters regarding Geddes' visits to German cities and his comparative conclusions; it also omits an intriguing interpretation of the life of a Paleotechnic Cinderella and her Neotechnic future. Mumford claimed that the selection in the revised edition actually emphasized the non-systematic side of Geddes' thinking. L. Mumford, "The Geddesian Gambit," in F. G. Novak, Jr. (ed.), *Lewis Mumford and Patrick Geddes: The Correspondence*, London and New York: Routledge, 1995, p. 370.

12 Tyrwhitt, introduction to *Cities in Evolution*, pp. ix, x.

13 "[N]ow that simultaneous thinking [. . .] has become insisted upon in the popular writings of philosophical scientists; [. . .] Now [. . .] that every book published on popular psychology, give overwhelming evidence of the profound effects of the opportunities available in the immediate environment upon the physical and mental development of the individual." Ibid., p. x.

14 A. Geddes, introduction to P. Mairet, *Pioneer of Sociology: The Life and Letters of Patrick Geddes*, London: Lund Humphries, 1957, p. xx.

15 Mairet, *Pioneer of Sociology*, pp. 69, 78–9,143, 216.

16 Ibid., p. 119.

17 Ibid., pp. 162, 167.

18 Ibid., p. 184; "Had the British administration grasped his vision and applied and widened his technique, the subsequent history of Palestine would have been very different." Ibid., p. 185.

19 F. R. Stevenson, "Pioneer of Sociology: The Life and Letters of Patrick Geddes, by Philip Mairet" (book review), *Journal of the Town Planning Institute* 44, 1957–8, 20.

20 Ibid.

21 *Sir Patrick Geddes Centenary Celebrations*, report of a symposium held in the Edinburgh College of Art on Friday, 1 October 1954, Heriot-Watt University. A radio broadcast was devoted to Sir Geddes: "The father of modern town planning, a centenary tribute to a practical visionary," BBC November 1954, NLS MS10608/62-89.

22 Sir W. Holford, foreword to Mairet, *Pioneer of Sociology*, p. xii.

23 Ibid.

24 *Sir Patrick Geddes Centenary Celebrations*, pp. 5–12.

25 Ibid., pp. 36–7. Two years later Fleure wrote, "some would consider the pioneering of Regional Survey as Geddes' most notable contribution to practical life." H. J. Fleure, "Patrick Geddes (1854–1932)," *The Sociological Review* New Series, December 1953, 5–13.

26 *Sir Patrick Geddes Centenary Celebrations*, p. 4.

27 They were funded by Forbes Trust, which was founded in 1953 "to study and re-assess the thought and writings of Geddes." *Journal of the Town Planning Institute* 11(5), 1954, 117–18. According to J. Earley, who in 1953 spent three months at the Outlook Tower sorting Geddes' papers, the Tower did not retain much evidence from Geddes' era, containing mainly boxes of papers and only several maps. "Sorting in Patrick Geddes' Outlook Tower," *Places* 7(3), 1991, 64–71.

28 T. F. L., "Outlook Towers," *Journal of the Town Planning Institute* 11(6), 1954, 145–6.

29 F. R. S., "The Relevance of Geddes To-day," *Journal of the Town Planning Institute* 11(6), 1954, 209–11.

30 "Geddes on Letchworth" (November 1905); "Geddes on Dispersal" (April 1906); "Geddes on Suburbs" (August 1906), *Town and Country Planning* 23(126), October 1954, 518, 524, 526.

31 G. Pepler, "Geddes' Contribution to Town Planning," *Town Planning Review* 26, 1955–6, 19–24.

32 Ibid., p. 24.

33 D. Chapman, "The Common Sense of Patrick Geddes," *Town and Country Planning* 13(52), 1945–6, 161–2, 181.

34 R. N. Rudnose Brown, "Scotland and Some Trends in Geography: John Murray, Patrick Geddes and Andrew Herbertson," (abridged from the Herbertson Memorial Lecture delivered to the Royal Scottish Geographical Society and the Edinburgh Branch of the Association on 5 March 1948) *Geography* 33, 1948, 110. Rudnose Brown studied botany under Arthur Thomson at Aberdeen University, 1899. H. Meller, *Patrick Geddes: Social Evolutionist and City Planner*, London: Routledge, 1990, p. 137.

35 P. Turnbull, "Patrick Geddes and the Planning Unit Today," reprinted from *Quarterly Journal of the R.I.A.S.*, 1947, T-GED 1/6/45.

36 G. B. Barker, "Plan for Central and South East Scotland," *Town and Country Planning* 17(65), 1949, 40–3. In the same volume Geddes and Thomson were quoted "on Gardening," following an article "The Flight from the Cities"; P. Geddes and J. A. Thomson, *Evolution*, London: Williams and Norgate, 1912, in ibid., p. 111. Another major regional plan conducted in Scotland then was made for the Clyde Valley; P. Abercrombie and R. H. Matthew, *The Clyde Valley Regional Plan 1946: A Report*, Edinburgh: HMSO, 1946.

37 W. Ashworth, *The Genesis of Modern British Town Planning: A Study in Economic and Social History of the Nineteenth Century*, London: Routledge & Kegan Paul, 1954; J. P. Reynolds, "The Genesis of Modern British Town Planning" (book review), *Town Planning Review* 25(3), 1954, 231.

38 Ashworth, *The Genesis of Modern British Town Planning*, pp. 175–6.

39 I. B. Whyte, "The Spirit of the City," in V. M. Welter, J. Lawson (eds), *The City after Patrick Geddes*. Bern: Peter Lang, 2000, pp. 15–32.

40 Eric Mumford claimed that "Tyrwhitt often used the Valley Section as a way of emphasizing the importance of region and topography in town planning." *The CIAM Discourse on Urbanism, 1928–1960*, Cambridge, MA, and London: The MIT Press, 2000, p. 332 [ref. 141]. On Tyrwhitt, who "worked willingly as the 'woman behind the man' – notably as a disciple of Patrick Geddes," and her contribution to the Modern Movement in planning, see E. Shoshkes, "Jacqueline Tyrwhitt: A Founding Mother of Modern Urban Design," *Planning Perspectives*, 21 April 2006, 179–97.

Another prominent figure of the APRR fascinated with Geddes was Max Lock who, after World War II, followed Geddes to India. He was mostly impressed with Geddes' "consultancy" relationship with the community, using similar visual means of public exhibitions and popular ads. S. G. Leonard, "The Context and Legacy of Patrick Geddes in Europe," in Welter and Lawson, *The City after Patrick Geddes*, p. 83.

41 CIAM 8, London/Hoddesdon 1951, Commission 2 (Giedion, Rogers, Batista, Roth, Bakema), "Reunion of the Arts at the Core," working paper. Ove Arup Collection, Churchill Archives Centre, Cambridge, file 5/17, quoted in Boyd Whyte, "The Spirit of the City," in Welter and Lawson, *The City after Patrick Geddes*, pp. 30–1.

42 Whyte, "The Spirit of the City," p. 19.

43 Mumford, *The CIAM Discourse on Urbanism*, pp. 238–41, 251.

44 V. M. Welter, "Arthur Glikson, Thinking-Machines, and the Planning of Israel," in Welter and Lawson, *The City After Patrick Geddes*, p. 212.

45 Ibid., pp. 213–14. Glikson, claims Boardman, emphasized Geddes' synoptic method and his comprehensive yet concrete intellectual synthesis. "[Lewis] Mumford told the author that he counts Glikson as P.G.'s most understanding critic and interpreter and active follower in this generation." *The Worlds of Patrick Geddes: Biologist, Town Planner, Re-educator, Peace-Warrior*. London, Henley and Boston: Routledge & Kegan Paul, 1978, pp. 438–40.

46 A. Glikson, *Regional Planning and Development: Six Lectures Delivered at the Institute of Social Studies, at the Hague*, Leiden: A. W. Sijthoff's Uitgeversmaatschappij 1953, p. 63, quoted in Welter, *The City after Patrick Geddes*, p. 221. His main point of interest when using the Valley Section, claims Welter, was the hierarchical network of settlements; ibid., p. 221.

47 "Glikson adapted and adjusted the diagram to his own needs and ultimately translated the thoughts embodied in Geddes' graphic thinking tool into the language of architects and planners . . . In doing so, Glikson followed the example set by his friend Lewis Mumford . . . although both started their respective engagements with Geddes' thoughts by interpreting a specific Geddesian Thinking Machine, the notation of Life, this tool was in the end dispensable." Ibid., p. 226.

48 G. Bell and J. Tyrwhitt (eds), *Human Identity in the Urban Environment*, Baltimore, MD: Penguin Books, 1972, pp. 15–28.

49 R. Glass, "Urban Sociology in Great Britain: A Trend Report," *Current Sociology (La Sociologie Contemporaine)* 4(4), 1955, 5–19. Meller claims that Glass, while being completely dismissive of the Geddes/Branford school, was actually proving Geddes' point that the study of place requires an emotional commitment and that the future is dominated by the cultural values of past and present. Meller, *Patrick Geddes*, pp. 303–4.

50 R. Glass, "The Evaluation of Planning: Some Sociological Considerations," *UNESCO International Social Science Journal* 11(3), 1959, 393–409; "*Geddes was definitely not anti-urban*;" Meller, *Victorian Studies* 16(3), 1973, 298.

51 R. J. Halliday, "The Sociological Movement, the Sociological Society and the Genesis of Academic Sociology in Britain," *The Sociological Review* New Series 16, 1968, 377–98.

52 H. Kendall, *Jerusalem the City Plan: Preservation and Development During the British Mandate, 1917–1948*, London: HMSO, 1948.

53 *Jerusalem Master Plan, 1968*, Jerusalem: Municipality, 1972.

54 A. T. A. Learmonth, "Urban Improvements: A Strategy for Urban Works. Observations of Sir Patrick Geddes with Reference to Old Lahore" (book review), *The Geographical Journal* 132(4), 1966, 538, commenting on: *Urban Improvements: A Strategy for Urban Works*, Government of Pakistan Planning Commission (Physical Planning & Housing Section), Study no. 21, June 1965.

55 K. L. Gillion, *Ahmedabad: A Study in Indian Urban History*, Berkeley: University of California Press, 1968.

56 B. Yosskovitz, "Tichnun vePituach Tel Aviv-Yaffo" (Planning and Development of Tel Aviv – Yaffo), *Tichnun Svivati* 57, 1999, 60–4.

57   See, for example, Moshe Landa and Amiram Oesemnik (eds), *Our City Tel Aviv*. Tel Aviv: Jaffa Municipality, 1959 (Hebrew); A. Vardi (ed.), *The City of Wonders*, Tel Aviv: Lema'an Hasefer, 1959 (Hebrew); Y. Yaari-Polskin, *Meir Dizengoff – His Life and his Deeds*, Tel Aviv: Yishuv Publications, 1936.

58   N. Dunevitz, *Holot SheHayu LeKrach* (Sands which have turned into City), Jerusalem and Tel Aviv: Shocken, 1959, p. 83.

3 The Humanist Perspective: The Return of Geddes, 1970s Onwards

1   W. Lesser, "Patrick Geddes: The Practical Visionary," *Town Planning Review* 45(3), 1974, 311; P. D. Goist, "Patrick Geddes and the City," *Journal of American Institute of Planners* 40(1), January 1974, 32; H. Meller, "Patrick Geddes 1854–1932," in G. Cherry (ed.), *Pioneers in British Planning*, London: Architectural Press, 1981, p. 46; P. Clavel, "Ebenezer Howard and Patrick Geddes: Two Approaches to City Development," in K. C. Parsons and D. Schuyler (eds), *From Garden City to Green City: The Legacy of Ebenezer Howard*, Baltimore, MD, and London: Johns Hopkins University Press, 2000, p. 54; P. Wilson, "French Dressing," *Building Design*, 12 March 2004, 18.

2   "For much of the time, during his lifetime and since, the world has been divided into the majority who regard Geddes as an interesting crank and the small bank of disciples for whom he is the inspiration and the light." H. Meller, "Understanding the European City Around 1900: The Contribution of Patrick Geddes," in *The City after Patrick Geddes*, Bern: Peter Lang, 2000, p. 37; H. Meller "Introduction and Note to Civics: As Applied Sociology," in *The Ideal City*, edited with an introduction by Helen E. Meller, Leicester University Press, 1979, pp. 9–46; 67–74.

3   These claims are practically unanimous amongst contemporary writers: B. T. Robson, "Geography and Social Science: the role of Patrick Geddes," in D. R. Stoddart (ed.), *Geography, Ideology and Social Concern*, London: Blackwell, 1981, pp. 195–6; *Town and Country Planning* September 1979, p. 181; P. Searby, "A Dreamer of Dreams': Patrick Geddes 1854–1932," Hughes Hall, Cambridge, the Wood Memorial Lecture, 1985, delivered in Hughes Hall on Saturday 5 October 1985, p. 3; K. Wheeler, "A Note on the Valley Section of Patrick Geddes," *Bulletin of Environmental Education* 33, 1974, 28; P. Hall, *Cities of Tomorrow: An Intellectual History of Urban Planning and Design in the Twentieth Century*, Oxford and New York: Basil Blackwell, 1988, p. 247; Goist, "Patrick Geddes and the City," p. 32; W. Stephen, "Patrick Geddes – the Legacy," in W. Stephen (ed.), *Think Global, Act Local: The Life and Legacy of Patrick Geddes*, Edinburgh: Luath Press, 2004, pp. 122, 125; H. Meller, "Understanding the European City Around 1900: The Contribution of Patrick Geddes," in V. M. Welter and J. Lawson (eds), *The City after Patrick Geddes*, Bern: Peter Lang, 2000; p. 53; G. Ferraro, *Reieducazione all Speranza: Patrick Geddes planner in India, 1914–1924*, Milano: Jaca Books, 1998, p. 25; C. Ward, "Old Prophets of New City-Regions," *Town and Country Planning* December 1990, 330; J. A. Hasselgren, "Introduction," in *Patrick Geddes: A Symposium*, 1 March 1982, Special Occasional Paper in Town and Regional Planning, Duncan of Jordanstone College of Art/University of Dundee (an event organized by the Department of Town and Regional Planning to celebrate the centenary of the foundation of the university); P. Boardman, "In defence of Patrick Geddes," *Town and Country Planning* September 1980, 270–1; Reviews: "The day Patrick Geddes blew his top", *Town and Country Planning* 52(2), 1983, 58–9.

4   P. Green, "Patrick Geddes," unpublished PhD thesis, University of Strathclyde, 1970; see also Green, "Patrick Geddes – Pioneer of Social Planning (1854–1932)," *Journal of Indian History* Golden Jubilee Volume, 1973, Department of History, University of Kerala, 847–62,

5   Many of the quotes constitute today the only evidence of their being written as many of were later lost. Meller agrees that Geddes' approach and techniques hardly changed and can be illustrated through a small selection of the reports. H. Meller, "Geddes and his Indian Reports," in *Patrick Geddes: A Symposium*, p. 7.

6   Green, "Patrick Geddes," p. 253.

7   Ibid., pp. 166–8, 172–80, 257.

8   Green, "Patrick Geddes – Pioneer of Social Planning," pp. 848, 860.

9 Ibid., p. 861; Green, "Patrick Geddes," p. 257.

10 Green, "Patrick Geddes – Pioneer of Social Planning," pp. 847–62.

11 Green, "Patrick Geddes," pp. 85, 92, 94, 119–21, 107–8, 209–1, 317.

12 Ibid., pp. 248–52. Green shows how Geddes' work in Cyprus and in Aden introduced the idea of a *central place*, arousing the importance of the development of a regional center as well as aesthetic considerations. Ibid., pp. 69, 270–3.

13 Ibid., pp. 243–7.

14 P. Green, "Cities in Evolution" (3rd edn) by Patrick Geddes (Book Review), *Town Planning Review* 41(3), July 1970, 293.

15 Green, "Patrick Geddes," p. 318.

16 Meller, *Patrick Geddes*; Meller, "Patrick Geddes 1854–1932," in Cherry, *Pioneers in British Planning*, p. 52. Meller claims that this theme in Geddes' work had been totally ignored due to the ideology adopted from the Modern Movement; while planning students were still trained in Geddesian techniques, survey, diagnosis, and plan, the most essential elements of Geddes' message, the critical relationship between social processes and spatial form, was ignored in relation to the existing environment. Thus, new amenities were provided with no reference to history and Geddes' message was overall ignored. Meller, *Patrick Geddes*, pp. 323–4.

17 H. Meller, "Cities and Evolution: Patrick Geddes as an International Prophet of Town Planning before 1914," in A. Sutcliffe (ed.), *British Town Planning: The Formative Years*, Leicester: Leicester University Press, 1981, pp. 199–219.

18 Meller, *Patrick Geddes*, p. 157, 63.

19 H. E. Meller, *Leisure and the Changing City 1870–1914*, London, Henley and Boston: Routledge & Kegan Paul, 1976; Meller, *Patrick Geddes*, p. 317.

20 Ibid., p. 103.

21 Ibid., pp. 134, 290, 321.

22 H. Meller, "Conservation and Evolution: The Pioneering Work of Sir Patrick Geddes in Jerusalem, 1919–1925," *Planning History Bulletin* 9, 1987, 42–9.

23 Meller, *Patrick Geddes*, p. 157.

24 Ibid., pp. 317, 322.

25 Meller, "Patrick Geddes 1854–1932," in Cherry, pp. 58–60.

26 Ibid p. 56; Meller, *Patrick Geddes*, pp. 44; 20; H. Meller, "Philanthropy and Public Enterprise: International Exhibitions and the Modern Town Planning Movement, 1889–1913," *Planning Perspectives* 19, 1995, 297.

27 Ferraro, *Patrick Geddes Planner in India*, p. 27.

28 Ibid., p. 195; Ferraro, "Il gioco del piano. Patrick Geddes in India 1914–1924," *Urbanistica* 103, 1995, 136. See also Ferraro, G. Ferraro, "Patrick Geddes, *Cities in Evolution*," *Urbanistica* 108, 1997, 157–61.

29 Ferraro, "Il gioco del piano," pp. 137–8, 143–4.

30 Ibid., p. 148.

31 Ferraro, *Patrick Geddes Planner in India*, pp. 199, 257.

32 Ferraro, "Il gioco del piano," p. 139; Ferraro, *Patrick Geddes Planner in India*, p. 223.

33 Ferraro, "Il gioco del piano," p. 152.

34 Ferraro, *Patrick Geddes Planner in India*, p. 29. Ferraro demonstrates this change in the language of Geddes' writings, moving from simplistic study in his early theoretical writings to accentuating the spiritual and moral energies in Indore Report to the need to reach the heart of the community, the traditional Indian society, in the Indian reports. *Patrick Geddes Planner in India*, pp. 204–13.

35 Ibid., pp. 59–61, 217.

36 Indian Dharma thus represents the moral laws and the goodwill rooted in the common sense, the practical end which is common to all world religions. Ibid., pp. 259–61.

37 Ferraro, "Il gioco del piano," p. 143.

38 Ibid., p. 144; Ferraro, *Patrick Geddes Planner in India*, pp. 223, 262.

39 Ibid., p. 231.

40 J. P. Reilly, "The Early Social Thought of Patrick Geddes," PhD thesis, Columbia University, 1972, pp. 198–9; Robson, "Geography and Social Science," in Stoddart, p. 187.

41 Wheeler, "A Note on the Valley Section of Patrick Geddes," p. 127. Although Jacobs herself gives Geddes no such credit; J. Jacobs, *The Death and Life of Great American Cities*, Harmondsworth: Penguin in association with Jonathan Cape 1994 (1961).

42 Ibid., p. 27.

43 Goist, "Patrick Geddes and the City," p. 32.

44 Leonard, "Finding Geddes Abroad," in Stephen, p. 60.

45 C. Ward, "Old Prophets of New City-Regions," *Town and Country Planning* December 1990, 329.

46 Reilly, "The Early Social Thought of Patrick Geddes," p. 49; Wheeler, "A Note on the Valley Section," p. 127; Robson, "Geography and Social Science," p. 196; Ward, "Old Prophets of New City-Regions," p. 329.

47 W. I. Stevenson, "Patrick Geddes and Geography: Biobibliographical Study," Occasional Papers 27, 1975, Department of Geography, University College: London, p. 7.

48 C. Ward, "The Outlook Tower, Edinburgh: Prototype for an Urban Studies Centre," *Bulletin of Environmental Education* 32, 1973. In June 1985 the Patrick Geddes Centre was opened by the University of Edinburgh, aimed to develop as "a Centre for Planning Studies," its roles including acting as a center and focus of planning and environmental ideas in Edinburgh and as headquarters for other countries; to cooperate with Edinburgh Conservation and Renewal committee; to promote symposia, lectures and summer schools at the Outlook Tower; to organize a society of Friends of Geddes' to stimulate support; and to publish books of Geddes where were out of print as well as results of research done in connection with the center. S. Leonard, "Patrick Geddes Centre For Planning Studies," *Planning History* 10(1), 1988, 26.

49 Ward, "Old Prophets of New City-Regions," p. 329.

50 C. Mercer, 'Geographies for the Present: Patrick Geddes, Urban Planning and the Human Sciences," *Economy and Society* 26(2), 1997, 211–24.

51 Leonard, "The Context and Legacy of Patrick Geddes in Europe," in Welter and Lawson, pp. 79–81.

52 H. G. Simmons, "Patrick Geddes – Prophet without Politics," *Studies in Modern European History and Culture* 2, 1976, p. 159; Searby, "A Dreamer of Dreams," p. 20.

53 Robson, "Geography and Social Science," in *Geography, Ideology and Social Concern*, pp. 195–6; Goist, "Patrick Geddes and the City," p. 31.

54 P. Hall, *Cities of Tomorrow: An Intellectual History of Urban Planning and Design in the Twentieth Century*, Oxford and New York: Basil Blackwell, 1988, p. 242.

55 W. Stephen, "Think Global, Act Local – The Life and Legacy of Patrick Geddes," in Stephen (ed.), p. 13.

56 Goist, "Patrick Geddes and the City," p. 32.

57 Robson, "Geography and Social Science," p. 198; "Happy Birthday, Patrick Geddes," *Town and Country Planning*, September 1979, p. 181.

58 Stevenson, "Patrick Geddes and Geography," p. 6.

59 B. Edwards, "Edinburgh Debates Mumford's Distortion of Geddes' Ideas," *Architects' Journal*, 16 November 1995, p. 16.

60 M. Cuthbert, "The Concept of the Outlook Tower in the Work of Patrick Geddes," MPhil, University of St. Andrews, 1987, p. 190; Wheeler, "A Note on the Valley Section of Patrick Geddes," p. 128.

4 The Appreciation of Patrick Geddes as a Planner Today

  1 S. Leonard, "The Regeneration of the Old Town of Edinburgh by Patrick Geddes," *Planning History* 21(2), 1999, pp. 33–47.

Notes

2   R. Pinkerton, "Patrick Geddes Hall: Scotland's First Hall of Residence" [n.p.], 1978; J. Brine, "Ramsay Gardens, Patrick Geddes Centre," *Planning History* 11(3), 1989, 25.

3   A. Saint, "Ashbee, Geddes, Lethaby and the Rebuilding of Crosby Hall," *Architectural History* 34, 1991, 206–17.

4   A. Ponte, "Arte civica o sociologia applicata? P. Geddes e T. H. Mawson: due progetti per Dunfermline" (Civic Art or Applied Sociology? P. Geddes and T. H. Mawson: Two Plans for Dunfermline), *Lotus International* 30, 1981, 91–8.

5   M. J. Bannon, "The Genesis of Modern Irish Planning," in M. J. Bannon (ed.), *A Hundred Years of Irish Planning Vol. I: The Emergence of Irish Planning 1880–1920*, Dublin: Turoe Press, 1985, p. 197.

6   "A regional approach has failed to evolve as regional proposals all too often depend on the tolerance of conflicting petty local authorities;" The conservative surgery approach was replaced by the bulldozer; and from 1915 to the late 1960s Geddes' recognition of the need for community participation, as well as conservation in the use of resources, was largely disregarded by the planning profession. M. J. Bannon, "The Making of Irish Geography, III: Patrick Geddes and the Emergence of Modern Town Planning in Dublin," *Irish Geography* 11, 1978, 141, 143, 147.

7   Bannon, *A Hundred Years of Irish Planning*, p. 252.

8   Bannon, "Irish Geography," p. 147; idem, *A Hundred Years of Irish Planning*, p. 230; Bannon, "Dublin Town Planning Competition: Ashbee and Chettle's 'New Dublin – A Study in Civics'," *Planning Perspectives* 14, 1999, 145–62.

9   D. Goodfriend, "Nagar Yoga: The Culturally Informed Town Planning of Patrick Geddes in India 1914–1924," *Human Organization* 38(4), 1979, 345; H. Meller, "Geddes and his Indian Reports," in *Patrick Geddes: A Symposium*, Special Occasional Paper in Town and Regional Planning, Duncan of Jordanstone College of Art/University of Dundee, 1 March 1982, p. 8; G. Ferraro, "Il gioco del piano. Patrick Geddes in India 1914–1924," *Urbanistica* 103, 1995, 151; A. Petruccioli, "Patrick Geddes in Indore: Alcune questioni di metodo (some questions of method)," *Lotus International* 34, 1982, 109.

10 J. Toppin, "History of Working Abroad," *The Architects' Journal* July 1982, 31; H. Meller, *Patrick Geddes: Social Evolutionist and City Planner*, London: Routledge, 1990, p. 203; Ferraro, "Il gioco del piano," p. 151.

11 Ibid., p. 144.

12 Toppin, "History of Working Abroad," p. 31; Meller, "Geddes and his Indian Reports," p. 5.

13 Meller, "Geddes and his Indian Reports," p. 7. In Madras, he had already found a framework for solving all the problems he was to encounter; ibid., pp. 4–25; Meller, *Patrick Geddes*, p. 7; in Lucknow, he expands on "planning for people"; Meller, "Geddes and his Indian Reports," pp. 13–16. Similarly, his thesis of public participation is fully developed in Indore, Green, *Patrick Geddes*, p. 266; "His episode [in Indore] . . . gives a better idea than any comment of the personality of Patrick Geddes," Petruccioli, "Patrick Geddes in Indore," p. 109.

14 H. E. Meller, "Urbanization and the Introduction of Modern Town Planning Ideas in India, 1900–1925," in K. N. Chaudhuri and C. J. Dewey (eds), *Economy and Society Essays in Indian Economic and Social History*, Delhi: Oxford University Press, 1979, p. 342; Toppin, "History of Working Abroad," p. 31.

15 Toppin, ibid., p. 31; Goodfriend, "Nagar Yoga," p. 351; Meller, "Geddes and his Indian Reports," p. 8; Petruccioli, "Patrick Geddes in Indore," p. 109, 113; T. G. McGee, "Planning the Asian City: The Relevance of 'Conservative Surgery' and the Concept of Dualism," in J. J. Ferreira and S. S. Jha (eds), *The Outlook Tower: Essays on Urbanization in Memory of Patrick Geddes*, Department of Sociology, University of Bombay, Bombay: Popular Prakashan, 1976, p. 266; see also Green, *Patrick Geddes*, Chapter 3.

16 "including a fine park and a zoological garden, a racecourse and a polo ground." Leonard, "Finding Geddes Abroad," in Stephen (ed.), p. 56.

17 Ibid., p. 56.

18   G. Ferraro, "Il gioco del piano. Patrick Geddes in India 1914–1924," *Urbanistica* 103, 1995, 153.

19   Goodfriend, "Nagar Yoga," p. 344; Petruccioli, "Patrick Geddes in Indore," p. 109; Meller, "Geddes and his Indian Reports," pp. 211–12; Ferraro, "Il gioco del piano," p. 153; McGee, "Planning the Asian City," p. 266; N. Gupta, "A Letter from India," in W. Stephen (ed.), *Think Global, Act Local: The Life and Legacy of Patrick Geddes*, Edinburgh: Luath Press, 2004, p. 118.

20   Meller, "Geddes and his Indian Reports," p. 8; Goodfriend, "Nagar Yoga," pp. 350, 354.

21   G. Ferraro, *Rieducazione alla Speranza: Patrick Geddes Planner in India, 1914–1924*, Milano: Jaca Books, 1998, p. 210.

22   Goodfriend, "Nagar Yoga," p. 355; Gupta, "A Letter from India," p. 117.

23   Petruccioli, "Patrick Geddes in Indore," p. 111.

24   Meller, *Patrick Geddes*, p. 218.

25   Ibid., p. 240; Toppin, "History of Working Abroad," p. 31; Petruccioli, "Patrick Geddes in Indore," p. 109. Goodfriend finds resonance between Geddes' theme of preservation and renewal and the Hindu notion of the cycle of *yugas* – epochs of time ruled successively by Vishnu the preserver, Shiva the destroyer and Brahma the creator and renewer (together known as Trimurti). Goodfriend, "Nagar Yoga," p. 346. Gupta claims that Lanchester's report for Delhi proclaims Geddes' idea to combine the New Delhi with the old one and to insist the architecture in the area must be Indian Vernacular; N. Gupta, *Delhi between Two Empires 1803–1931: Society, Government and Urban Growth*, Delhi: Oxford University Press, 1981, p. 182.

26   Gupta, "A Letter from India," p. 118.

27   Ibid., p. 119; see also N. Gupta, "Twelve Years on: Urban History in India," *Urban History Yearbook*, 1981, pp. 76–9.

28   McGee, "Planning the Asian City," pp. 266, 280–1.

29   "I make the same assumption as Geddes, but for different reasons: it is impractical and inefficient to rebuild the urban shell while the economic structure of the city cannot cope with it." Ibid., p. 269.

30   Petruccioli, "Patrick Geddes in India," p. 109; Goodfriend, "Nagar Yoga," p. 352; Meller, "Patrick Geddes and his Indian Reports," pp. 13–16.

31   Green, *Patrick Geddes*, pp. 276, 282, 284.

32   Ibid., p. 294.

33   Ibid., pp. 302, 307. The report is missing today.

34   B. Hyman, "British Planners in Palestine, 1918–1936," PhD thesis, London School of Economics and Political Science, 1994.

35   G. Herbert and S. Sosnovsky, *Bauhaus on the Carmel and the Crossroads of Empire: Architecture and Planning in Haifa during the British Mandate*, Jerusalem: Yad Yizhak Ben–Zvi, 1993, p. 73; N. I. Payton, "The Machine in the Garden City: Patrick Geddes' Plan for Tel Aviv," *Planning Perspectives* 19(4), 1995, 363; M. Shapira, "The University and the City: Patrick Geddes and the First Master Plan for the Hebrew University, 1919," in S. Katz and M. Heyd (eds), *The History of the Hebrew University in Jerusalem: Roots and Beginnings*, Jerusalem: Magnes Publishers, 1997, pp. 201–35 (Hebrew); G. Biger, "A Scotsman in the First Hebrew City: Patrick Geddes and the 1926 Town Plan for Tel Aviv," *The Scottish Geographical Magazine* 108(4), 1992, 4; Hyman, "British Planners in Palestine," p. 300; I. Troen, "Tel Aviv: Vienna on the Mediterranean," in *Imagining Zion: Dreams, Designs, and Realities in a Century of Jewish Settlement Zion*, New Haven: Yale University Press, 2003, pp. 85–111.

36   Payton, "The Machine in the Garden City," p. 363.

37   R. Kallus, "Patrick Geddes and the Evolution of a Housing Type in Tel-Aviv," *Planning Perspectives* 12, 1997, 290; Payton, "The Machine in the Garden City," pp. 364, 372; Hyman, "British Planners in Palestine," p. 362; Herbert and Sosnovsky, *Bauhaus on the Carmel*, pp. 68–73, 75–6. See also Y. Ogen (ed.), *Asher Haya*, Tel Aviv: n.p., 1959, celebrating the accomplishments of Asher Ehrlich, one of the founders of the Jewish garden suburb in Tiberius and his work with Geddes.

38 H. Meller, "Conservation and Evolution: The Pioneering Work of Sir Patrick Geddes in Jerusalem, 1919–1925," *Planning History Bulletin* 9, 1987, 44; Meller, *Patrick Geddes*, p. 278.

39 Herbert and Sosnovsky, *Bauhaus on the Carmel*, p. 75.

40 Meller, *Patrick Geddes*, pp. 229–77.

41 S. Shapiro, "Planning Jerusalem: The First Generation, 1917–1968," in *Urban Geography of Jerusalem: A Companion Volume to the Atlas of Jerusalem*, D. Amiran, A. Shachar and I. Kimhi (eds), Jerusalem: Massada Press, 1973; E. Efrat, "British Town Planning Perspectives of Jerusalem in Transition," *Planning Perspectives* 8, 1993, 377–93; Y. Ben-Arieh, "The Planning and Conservation of Jerusalem during the Mandate Period in Israel 1917–1926: A Land Reflected in its Past," in R. Aharonsohn and H. Lavsky (eds), *Studies in [the] Historical Geography of Israel*, Jerusalem: Magnes Press, Yad Ben-Zvi Press, 2001, pp. 441–93 (Hebrew).

42 S. E. Cohen, "Greenbelts in London and Jerusalem," *Geographical Review* 84(1), 1994, 74–89.

43 M. Shapira, "The University and the City," in Katz and Heyd (eds), *The History of the Hebrew University in Jerusalem*, p. 201.

44 D. Dolev, "The Architectural Master Plans of the Hebrew University, 1918–1948," in Katz and Heyd (eds), p. 264 (Hebrew). See also D. Dolev, "Architecture and Nationalist Ideology: The Case of the Architectural Master Plans for the Hebrew University in Jerusalem (1919–1974) and their Connections with Nationalist Ideology," PhD thesis, University College: London, 2001; Shapira, "The University and the City," p. 201; Meller, "Conservation and Evolution," p. 46.

45 Y. Shavit and G. Biger, *Ha'historya shel Tel Aviv 1: Leydata shel ir (1909–1936) (The History of Tel Aviv Vol. 1: The Birth of a Town (1909–1936))*, Tel Aviv: Ramot Press, Tel Aviv University, 2001, p. 33; M. Azrayahu, *Tel Aviv: Ha'ir Ha'Amitit (Tel Aviv: Mythography of a city)*, Beer Sheva: Ben Gurion University of the Negev, 2005, p. 115.

46 Biger, "A Scotsman in the First Hebrew City," p. 4. In fact, claim Marom, of all Tel Aviv's planners over the years, Geddes is the only one known to the public, and celebrated in any way. N. Marom, *Ir im Conceptsia: Metachnenim et Tel-Aviv (A City with a Concept: Planning Tel-Aviv)*, Tel Aviv: Babel, 2009, p. 9.

47 Kallus, "Patrick Geddes and the Evolution of a Housing Type in Tel-Aviv," p. 290; Payton, "The Machine in the Garden City," p. 359.

48 Kallus, ibid., p. 290; Payton, ibid., p. 361.

49 E. Zandberg, "Halbinu et Ha'ir HaLevana" (Bleach the White City), *Haaretz (The Country)*, Gallery section (14 February 1999) quoted in Shavit and Biger *The Birth of a Town*, p. 34.

50 Geddes' plan was commended for its comprehensive approach, its attention to private and public open spaces, and the high priorities it gave to environmental issues, such as providing for low level of vehicles. The pedestrian-scaled city, together with an appropriate mixture of land uses, supported an active civic life and promoted a great sense of community, both of which were found crucial to the city's identity. B. Yosskovitz, "Tichnun vePituach Tel Aviv-Yaffo" (Planning and Development of Tel Aviv-Yaffo), *Tichnun Svivati (Environmental Planning)* 57, 1999. 60–4; On similar grounds, the strategic planning process which started in 2000 is carried out under the slogan of "Public Participation in Planning" following in Geddes' footsteps; T. Gavrieli, "Hatochnit Ha'estratgit leTel Aviv-Yafo: Ekronot, Tahalich, Matrot Tichnun, Yissum" (The Strategic Plan for Tel Aviv-Jaffa: Principles, Process, Plan Targets, Implementation), in B. A. Kipnis (ed.), *Tel Aviv-Yafo: Me'ir Ganim le'ir Olam: Mea Hashanim Harishonot (Tel Aviv-Yafo: from a garden city to a world city. The first one hundred years)*, Tel Aviv: Pardes Publishing, 2008, p. 44. See also Kallus, "Housing Type in Tel Aviv," pp. 290, 293; Payton, "The Machine in the Garden City," p. 359.

51 Payton, ibid., p. 361.

52 UNESCO, 2003 *27COM 8C.23 – White City of Tel-Aviv – the Modern Movement (Israel)*. Available online at: http://whc.unesco.org/en/decisions/718 (accessed 15 March 2010); also quoted in N. Szmuk, *Tel-Aviv's Modern Movement: The White City of Tel Aviv, A World Heritage Site* ('Living on the Dunes' Exhibition Catalogue, Tel Aviv Museum), The Municipality of Tel Aviv-Yafo: Tel Aviv, 2004.

53 Szmuk, *Living on the Dunes*, pp. 19–20. A "lack of reference in Geddes' report to an architectural code or any other system made all options possible"; ibid., p. 35.

54 Kallus, "Housing Type in Tel Aviv," p. 381. As a city planned "while Le Corbusier was working on the Plan Voisin for Paris," according to G. Confurius, "Tel Aviv und die Transportfähigkeit der Moderne" (Tel Aviv and the Transportability of the Modern Movement), *Daidalos* 54, 15 December 1994, 55, the international style apparently "could hardly have found a better place to develop"; C. Weill-Rochant, "Tel-Aviv des années trente: béton bland sur la terre promise," *l'architecture d'aujourd'hui* 293, June 1994, 41.

5 Discussion: Geddes' Historiography as a Reflection of the History of Town Planning

1 One example which should be pointed out is that both Green and Ferro insist on Geddes' pronounced Public Participation, yet they both end up describing an ideal scheme which no one, including Geddes himself, has ever practiced. Eventually they reduce the expected result to the planner presenting his plans to the public and allowing for responses. Another inconsistency can be spotted in the writing regarding Geddes' work in Palestine, where it seems that the reasons listed for Geddes' commission were also the reason for his downfall, and his overall admiration in Tel Aviv since the 1970s in spite of the obvious contradictions.

2 For example, "Only Mumford was able to breathe life into the bare bones of the ideas scattered through . . . those who read Geddes expecting to be overwhelmed by the master, because dazzled by the student Mumford, will be sorely disappointed. In the end, one can almost get a better idea of what Geddes was all about from reading Mumford." H. G. Simmons, "Patrick Geddes: Prophet without Politics," *Studies in Modern European History and Culture* 2, 1976, 184.

3 "Geddes' influence will never be known to the world at large . . . it is sort of vital idea – a divine inoculation that goes on spreading its infusion," P. Abercrombie, "Geddes as Town Planner," in A. Defries, *The Interpreter Geddes: The Man and his Gospel*, foreword by Rabindranath Tagore, introduction by Israel Zangwill. London: George Routledge & Sons, 1927, pp. 323, 324.

4 M. Hebbert, "Patrick Geddes Reconsidered," *Town and Country Planning*, January 1980, 16.

5 "Even Geddes' oldest and closest colleagues had faced this difficulty; and though some of them could repeat his graphs and explanations from memory – they did not in fact make use of them except in paying homage to Geddes." L. Mumford, "The Geddesian Gambit," in F. G. Novak, Jr. (ed.), *Lewis Mumford and Patrick Geddes: The Correspondence*, London and New York: Routledge, 1995, p. 538. Boardman described one incident which seems to be representing the overall impression: "Things went along smoothly as long as it was a question of historical charts [. . .] But then came A, B, C, with their six combinations, followed by a similar game with O, F, E [. . .] and then the parallel Place, Work, Folk of sociology. P. G. proceeded to fold and refold sheets and to scribble words in the squares thus formed, but the words were often so abbreviated as to be unintelligible until explained. And since the process of turning out these thinking-machines was more engrossing to their producer than mere explanation of what he had meant to write, many of the square's labels remained undeciphered . . ." P. Boardman, quoted in J. Tyrwhitt, "Introduction," in *Cities in Evolution by Patrick Geddes*, edited by the Outlook Tower Association Edinburgh and the Association for Planning and Regional Reconstruction, London. New and revised edition, London: Williams & Norgate, 1949, pp. xiv–xv.

6 H. Meller, *Patrick Geddes: Social Evolutionist and City Planner*, London: Routledge, 1990, p. 290; Meller, *Towns, Plans and Society in Modern Britain*, prepared for the Economic History Society, Cambridge: Cambridge University Press, 1997, pp. 48–9.

7 Hebbert suggests a periodical differentiation: "In the 1940s he was read by architects as an exponent of ambitious schemes of drawing-board social engineering. In the 1960s, he was hailed as a proto-technocrat." P. Hebbert, "Retrospect on the Outlook Tower," in *Patrick Geddes: A Symposium*, 1 March 1982, Special Occasional Paper in Town and Regional Planning, Duncan of

Jordanstone College of Art/University of Dundee (An Event Organized by the Department of Town and Regional Planning to celebrate the Centenary of the foundation of the University), p. 55.

8 I. B. Whyte, "The Spirit of the City," in V. M. Welter and J. Lawson (eds), *The City after Patrick Geddes*, Bern: Peter Lang, 2000, pp. 15–32.

9 "When . . . there was a reaction against the bulldozer concept of urban renewal, Geddes' work in Edinburgh and India was justifiably invoked as the model of a more sensitive, remedial approach." Hebbert, "Retrospect on the Outlook Tower," p. 56.

10 Writings on Geddes are piling on, generally following the above described lines. Several new strands have been detected since the completion of the present research: as a planner, Geddes has been accredited as a precursor of New Urbanism: E. Talen, "Beyond the Front Porch: Regionalist Ideals in the New Urbanism Movement," *Journal of Planning History* 7(1), 2008, 20–47; he had also been linked with modern information and knowledge management: B. Jones, "European Modernism and the Information Society: Review Article," *Australian Academic and Research Libraries* 39(3), 2008, 207–13; finally, Geddes' urban and regional theory has been used to identify best practices in eco-efficient development of regions to form a "new concept for housing foresight, Slow Housing, in analogy to slow food and as a contrast to hectic urban life:" S. Heinonen, "Slow Housing – Competitive Edge for Innovative Living Environments," *Fennia* 184(1), 2006, 91–104. Geddes has also been strongly incorporated in the project of reinscribing British sociology: C. Renwick and R. C. Gunn, "Demythologizing the Machine: Patrick Geddes, Lewis Mumford, and Classical Sociological Theory," *Journal of the History of the Behavioral Sciences* 44(1), 2008, 59–76, claim classical sociological theory to be the only true way to appreciate the work of the two polymaths; a vigorous discussion has taken place concerning environmental sociology between Maggie Studholme, "Patrick Geddes and the History of Environmental Sociology in Britain," *Journal of Classical Sociology* 8(3), 2008, 367–91; M. Studholme, J. Scott and C. T. Husbands, "Dopplegängers and Racists: On Inhabiting Alternative Universes. A Reply to Steve Fuller's 'A path better not to have been taken'," *The Sociological Review* 55(4), 2007, 816–22, calling for sociologists to reclaim Geddes and to recover "the potential value of [his] proto-environmentalist insights and their ecological sensibilities," and Steve Fuller ("A Path Better not to Have Been Taken," *The Sociological Review* 55[4], 2007, 805–15) who, by examining Geddes' concepts of eugenics and evolution, claimed that others have "cast them in a politically correct light." See also T. Osborne, N. Rose and M. Savage, "Editors' Introduction Reinscribing British Sociology: Some Critical Reflections," *The Sociological Review* 56(4), 2008, 519–34; A. Law, "The Ghost of Patrick Geddes: Civics as Applied Sociology," *Sociological Research Online* 10(2), 2005. Available online at: http://www.socresonline.org.uk/10/2/law.html (accessed May 2010); L. Goldman, "Foundations of British Sociology 1880–1930: Contexts and Biographies," *The Sociological Review* 55(3), 2007, 431–40.

11 H. Meller, *Patrick Geddes: Social Evolutionist and City Planner*, London: Routledge, 1990, pp. 2, 68; G. Ferraro, *Rieducazione alla Speranza: Patrick Geddes Planner in India, 1914–1924*, Milano: Jaca Books, 1998, p. 26; Simmons, "Prophet without Politics," 163; J. P. Reilly, "The Early Social Thought of Patrick Geddes," PhD, Columbia University, 1972, p. iv.

12 Meller, *Patrick Geddes*, p. 50; Meller, "Cities and Evolution: Patrick Geddes as an International Prophet of Town Planning before 1914," in A. Sutcliffe (ed.), *British Town Planning: The Formative Years*, Leicester: Leicester University Press, 1981, pp. 199–219; Reilly, "The Early Social thought of Patrick Geddes," p. 49.

13 By going to India at the outbreak of the First World War, claims Meller, Geddes had taken himself out of the mainstream of the development of modern town planning, which was concentrated on the phenomenon of rapid urbanization in the west. Meller, *Patrick Geddes*, pp. 203, 317; Ferraro, *Patrick Geddes Planner in India*, p. 26; S. Leonard, "Finding Geddes Abroad," in W. Stephen (ed.), *Think Global, Act Local: The Life and Legacy of Patrick Geddes*, Edinburgh: Luath Press, 2004, pp. 41–60.

14 Meller, *Patrick Geddes*, pp. 7, 56; Meller, *Towns, Plans and Society in Modern Britain*, prepared for the Economic History Society, Cambridge: Cambridge University Press, 1997, p. 53; V. M. Welter, *Biopolis: Patrick Geddes and the City of Life*, Cambridge, MA: The MIT Press, 2002, pp. 1–2; P. Searby, "A Dreamer of Dreams: Patrick Geddes 1854–1932," Hughes Hall, Cambridge, the Wood Memorial Lecture 1985, delivered 5 October 1985, p. 11.

15 Meller, *Patrick Geddes*, p. 49.

16 Meller, *Patrick Geddes*, p. 45; 317; B. T. Robson, "Geography and Social Science: The Role of Patrick Geddes," in D. R. Stoddart (ed.), *Geography, Ideology and Social Concern*, London: Blackwell, 1981; W. Lesser, "Patrick Geddes: The Practical Visionary," *Town Planning Review* 45(3), 1977, 311–27; Ferraro, *Patrick Geddes Planner in India*, p. 153.

17 P. Boardman, *The Worlds of Patrick Geddes: Biologist, Town Planner, Re-educator, Peace-Warrior*. London, Henley and Boston: Routledge & Kegan Paul, 1978, p. 233.

18 Meller, *Patrick Geddes*, p. 103; Meller, "Patrick Geddes 1854–1932," in G. Cherry (ed.), *Pioneers in British Planning*, London: The Architectural Press, 1981, pp. 46–71; Reilly, "The Early Social Thought of Patrick Geddes," p. 48; Lesser, "Patrick Geddes: The Practical Visionary," p. 311.

19 Reilly, "The Early Social Thought of Patrick Geddes," p. 111; Meller, *Patrick Geddes*, p. 56; S. Leonard, "The Context and Legacy of Patrick Geddes in Europe," in V. M. Welter and J. Lawson (eds), *The City after Patrick Geddes*. Bern: Peter Lang, 2000, p. 77.

20 Ferraro, *Patrick Geddes Planner in India*, p. 25.

21 P. Green, "Patrick Geddes – Pioneer of Social Planning (1854–1932)," *Journal of Indian History* Golden Jubilee Volume 1973, Department of History, University of Kerala, 851, 861; Meller, *Patrick Geddes*, p. 318; D. Shillan, "Biotechnics: The Practice of Synthesis in the Work of Patrick Geddes," New Atlantis Foundation, Sixteenth Foundation Lecture, Richmond: New Atlas Foundation, 1972, p. 19; Searby, "A Dreamer of Dreams," p. 2; P. Hall, *Cities of Tomorrow: An Intellectual History of Urban Planning and Design in the Twentieth Century*, Oxford and New York: Basil Blackwell, 1988, p. 247.

22 W. I. Stevenson, "Patrick Geddes and Geography: Biobibliographical Study," Occasional Papers 27, 1975, Department of Geography, University College London; Ferraro, *Patrick Geddes Planner in India*.

23 Robson, in *Geography and Social Sciences*, p. 203; Ferraro, *Patrick Geddes Planner in India*, p. 269.

24 Robson, ibid.; C. Ward, "Old Prophets of New City-Regions," *Town and Country Planning*, December 1990, 329.

25 Ferraro, *Patrick Geddes Planner in India*, p. 26.

26 P. Clavel, "Ebenezer Howard and Patrick Geddes: Two Approaches to City Development," in K. C. Parsons and D. Schuyler (eds), *From Garden City to Green City: The Legacy of Ebenezer Howard*, Baltimore and London: Johns Hopkins University Press, 2002, p. 54.

27 R. Cowan, "Planners, Gardeners and Patrick Geddes," *Town and Country Planning* 45(7–8), 1977, 348–51.

28 Robson, in *Geography and Social Sciences*, p. 188; Green, *Patrick Geddes*, p. 318.

29 Meller, *Patrick Geddes*, p. 321; Meller, *Towns and Plans*, pp. 53, 55; see also M. Dehaene, "Urban Lessons for the Modern Planner: Patrick Abercrombie and the Study of Urban Development," *Town Planning Review* 75(1), 2004, 1–30.

30 G. E. Cherry, *Town Planning in Britain Since 1900,* Making Contemporary Britain Series, Oxford and Cambridge, MA: Blackwell Publishers, 1996, p. 42.

31 Meller, in *British Town Planning*, p. 220.

32 Meller, *Patrick Geddes*, p. 321.

33 Ferraro, *Patrick Geddes Planner in India*, p. 25.

34 Hebbert, "Retrospect on the Outlook Tower," p. 56; Hebbert, "Patrick Geddes Reconsidered," *Town and Country Planning* January 1980, 16.

35 "Patrick Geddes: A Symposium," ibid.

36 Simmons, "Prophet without Politics," pp. 177–8.

37 Ibid., pp. 159–91; M. Cuthbert, "The Concept of the Outlook Tower in the Work of Patrick Geddes," MPhil thesis, University of St. Andrews, 1987, p. 191.

38 Hasselgren, in *Patrick Geddes: A Symposium*, p. 40; Simmons, "Prophet without Politics," p. 189.

39 Leonard, "The Context and Legacy of Patrick Geddes in Europe," Welter and Lawson (eds).

40 Simmons, "Prophet without Politics," p. 169; Leonard, ibid., p. 77.

41 J. B. McLoughlin, *Urban and Regional Planning: A Systems Approach*, London: Faber and Faber, 1969, p. 125; A. Ravetz, *The Government of Space: Town Planning in Modern Society*, London: Faber and Faber, 1986, p. 52, both in J. Muller, "From Survey to Strategy: Twentieth Century Developments in Western Planning Method," *Planning Perspectives* 7(2), 1992, 127. These themes will be elaborated in Part II.

42 Hebbert, "Retrospect on the Outlook Tower," p. 51; Hebbert, "Patrick Geddes Reconsidered," p. 16.

43 Hebbert, "Retrospect on the Outlook Tower," pp. 53, 62.

44 Hebbert, "Patrick Geddes Reconsidered," p. 16.

45 Simmons, "Prophet without Politics," p. 171; see also: K. D. Lilley, "On Display: Planning Exhibitions as Civic Propaganda or Public Consultation?" *Planning History* 25(3), 2003, 3–8.

46 Hebbert, "Retrospect on the Outlook Tower," p. 57.

47 For example, an early criticism by Thomas Adams: "Professor Patrick Geddes has the credit of initiating regional and civic surveys on comprehensive lines, although perhaps covering a wider field of investigation than necessary for town planning purposes . . . These surveys have had an educational value for students of history and sociology but do not contain a great deal of data for purposes of practical town planning." *Recent Advances in Town Planning*, London: J. and A. Churchill, 1932, quoted in Muller, "From Survey to Strategy," p. 131. See also M. Dehaene, "Urban Lessons for the Modern Planner: Patrick Abercrombie and the Study of Urban Development," *Town Planning Review* 75(1), 2004, 1–30 on the differences between Geddes' and Abercrombie's Survey and their manifestation in the reports; see descriptions above (Part I, Chapter 2) regarding Arthur Glicksons' adaptation of Geddes' Survey.

48 Hebbert, "Retrospect on the Outlook Tower," p. 58.

49 M. J. Breheny, "In Search of Survey-Analysis Plan," *The Planner* 75(6), 1989, 23.

50 Simmons, "Prophet without Politics," p. 159.

51 Welter, *Biopolis*, p. 50.

52 Hebbert, "Patrick Geddes Reconsidered," p. 17.

53 Hasselgren, introduction to *Patrick Geddes: A Symposium*, p. 39; Hebbert, ibid., p. 17.

54 Meller, *Patrick Geddes*, p. 103.

55 Hebbert, "Retrospect on the Outlook Tower," p. 61.

56 Simmons, "Prophet without Politics," pp. 184–5.

57 Hebbert, "Retrospect on the Outlook Tower," p. 51.

58 Ibid., p. 16. Hasselgren agrees, claiming that we cannot regard Geddes as "the Marx or the Max Weber of town planning" as he did not change the way in which we view the world. "Introduction," p. 26.

59 Hebbert, "Retrospect on the Outlook Tower," p. 49.

60 Meller, *Patrick Geddes*, p. 103.

61 Hasselgren, introduction to *Patrick Geddes: A Symposium*, p. 44.

6 Geddes' Urban Conceptual Framework

1 P. Geddes, *Co-operation versus Socialism*, reprinted from *The Co-operative Wholesale Societies Annual* for 1888, Manchester: Co-operative Printing Society, p. 24.

2 P. Geddes, "City Surveys for Town Planning: And the Greater Cities," A Paper Read at the Birkenhead Congress, 1910, Edinburgh: Geddes and Colleagues, 1911, p. 1, T-GED 1/6/52; *Cities in Evolution: An Introduction to the Town Planning Movement and to the Study of Civics.*

London: Williams & Norgate, 1915, pp. 129–30, 148–9; "The Twofold Aspect of the Industrial Age: Paleotechnic and Neotechnic," *Town Planning Review* 3(3), 1912, 182. In a chapter which was omitted from the later edition of *Cities in Evolution*, Geddes dwelt on the faults of London's new neighborhoods, which he claimed caused similar defects. Ibid., pp. 116, 124, 147.

3   "The Joint Secretaries of the Cities Committee, The Doctrine of Civics," *The Sociological Review* 10(1), 1918, 61; "In an Old Scots City," *Contemporary Review* 82, January–June 1903, 562.

4   "Every Man his own Art Critic: Glasgow Exhibition, 1888," Edinburgh: William Brown, and Glasgow: John Menzies, 1888, p. 54.

5   These subjects were elaborated regarding the betterment of the home in a modern fable omitted from later versions of *Cities in Evolution*: "Cinderella . . . her future in the adequate Neotechnic home, characterised by electricity and its labour-saving, by hygiene, and by art, is thus as true princess, that is, lady commanding assured wealth, effective service, adequate leisure, and thus with no limit to her refinement and her influence," 1915, p. 129; on the construction of new docks in London and in Frankfurt (again, omitted from later versions) ibid., pp. 192, 215–17. See also "A Symposium on Town-Planning," Supplement to the *New Age* 8(1), 1910, T-GED 1/6/53; "Co-operation versus Socialism," p. 23; "Every Man his own Art Critic at the Manchester Exhibition," Manchester and London: John Heywood, 1887, p. 23, T-GED 5/3/1.

6   "The Doctrine of Civics," p. 61.

7   *Cities in Evolution by Patrick Geddes*, edited by the Outlook Tower Association Edinburgh and the Association for Planning and Regional Reconstruction, London, new and revised edition, London: Williams & Norgate, 1949, p. 51; "In an Old Scots City," p. 568.

8   *Cities in Evolution*, 1949, p. 104.

9   "Civics: As Applied Sociology," Part I, *Sociological Papers* I, published for the Sociological Society, London: Macmillan & Co., 1905, pp. 103–44; "Civics: As Concrete and Applied Sociology," Part II, *Sociological Papers* II, published for the Sociological Society, London: Macmillan & Co., 1906, pp. 57–119; "A Suggested plan for a Civic Museum (or Civic Exhibition) and its Associated studies," read at a Research Meeting of the Sociological Society, at the School of Economics and Political Science (University of London) 19 March 1906, James Oliphant, Esq., in the Chair. *Sociological Papers* III, published for the Sociological Society, London: Macmillan & Co., 1907, pp. 199–240.

10   *Cities in Evolution*, 1949, p. 104.

11   "Civics: As Applied Sociology," pp. 107–08. "Our modern town . . . no mere vacant site, but enriched and encumbered by the surviving traditions of the past [. . .] the historic glories . . . may long shed radiance and glamour upon its town, and linger in the world's memory long after not only these have faded, but their very folk have vanished, their walls fallen, nay their very site been buried or forgotten;" "Civics: As Concrete and Applied Sociology," p. 94.

12   P. Geddes and V. Branford, *The Coming Polity, The Making of the Future*, Westminster: Le Play House Press, 1919, pp. 155–6.

13   "In an Old Scots City," p. 568; *Cities in Evolution*, 1949, p. 153.

14   *Cities in Evolution*, p. 103.

15   "From our marvelous modern recovery of selective skill . . . the idea has been suggesting itself – why not consider whether we may not also ameliorate and ennoble our own human stocks, in which there is plainly so much room for improvement?" *Syllabus of a Course of Ten Lectures on Evolutionary Ethics, Based on Natural Science and Sociology*, University of London (University Extension Lectures), London: W. Bishop [Hampton & Co.], 1905, p. 9, T-GED 3/6/5. Moreover, eugenics also has a Greek origin and set ideal: "To image anew such types of beauty and perfection for our own race and its coming generations . . . is thus no fantastic dream; but at once a forecast and an element of the revival of classic studies, and of the approach of a more eugenic order." *Syllabus of a Course of Ten Lectures on Evolution in Life, Mind, Morals and Society*, University of London, 1910, pp. 15–16.

16 *Syllabus of a Course of Ten Lectures on: Contemporary Social Evolution*, University of London (University Extension Lectures), W. Bishop [Hampton & Co.], 1906, p. 10, T-GED 3/2/34; "Simplistic Darwinism would avoided by proper matching of human types to local regional growth;" ibid., pp. 9–10.

17 H. Meller, *Patrick Geddes: Social Evolutionist and City Planner*, London: Routledge, 1990; P. Chabard, "Towers and Globes: Architectural and Epistemological Differences between Patrick Geddes' Outlook Towers and Paul Otlet's Mundaneums," in B. Rayward (ed.), *European Modernism and the Information Society, Informing the Present, Understanding the Past*, London: Ashgate, 2008, pp. 105–26. See Appendix.

18 It is difficult to find a full description of the Valley Section concept; see mainly lecture given at the New School of Social Research in New York City in 1923, quoted in J. Tyrwhitt, introduction to *Cities in Evolution*, 1949, pp. xvi–xxviii. See also "The Influence of Geographical Conditions on Social Development," pp. 582–5; "Civics: As Concrete and Applied Sociology," pp. 60–1; "Country and Town," pp. 6–8; "A Rustic View of War and Peace," p. 5; and many more. The notion was based on social-regional ideas of Frederic Le-Play and Elisée Reclus; Meller, *Patrick Geddes*, pp. 34–43.

19 In his analysis, Geddes often turned to Edinburgh and its region; but also provided many examples over time and space. See, for example, "Edinburgh and its Region, Geographic and Historical," *Scottish Geographical Magazine* 18, 1902, 302–12; "The Civic Survey of Edinburgh," *Transactions of the Town Planning Conference London 10–15 October 1910*, London: Royal Institute of British Architects, 1911, pp. 538–68; "Beginnings of a Survey of Edinburgh," *The Scottish Geographical Magazine*, 35, 1919, 298–327.

20 This notion was greatly emphasized and elaborated in the years following World War I. See for example: P. Geddes and V. Branford, *The Coming Polity, The Making of the Future*, Westminster: Le Play House Press, 1919.

21 "The mass or the average of the civilized communities of our age . . . is [defined by] the term Occident." "City Deterioration and the Need of City Survey," reprinted from *The Annals of the American Academy of Politician and Social Science*, July 1909, Publication of the American Academy of Political and Social Science no. 579, Philadelphia, the American Academy of Political and Social Science, p. 57, T-GED 1/6/48, as one example.

22 *The Masque of Learning and its Many Meanings, Devised and Interpreted by Patrick Geddes*. Edinburgh: Patrick Geddes and Colleagues, Outlook Tower and Chelsea, 1912, p. vi; see also *The Masque of Medieval and Modern Learning and its many meanings: a Pageant of Education from Medieval to Modern Times, Devised and Interpreted by Patrick Geddes*, The Outlook Tower, Edinburgh: Patrick Geddes & Colleagues, 1913.

23 The Tree was painted by one of Geddes' students in 1892 and reproduced repeatedly, from "paper on geographic survey," 1894, pp. 3–5, T-GED 1/5/1; P. Geddes and G. Slater, *Ideas at War*, London: Williams & Norgate, 1917, pp. 23–7.

24 *Biopolis: Patrick Geddes and the City of Life*, Cambridge, MA: the MIT Press, 2002, p. 89.

25 "Israel from age to age has renewed the searchings after Unity, as do indeed so many of her children to this day;" *The Masque of Learning*, pp. 74–5; "Country and Town: In Development, Deterioration, and Renewal," [n.d.] T-GED 3/7/37, p. 19.

26 *The Higher Uses of Geography: A Course of Lectures*. The Outlook Tower [n.d.] pp. 1, 2, T-GED 13/1/17.

27 "Civics: As Applied Sociology," p. 107.

28 ". . . Zeus-like maturity and strength, as with each environment, each true mastery of it, was associated for the Greek a corresponding invigoration of the body and development of the mind." *The Masque of Learning*, pp. 16–18, 21.

29 *Ten Lectures on Evolutionary Ethics*, p. 3; *The Masque of Learning*, pp. 21, 74–5; "Civics: As Applied Sociology," p. 107; "Athens, Notes," [n.d.] T-GED 1/6/26/1a.

30 "How grand and spacious were its markets and public places, how ample its gardens, even how broad and magnificent were the thoroughfares;" *Cities in Evolution*, 1949, p. 5.

31 This is symbolized in the Tree of history by the branches attached to each civilization, representing the quadruple social division in each. Relying on August Comte, society was divided into *People* "in their working everyday life;" *Chiefs*, "whether mediaeval barons or modern employers;" *Intellectuals*, "represented by ancient philosophers or by mediaeval doctors, by monkish scholars or by modern men of science" and *Emotionals*, "the minister busy among his flock, the true teacher among his pupilsw" as well as mothers to their children. "A Suggested Plan for a Civic Museum," pp. 215–17; see also V. M. Welter, *Biopolis: Patrick Geddes and the City of Life*, Cambridge, MA: The MIT Press, 2000, pp. 88–92.

32 "Here then, plain enough, were the chiefs in their castles, the people in their towns and town-houses, the intellectuals in their abbeys, and the emotional forces of the time centering around the cathedral; and thus it is that town-house and castle, cloister and cathedral are all needed to understand and express the main life of the cities in the medieval time." Geddes, "A Suggested Plan for a Civic Museum," pp. 217–18; *Cities in Evolution*, 1949, pp. 172–8.

33 Geddes, "Country and Town," p. 11.

34 Geddes, *The Masque of Learning*, pp. 7–8; see also, for example, *Syllabus of a Course of Five Lectures on the History of Learning*, at Crosby Hall, Cheyne Walk, Chelsea, London: University of London Press, 1913.

35 Geddes, *The Masque of Learning*, pp. 12, 74–5; "The Twofold Aspect of the Industrial Age," pp. 176–87. Working in India alongside with his father, Arthur Geddes suggested a "corresponding picture, symbol or diagram for India," demonstrating similar notions as the Occidental Tree, including a fourfold division of the Indian society; Arthur Geddes, "Suggestion towards a Visual & Symbolic Presentment of History for India," [n.d.] T-GED 4/3/8.

36 "Town Planning and City Design – in Sociology and in Citizenship," 1908, p. 4, T-GED 3/6/7. See Welter for discussion of theoretical sources for Geddes' suggested typologies, *Biopolis*, pp. 92–9, 131–3.

37 P. Geddes, *The Masque of Learning*, pp. 50, 73.

38 Ibid., p. 72 and many other references. See also "The Twofold Aspect of the Industrial Age," pp. 176–87.

39 P. Geddes, "Two Steps in Civics: 'Cities and Town Planning Exhibition' and the 'International Congress of Cities'," Ghent International Exhibition, 1913, p. 5, T-GED 1/5/40.

40 Geddes, *Country and Town*, p. 21; *The Making of the Future: A Manifesto and a Project*, reprinted from *The Sociological Review*, May 1917, 4–5.

41 Geddes, "A Suggested Plan for a Civic Museum," pp. 212–13.

42 Geddes, "A Rustic View of War and Peace," *The Sociological Review* 10(1), 1918, 12–13. A full description of the process is provided in Geddes' final article about Civics (1906).

43 Geddes, "A Suggested Plan for a Civic Museum," p. 220. The cloister is "a centre of learning, a creative home of art, and above all these a radiant centre of moral and social idealism." "Chelsea, Past and Possible," in D. Hollins (ed.) *Utopian Papers*, London: Masters and Co., 1908, p. 12.

44 "Civics: As Concrete and Applied Sociology," pp. 83, 86.

45 Society's role in stimulating sympathetic understanding was stressed in 1918 although it had been mentioned already in 1888: "we are passing out of the age of competition into that of – co-operation; out of individual isolation for personal winnings into social reunion for the public weal." *Co-operation versus Socialism*, p. 17; and later, in "A Rustic View of War and Peace," p. 16.

46 "Civics: As Concrete and Applied Sociology," pp. 85, 91.

47 See, for example, a late account in "Regional and City Surveys as Affording Policy and Theory for Town Planning and City Design," *Town Planning Institute Papers and Discussions* 3, 1920–1, 121.

48 Geddes, "Town Planning and City Design," p. 2.

49 Geddes, "Country and Town," p. 21.

50 Geddes, *Cities in Evolution*, 1915, p. 211.

51 Defries, *The Interpreter Geddes*, p. 56.

52 *A Course of Three Lectures on Inland Towns and Cities: Their Main Origins*, Royal Geographical Society [n.d.] T-GED 1/5/25; "Edinburgh Summer Meeting (1–27 August 1904)," *The Geographical Teacher*, 229–30.

53 "City Surveys for Town Planning," p. 5; P. Geddes and V. Branford, "Rural and Urban Thought: A Contribution to the Theory of Progress and Decay," *The Sociological Review* 21(1), 1929 [presented to the Meeting of the International Association for the Improvement of Industrial Relations, held at Girton College, Cambridge], p. 7; "Civic Education and City Development," *The Contemporary Review* 87, 1905, 426.

54 Geddes, *Cities in Evolution*, 1949, pp. 9, 29.

55 Geddes, "Cities, and the Soils they Grow From: Talks From My Outlook Tower," *The Survey*, 1925, 41, T-GED 23/3/9.2. This notion was affected by the tides of war and the regional crisis in the UK. See Geddes and Branford, "Rural and Urban Thought," 11; "The Making of Our Coal Future" [Part I of "Coal: Ways to Reconstruction," *Ways of Approach: The Regional Planner's Way.*] *The Sociological Review* 18(3), 1926, 178–85; "Rural and Urban Thought," 6–11; "Ways of Transition – Towards Constructive Peace," *The Sociological Review* 22(1), 1930, 29; "The Village World: Actual and Possible," *The Sociological Review* 19(2), 1927, 108–19.

56 "Programme of Conference on Regional Survey during the Easter Vacation at the Outlook Tower," The Regional Association, 6–13 April 1920, T-GED 1/6/42.1; "Ways of Transition," p. 6.

57 Geddes, *Cities in Evolution*, 1915, pp. 223, 241.

58 Geddes, "The Village World," pp. 108–19; "Ways of Transition," pp. 24–7.

59 "[W]hen we ascend the vale to the mountains, or descend again to the sea, we are for the time freed from our imperial or national cares"; "Civic Education and City Development," p. 426; Geddes and Branford, "Rural and Urban Thought," 4–5.

60 Geddes, "The Twofold Aspect of the Industrial Age," pp. 185–6;

61 "What better training in citizenship, as well as opportunity of health, can be offered any of us than in sharing in the upkeep of our parks and gardens?" *Cities in Evolution*, 1949, p. 54. More on this ahead.

62 Geddes, *Cities in Evolution*, 1949, p. 53.

63 Geddes and Branford, "Rural and Urban Thought," 10.

64 Geddes, *Cities in Evolution*, 1915, pp. 154–5.

65 Ibid., pp. 160, 158.

66 Geddes, *Cities in Evolution*, 1949, p. 78.

67 Geddes, *Cities in Evolution*, 1915, p. 207; "A Rustic View of War and Peace," p. 16.

68 P. Geddes, "Introduction," in L. R. Latter, *School Gardening for Little Children*, London: Swan Sonnenschein & Co., 1906, p. xiv.

69 Geddes, *Cities in Evolution*, 1949, pp. 116, 120.

70 Geddes, "Civic Education and City Development," 420.

71 Geddes, *Cities in Evolution*, 1915, p. 212.

72 Geddes, "Civic Education and City Development," 418–19.

73 More on this ahead in Part III.

7 Geography and Education: The Planning Tools

1 Geddes, "Civic Education and City Development," *The Contemporary Review* 87, 1905, 415.

2 "[T]he geographer's is thus the comprehensive concrete mind . . . He takes all the various results of the different sciences and reunites them into a series of living and characteristic world-scenes." P. Geddes, *City Development, a Study of Parks, Gardens, and Culture-Institutes, a Report to the Carnegie Dunfermline Trust*, Edinburgh: Geddes and Company, Outlook Tower, Westminster, and Birmingham: The Saint George Press, Bournville, 1904, pp. 112–13. See also "The Outlook Tower as an Embryonic School and College: On the Tower's Aim of Training Students as Social Minders and Socialised Men and the Women of Action," 24/12/02, 1892, p. 2, T-GED 7/4/8; "The Influence of Geographical Conditions on Social Development," *The Geographical Journal* 12(6), 1898, 584; "Nature Study and Geographical Education," *Scottish Geographical Magazine* 18, 1902, 525; "City

Deterioration and the Need of City Survey," reprinted from *The Annals of the American Academy of Politician and Social Science*, July 1909, publication of the American Academy of Political and Social Science no. 579, Philadelphia: American Academy of Political and Social Science, p. 56, T-GED 1/6/48; "Essentials of Sociology in Relation to Economics," *Indian Journal of Economics* 3, 1920, Part 1, 21.

3 "Programme of Conference on Regional Survey during the Easter 1915 at the Outlook Tower, Provisional Committee for the Development of Regional Survey," 2–5 April, T-GED 1/6/42.2.

4 For example, "The outlooks of London may be viewed as so many widening circles: city or Westminster; L.C.C. area; Suburb Dormitories; Metropolitan (South-East); England; its northern and Western Provinces; Ireland and Scotland. (With those of Colonies; U.S.A.; India; Continent; and remainder of the world . . .);" "Country and Town: In Development, Deterioration, and Renewal" [n.d.] pp. 3–4, T-GED 3/7/37.

5 Geddes, "Note on Draft Plan for Institute of Geography," *Scottish Geographical Magazine* 18, 1902, 143–4.

6 Geddes, "The Influence of Geographical Conditions on Social Development," *The Geographical Journal* 12(6), 1898, 580.

7 These notions were elaborated quite early in Geddes' guides to art exhibitions: "Every Man his Own Art Critic at the Manchester Exhibition," Manchester and London: John Heywood, 1887, pp. 9–15, T-GED 5/3/1; "Every Man his Own Art Critic: Glasgow Exhibition, 1888," Edinburgh: William Brown, and Glasgow: John Menzies, 1888, pp. 22, 24; and later on, in a "Paper on the Power of Sight, the Art of Seeing and the Camera Obscura," [n.d.] T-GED 7/4/5.

8 Geddes, "Every Man his Own Art Critic at the Manchester Exhibition," pp. 18, 24; *Cities in Evolution by Patrick Geddes*, edited by the Outlook Tower Association Edinburgh and the Association for Planning and Regional Reconstruction, London. New and revised edition, London: Williams & Norgate, 1949, p. 97.

9 "Facilities for nature study, school excursions and school journeys, school gardens and the rest – these are now in the first rank of immediate educational desiderata. Here then is at once a theoretic and a practical strategic point for the geographical educationist." "Nature Study and Geographical Education," p. 527; *Syllabus of a Course of Ten Lectures on Evolutionary Ethics, Based on Natural Science and Sociology*, University of London (University Extension Lectures), London: W. Bishop [Hampton & Co.], 1905, p. 7, T-GED 3/6/5; "The Museum and the City: A Practical Proposal" [Read at the Dundee Conference, 1907], reprinted from *The Museums Journal*, 1908, 378–9, T-GED 5/3/26; "Scouting and Woodcraft – Present and Possible," *The Sociological Review* 22(3), 1930, 274–7; and more.

10 Geddes, "Nature Study and Geographical Education," pp. 528, 531, 535.

11 "On Universities in Europe and in India: And a Needed Type of Research Institute, Geographical and Social, Five Letters to an Indian Friend," reprinted from *The Pioneer* (14 August 1901) and from *East and West* (September 1903), Madras: National Press, p. 27, T-GED 12/2/449; [Letter] to the Secretary, Scotch Education Department, 5 March 1903, T-GED 5/3/55.

12 These were described in numerous pamphlets, courses syllabi, papers and finally books. See, for example, *Observation and Method in Sociological Studies, Synopsis of a Course of Lectures for the Second Term*, School of Sociology and Social Economics, Spring 1904, p. 2, T-GED 3/5/49; "Two Steps in Civics: 'Cities and Town Planning Exhibition' and the 'International Congress of Cities'," Ghent International Exhibition, 1913, p. 13, T-GED 1/5/40; "Sociological Society – Cities Committee, Memorandum on the Need of City Survey Preparatory to Town Planning," February 1911, p. 6, T-GED 1/6/34; "Town Planning and City Design – in Sociology and in Citizenship," 1908, p. 2, T-GED 3/6/7; and more below.

13 Geddes, "The City Survey: A First Step: I, II, II," *Garden Cities and Town Planning* 1(1–3), 1911. See also "Memorandum on the Need of City Survey Preparatory to Town Planning."

14 "Our endeavour is first and foremost to 'see the thing as it is,' and next to coordinate it with other things, until we reach a mental picture of each of our regions and communities in all the

elaborations of their place, work and people." *Cities in Evolution*, 1949, pp. xxvii, 136; "Edinburgh Summer Meeting (August 1–27, 1904)," *The Geographical Teacher*, 229; "The Movement Towards Synthetic Studies, and its Educational and Social Bearings," *The Sociological Review* 20(3), 1928, 223, T-GED 1/6/30.

15 "And thus via surveys we shall reach the modern civic problems." "Civics: As Applied Sociology," p. 108.

16 *Cities in Evolution*, 1949, p. 81.

17 "The Museum and the City," p. 376.

18 For example, the study of Edinburgh compared its location to that of Athens, and marked out many medieval houses; "Edinburgh and its Region, Geographic and Historical," *Scottish Geographical Magazine* 18, 1902, pp. 302–12; while in Chelsea, Thomas More's Garden provided local Renaissance memoirs; P. Geddes, "Chelsea, Past and Possible," in D. Hollins (ed.) *Utopian Papers*, London: Masters and Co., 1908, pp. 10–13. Similar analysis of Paris in "Lecture Notes by Patrick Geddes on the Synthetic Approach to Study, Especially History," 15 May 1900 [Paris], p. 11, T-GED 6/2/1.

19 "Observation and Method in Sociological Studies," 1904, p. 5.

20 "Conference on Regional Survey," 1920.

21 A Greek notion, in which education was "specialised perfecting of the body in youths . . . and with this the attuning of the spirit also." *The Masque of Learning*, 1912, pp. 16–18.

22 "Civics: As Applied Sociology," 1905, p. 113.

23 "Observation and Method in Sociological Studies," pp. 6–7; *Ten Lectures on Evolutionary Ethics*, p. 10; *Cities in Evolution*, 1949, p. 150.

24 See, for example, "Country and Town," pp. 30–1; *Cities in Evolution*, 1949, p. 103.

25 "Nature Study and Geographical Education," 527, 534–5. Geddes illustrated how the survey was already being used throughout the empire, mentioning the work of H. V. Lanchester, Aston Webb, Raymod Unwin and Geddes himself in his work in India. "Programme of Conference on Regional Survey," 1915.

26 "The Town Planning Bill," *Garden Cities and Town Planning* 3(28), May–June 1908, 72; "Programme of Conference on Regional Survey during the Easter Vacation at the Outlook Tower, the Regional Association," 6–13 April 1920, T-GED 1/6/42.1. Detailed headlines for the final report are listed in the third article of Geddes' advocatory series on surveys, "The City Survey: a First Step," p. 56; and shortly after, discussing the suggested "Cities Committee."

27 'Edinburgh and its Region, Geographic and Historical'; 'The Civic Survey of Edinburgh', *Transactions of the Town planning conference London 10–15 October 1910*, London: Royal Institute of British Architects, 1911, 538–68; 'Beginnings of a Survey of Edinburgh', *The Scottish Geographical Magazine*, 35, 1919, 298–327.

28 "Let us obtain photographs, pictures, engravings; we shall soon have a really adequate presentment of our city's recent growth, its advantages and disadvantages, its beauties and its ugliness. Let us collect statistics too of the city's life in every shape, vital, industrial, educational, and all else; let us ransack the Registrar's Office, the Chamber of commerce, the Town House, the School Board Offices, the College, and the rest, our City Library above all, and so enrich it also . . ." "The Museum and the City: A Practical Proposal" [Read at the Dundee Conference, 1907], reprinted from *The Museums Journal*, 1908, 373, T-GED 5/3/26; "What a Local Museum Might Be," [n.d.] T-GED 5/1/7.

29 "A Suggested Plan for a Civic Museum," p. 224; "Cities Committee," p. 3.

30 "A Suggested Plan for a Civic Museum," p. 235.

31 [Letter] to the Secretary, Scotch Education Department, 5 March 1903.

32 *The Masque of Learning*, 1912, pp. 18–19.

33 "The Museum and the City," p. 353; "Chelsea, Past and Possible," p. 7.

34 "Town Planning and City Design," p. 3.

35 "Nature Study and Geographical Education," p. 529.

36 [Letter] to the Secretary, Scotch Education Department, 5 March 1903.

37 *Cities in Evolution*, 1949, pp. 106–7. Regarding the index museum in Edinburgh as an entrance hall of a large museum; "Town Planning and City Design," p. 3.

38 "A Suggested Plan for a Civic Museum," pp. 200, 213–14.

39 "The Town Planning Bill," p. 71. "In this way our civic museum is growing, from its small individual beginnings, its small local dimensions, to absorb the essentials of all other museums; it is thus becoming each of its successive rooms having to furnish a summary and a signpost to the great culture resources around us here . . . to represent our rich and varied heritage from all the civilisations;" "A suggested plan for a Civic Museum," pp. 212–13.

40 "Two Steps in Civics." It was also described by Defries, *The Interpreter Geddes*, pp. 57–68. Texts drawn from the Catalogue to the first exhibition (1910) illustrated with a selection from the second exhibition were incorporated in the 1949 edition of *Cities in Evolution*, pp. 162–89. See also V. M. Welter, "Stages of an Exhibition: The Cities and Town Planning Exhibition of Patrick Geddes," *Planning History* 20(1), 1998, 25–35, discussed in Chapter 8.

41 "In this way, amid our City's Exhibition of Past and Present, the needful suggestions for the practical realisation of this future would not be lacking. These would come from all sides and form a new, a vital, a stimulating and suggestive section of the exhibition, one not only provoking criticism, but eliciting originality and power . . . and with these before us it would be hard if we did not, here and there, devise something no less worthy for our own town." "The Town Planning Bill," pp. 71–2; "Town Planning and City Design," p. 3. See also *Cities in Evolution*, 1949, pp. 92–3; 163–5.

42 "[T]he above description has been given in some detail, because it differs so largely from the 18th and 19th c. misrepresentations of the Middle Ages, in which so many of us were brought up." *Cities in Evolution*, 1949, pp. 173–7.

43 "Two Steps in Civics," p. 9.

44 "Two Steps in Civics," pp. 8, 16; *Cities in Evolution*, 1949, pp. 75–96, 162–89.

45 "Two Steps in Civics," p. 4.

46 *Cities in Evolution*, 1949, pp. 94–5.

47 "Two Steps in Civics," pp. 12–13.

48 *The Masque of Learning*, 1912, pp. 40–1.

49 "The Outlook Tower as an Embryonic School and College: On the Tower's Aim of Training Students as Social Minders and Socialised Men and the Women of Action." 24/12/02, 1892, pp. 1–2, T-GED 7/4/8; "Country and Town," pp. 30–31; "Observation and Method"; "Education for Citizenship." See also P. Chabard, "Towers and Globes: Architectural and Epistemological Differences between Patrick Geddes' Outlook Towers and Paul Otlet's Mundaneums," in B. Rayward (ed.), *European Modernism and the Information Society, Informing the Present, Understanding the Past*, London: Ashgate, 2008, p. 114.

50 "On Universities in Europe and in India." These were written and published upon the intention of Mr. Tata, an Indian iron and steel magnate, to fund a new-style scientific institute in India ("But Mr. Tata's choice was not for Geddes' plans and the institute set up at Bangalore was on more conventional lines"). Meller, *Patrick Geddes*, p. 223.

51 "[T]his highest outlook upon the beauty of the landscape and city deepens in appreciation. We not only see and feel what is without; but at other times and in other moods we feel and see it anew and transformed within . . ."; "On Universities in Europe and in India," p. 28. See also "Paper on the Power of Sight, the Art of Seeing and the Camera Obscura" [n.d.] T-GED 7/4/5.

52 "Education for Citizenship."

53 "The Influence of Geographical Conditions on Social Development," p. 585; "Note on Draft Plan for Institute of Geography," *Scottish Geographical Magazine* 18, 1902, 143; "On Universities in Europe and in India," 1903, p. 25. See also "A Suggested Plan for a Civic Museum," pp. 207–9.

54 "On Universities in Europe and in India," 1903, p. 25; "The Influence of Geographical Conditions," p. 582.

Notes

55 *Cities in Evolution*, 1949, p. 117.

56 "On Universities in Europe and in India," 1903, p. 23.

57 Ibid., p. 25. In his "letter to an Indian friend" Geddes elaborated upon the unity of Occident and Orient as well as on their differences, foreshadowing "that ever completer philosophy which is the united problem of humanity to attain;" ibid., p. 27. For Geddes, the West accentuated the individuality of the moment, while the East was collective and enduring. The Tower is merited for providing 'the long perspective headed by the ever-continued ancestral past, followed by the unborn future . . .'; yet "may not our activity in turn recall him to an intenser grasp of life?" p. 30. Similarly, the West was scientific, holding practical applications; the Tower, being westernly practical, expressed "our eager ambition of knowing and doing in the concrete world; our spirit of self assertion and self-realisation therefore" (pp. 29, 32–3). The Orient is spiritual, being more related to thought and to feeling, traits which the West should nevertheless aspire for. The East is also closer to its constituting mythologies: "As we descend we see developing a deeper spirit than that of our ever-widening scientific survey . . . a view expressed in two of our noblest Western myths, Greek and Mediaeval;" pp. 32–3. The interchange between East and West is embodied in the Tower. Thus, Geddes concludes: "I now see it no longer as a resultant and an expression of our Western sociology and our practical economics, not even of our philosophy and of our morals, but as a meeting-place with Eastern thought as well. It remains a Western observatory and laboratory, yet it has an Eastern cloister; it is an outlook, yet a minaret; designed as a teaching and guiding lighthouse, it has also place for an altar of the Sacred Fire;" p. 34.

58 Various sources: "Eve . . . the mother-church of the west, and also Sibyl . . . oracle with counsel . . . signified in the present by colleges and institutes; nature and labour, brought in by Science, physical and organic; as of engineering, civil, and mechanical." *The Masque of Learning*, 1912, pp. 67–9; and various other manifestations of the university prototype. "University Systems, Past and Present," pp. 527–30; *The Masque of Learning*, 1912, pp. 45–6.

59 "With regard to the duty of universities to conserve their vast and glorious heritage from the past, it has assuredly been the central strength of universities to be also in direct association with the needs and life of their communities and a constant source of weakness and decay to forget this." "University Studies and University Residence: An Address to the University Extension Students' Guild," at the University of London, South Kensington, February 1906, in P. Geddes, W. Seton, J. W. Graham, A. C. Ward, W. McDougall and T. B Whitson, *Halls of Residence for University Students*, with extract from reports by Inter-Universities Halls of Residence Committee. Edinburgh: Geddes and Colleagues, 1906, p. 3.

60 *The Proposed University for Central India, at Indore*, a reprint from *Town Planning Towards City Development*, a report to The Durbar of Indore, Indore: Holkar State Printing Press, 1918.

61 *The Masque of Learning*, 1912, pp. 74–5.

62 *The Making of the Future: A Manifesto and a Project*, reprinted from *The Sociological Review*, May 1917, p. 6.

63 *Cities in Evolution*, 1949, pp. 116–17.

64 *The Masque of Learning*, 1912, pp. 67–71.

65 "On Universities in Europe and in India," 1901, p. 6.

66 "University Studies and University Residence," pp. 14, 18–19. Examples include the University Hall of Residence in Edinburgh, built by Geddes (*The Masque of Learning*, 1912, p. 71) and Crosby Hall in Chelsea: *University Hall of Residence & Crosby Hall, Chelsea* (Officially recognized by the University of London), Warden: Professor Patrick Geddes, Visitor: The Principal of the University of London, the University and City Associates of London [Directors: James Martin White, Sir Thomas Barclay, N. P. W. Brady, Sir William Henry Dunn, Professor Patrick Geddes, Thomas Waterman Hellyer, George Montagu, R. C. Norman. Secretary: John Ross] [1911?].

67 "University Studies and University Residence," 1906, p. 14.

68 "Civics: As Concrete and Applied Sociology," 1906, p. 92.

69 *Cities in Evolution*, 1949, p. 98.

70 According to Welter, *Biopolis*, p. 232.

71 Ibid., pp. 234–5.

72 Book II of the report, describing Museums and Institutes included an astronomic museum; a geology museum including oceanography and meteorology; museum of biology and zoology; museum of the human world and an Open-air museum. "City Development, a Study of Parks, Gardens, and Culture-Institutes, a report to the Carnegie Dunfermline Trust," Edinburgh: Geddes and Company, Outlook Tower, Westminster, and Birmingham: The Saint George Press, Bournville, 1904, pp. 116–17, 122–5. A crafts village as well as a Primitive Village were recommended as open-air museums, ibid., p. 121; and a Nature Palace, being basically a Museum of Geography, ibid., pp. 112–13; a "temple of geography," according to Welter (2002), pp. 200, 202. Complementing all would be a Palace of History, as well as a historic reference museum and a History Garden; ibid., pp. 143, 152, and the art institutes would include exhibitions, studios, an art library, lending museums, an arena and a stage. The list of parks included a children's park, men's gymnasium, women's pavilion and open-air theatre, a Japanese garden, a rock garden ("evolutionary and geological"), conservatories, school gardens, a formal garden, botanic gardens and finally, playing fields; ibid., pp. 44–5.

73 Ibid., pp. 36–40.

8 Geddes' Planning Theory: Critical Evaluations

1 P. Geddes, "Cities, and the Soils They Grow From," (The Second of the Talks from the Outlook Tower) *The Survey Graphic*, 1925, 40, T-GED 23/3/9.2.

2 G. Ferraro, "'Il gioco del piano. Patrick Geddes in India 1914–1924," *Urbanistica* 103, 1995, 136–52.

3 L. Mumford, "Introduction," in P. Boardman, *Patrick Geddes: Maker of the Future*, Chapel Hill: University of North Carolina Press, 1944, pp. xiii–xiv; Mumford, introduction to J. Tyrwhitt (ed.), *Patrick Geddes in India*, with a preface by H. V. Lanchester, London: Lund Humphries, 1947, pp. 7–13; Mumford, "Mumford on Geddes," *The Architectural Review* special number, July 1950, pp. 81–7; Mumford, "The Disciple's Rebellion: A Memoir of Patrick Geddes," *Encounter* 27(3), 1966, 11–21.

4 Mumford, introduction to Tyrwhitt (ed.), *Patrick Geddes in India*, p. 7; Mumford, introduction to Boardman, *Maker of the Future*, p. xi; Mumford, "Mumford on Geddes," pp. 81–7.

5 Mumford, "The Disciple's Rebellion," p. 15.

6 Mumford, "The Geddesian Gambit," in F. G. Novak, Jr. (ed.), *Lewis Mumford and Patrick Geddes: the Correspondence*, London and New York: Routledge, 1995, p. 354. Apparently it was intended as a chapter in Mumford's biography but was never published.

7 Ibid.; see also F. G. Novak introduction to Novak, *The Correspondence*, pp. 27–8.

8 Mumford, "The Geddesian Gambit," in Novak, *The Correspondence*, pp. 361–2.

9 Mumford, "The Disciple's Rebellion," p. 18.

10 Arthur Geddes, 1968–7, quoted in P. Green, "Patrick Geddes," unpublished PhD thesis, University of Strathclyde, 1970, p. 5.

11 J. A. Hasselgren, "What is Living and What is Dead in the Work of Patrick Geddes? in University of Dundee, Special Occasional Paper in Town and Regional Planning," *Patrick Geddes: A Symposium* (1 March 1982), an event organized by the Department of Town and Regional Planning to celebrate the centenary of the foundation of the university, pp. 43–4.

12 Ibid., pp. 31, 33–6.

13 B. T. Robson, "Geography and Social Science: The Role of Patrick Geddes," in D. R. Stoddart (ed.), *Geography, Ideology and Social Concern*, London: Blackwell, 1981 p. 193.

14 H. G. Simmons, "Patrick Geddes – Prophet without Politics," *Studies in Modern European History and Culture* 2, 1976, 179.

15 V. M. Welter, *Biopolis: Patrick Geddes and the City of Life*, Cambridge, MA: The MIT Press, 2002, pp. 111–12.

16   V. M. Welter, "History, Biology and City Design – Patrick Geddes in Edinburgh," *Architectural Heritage* 6, 1995, 61–82; Welter, "The return of the Muses: Edinburgh as a *Museion*," in M. Giebelhausen (ed.), *The Architecture of the Museum: Symbolic Structures, Urban Contexts*, Manchester and New York: Manchester University Press, 1993, pp. 144–59. Welter claims that Geddes' interest in urban preservation did not emanate from reasons of beauty or sentiment, as he was simply interested in allowing contemporary citizens to embark on a new stage of city development; as such, one example of building of each period was enough. Similar criticism can be made of Geddes' practice of secondary use of past buildings.

17   A. Blunt and C. McEwan, "Introduction to Part 1: Postcolonial Knowledge and Networks," in A. Blunt and C. McEwan (eds), *Postcolonial Geographies*, New York and London: Continuum, 2002, p. 9.

18   M. Bell, R. Butlin and M. Heffernan (eds), *Geography and Imperialism 1820–1940*, Studies in Imperialism, New York: Manchester University Press, 1995, p. 4.

19   S. Naylor and G. A. Jones, "Writing Orderly Geographies of Distant Places: Regional Survey Movement and Latin America," *Ecumene* 4(3), 1997, 274. See also J. Duncan and D. Ley, introduction to J. Duncan and D. Ley (eds), *Place/Culture/Representation*, London and New York: Routledge, 1993, p. 1; D. Cosgrove and M. Domosh, "Author and Authority," in ibid., p. 28; A. Kobayashi, "Multiculturalism: Representing a Canadian Institution," in ibid., p. 207; T. Ploszajska, "Historiographies of Geography and Empire," in C. Nash and B. Graham (eds), *Modern Historical Geographies*, Essex: Pearson Education, 2002, pp. 126–7; F. Driver and G. Rose, introduction to F. Driver and G. Rose (eds), *Nature and Science: Essays in the History of Geographical Knowledge*, Historical Geography Research Series no. 28, London: Institute of British Geographers, 1992, p. 4; D. Matless, "Regional Surveys and Local Knowledges: The Geographical Imagination in Britain, 1918–39," *Transactions of the Institute of British Geographers*, New Series 17(4), 1992, 477.

20   Duncan and Ley, introduction to Duncan and Ley, *Place/Culture/Representation*, pp. 2, 4; W. J. T. Mitchell, *Iconology: Image, Text, Ideology*, Chicago and London: The University of Chicago Press, 1986, p. 38; O. Söderström, "Paper Cities: Visual Thinking in Urban Planning," *Ecumene* 3(3), 1996, 249–81.

21   C. Nash, "Cultural Geography: Postcolonial Cultural Geographies," *Progress in Human Geography* 26(2), 2002, 221.

22   G. Rose, "Geography as a Science of Observation: The Landscape, The Gaze and Masculinity," in *Nature and Science: Essays in the History of Geographical Knowledge*, Historical Geography Research Series no. 28, London: Institute of British Geographers, 1992, pp. 7, 11; J. S. Duncan, *The City as Text: The Politics of Landscape Interpretation in the Kandy Kingdom*, Cambridge: Cambridge University Press, 1990; D. Mitchell, *Cultural Geography: A Critical Introduction*, Oxford: Blackwell Publishers, 2000; Duncan and Ley, introduction to Duncan and Ley, *Place/Culture/Representation*, pp. 13, 17; D. Cosgrove and S. Daniels, (eds), *The Iconography of Landscape: Essays on the Symbolic Representation, Design and Use of Past Environments*, Cambridge: Cambridge University Press, 1988, p. 1.

23   Duncan and Ley, in *Place/Culture/Representation*, p. 13; Cosgrove and Domosh, ibid., p. 31.

24   Naylor and Jones, "Writing Orderly Geographies," 274–6.

25   Ibid., p. 275. For earlier criticism on surveys and fieldworks see J. B. Harley, "Maps, Knowledge and Power," in Cosgrove and Daniels (eds), *The Iconography of Landscape*, pp. 279–312; Duncan, "Sites of Representation," in Duncan and Ley, *Place/Culture/Representation*, pp. 42–3; Duncan and Ley, "Introduction," in ibid., p. 2; Rose, in "Geography as a Science of Observation," p. 9; Bell, Butlin and Heffernan, in *Geography and Imperialism*, p. 4; A. Godlewska, "Napoleon's Geographers (1797–1815): Imperialists and Soldiers of Modernity," in A. Godlewska and N. Smith, *Geography and Empire*, Oxford: Blackwell, 1994, pp. 31–54; M. L. Pratt, *Imperial Eyes: Travel Writing and Transculturation*, London: Routledge, 1992. For maps see mainly Harley, ibid.;

Ploszajska, "Historiographies of Geography and Empire," in Nash and Graham, *Modern Historical Geographies*, p. 125.

26 E. Said, *Orientalism*, New York: Pantheon Books, 1978, quoted in Duncan and Ley, *Place/Culture/ Representation*, p. 6; Duncan, "Sites of Representation," in ibid., p. 42.

27 M. C. Boyer, *The City of Collective Memory: Its Historical Imagery and Architectural Entertainments*, Cambridge, MA and London: The MIT Press, 1994; 2nd edn, 1998.

28 Ibid., pp. 210–14.

29 Ibid., pp. 204–5.

30 Matless, "Regional Surveys," p. 465.

31 Boyer, *The City of Collective Memory*, pp. 212, 221–2.

32 Naylor and Jones, "Writing Orderly Geographies," pp. 277–8.

33 Ibid., p. 280. See also D. N. Livingstone, "Never Shall Ye Make the Crab Walk Straight: An Inquiry into the Scientific Sources of Racial Geography," in Driver and Rose (eds), *Nature and Science*, pp. 38–40; "Moral numerology, *of course, turned out to be* moral geography *too*;" ibid., p. 40.

34 Naylor and Jones, ibid., p. 278.

35 B. Latour, *Science in Action: How to Follow Scientists and Engineers Through Society*, Cambridge, MA: Harvard University Press, 1987, ch. 6: "Centres of Calculation," pp. 215–57, in Naylor and Jones, ibid., p. 275.

36 P. Geddes, "Nature Study and Geographical Education," *Scottish Geographical Magazine* 18, 1902, 529.

37 Pratt, *Imperial Eyes*, p. 38; Duncan, "Sites of Representation," in Duncan and Ley, *Place/Culture/ Representation*, p. 42.

38 Boyer, *The City of Collective Memory*, pp. 221–2.

39 Naylor and Jones, "Writing Orderly Geographies," p. 276.

40 Ibid., pp. 275–6; Ploszajska, "Historiographies of Geography and Empire," in Nash and Graham, *Modern Historical Geographies*, p. 125; F. Driver, *Geography, Empire and Visualization*, Royal Holloway: Department of Geography Working Paper no. 1, 1994; D. Haraway, *Primate Visions*, London: Verso, 1989. On colonial exhibitions see Driver, ibid.; T. Mitchell, *Colonising Egypt*. Berkeley, CA: University of California Press, 1988, pp. 8–12; see also F. Driver, *Geography Militant: Cultures of Exploration in the Age of Empire*, Oxford: Blackwell 1999, 2nd edn, 2001, ch. 7: "Making Representation: From an African Exhibition to the High Court of Justice," pp. 146–69; P. Greenhalgh, *Ephemeral Vistas: A History of the Expositions Universelles, Great Exhibitions and World's Fairs, 1851–1939*, Manchester: Manchester University Press, 1988; P. A. Morton, *Hybrid Modernities: Architecture and Representation at the 1931 Colonial Exposition, Paris*, Cambridge, MA and London: The MIT Press, 2000.

41 Bell, Butlin and Heffernan, in *Geography and Imperialism*, p. 6; Ploszajska, "Historiographies of Geography and Empire," pp. 121–45; J. R. Ryan, "Visualizing Imperial Geography: Halford Mackinder and the Colonial Office Visual Instruction Committee, 1911," *Ecumene* 1(2), 1994, 157–76; F. Driver and A. M. C. Maddrell, "Geographical Education and Citizenship: Introduction," *Journal of Historical Geography* 22(4), 1996, 371–72; A. M. C. Maddrell, "Empire, Emigration and School Geography: Changing Discourses of Imperial Citizenship, 1880–1925," in ibid., 373–87; R. Walford, "Geographical Education and Citizenship: Afterword, in ibid., 440–2; T. Ploszajska, "Constructing the Subject: Geographical Models in English Schools, 1870–1944," in ibid., 388–98.

42 M. Bell, "Reshaping Boundaries: International Ethics and Environmental Consciousness in the Early Twentieth Century," *Transactions of the Institute of British Geographers* New Series 23, 1998, 164. The connection of citizenship to geography is long established, calling attention to the intersections of society, space and citizenship; J. Painter and C. Philo, "Spaces of Citizenship: An Introduction," *Political Geography* 14(2), 1995, 107–20. More specifically on Geddes' concerns to see geographical knowledge as a form of citizenship, being part of a national Scottish project, see C. Withers, *Geography, Science and National Identity: Scotland since 1520* (Cambridge Studies in Historical Geography), Cambridge: Cambridge University Press, 2006.

43 Bell, "Reshaping Boundaries," pp. 154, 159.

44 Ibid., pp. 155–8.

45 Ibid., p. 155, 162.

46 D. Matless, "Ordering the Land: The 'Preservation' of the English Countryside, 1918–1939," Vol. 1, unpublished PhD thesis, University of Nottingham, 1990; Matless, "Regional Surveys," pp. 464, 475; Bell, "Reshaping Boundaries," p. 151.

47 Bell, "Reshaping Boundaries," p. 151.

48 Ibid., pp. 155, 162.

49 Matless, D. "Regional Surveys," pp. 465, 466; Withers, *Geography, Science and National Identity*, pp. 225–32.

50 Bell, ibid., pp. 152, 154; D. Matless, "Visual Culture and Geographical Citizenship: England in the 1940s," *Journal of Historical Geography* 22(4), 1996, p. 425.

51 F. Driver, "Moral Geographies: Social Science and the Urban Environment in Mid-nineteenth Century England," *Transactions of the Institute of British Geographers* New Series 13, 1988, 276.

52 D. Matless, 'Forms of Knowledge and Forms of Belonging: Regional Survey and Geographical Citizenship," in V. M. Welter and J. Lawson (eds), *The City After Patrick Geddes*, Bern: Peter Lang, 2000, p. 93.

53 Ibid., p. 110; Matless, "Regional Surveys," p. 471; see also Naylor and Jones, "Writing Orderly Geographies," pp. 273–99.

54 Matless, "Regional Surveys," p. 472.

55 Idem, "Visual Culture and Geographical Citizenship," pp. 425, 428, 433.

56 Naylor and Jones, "Writing Orderly Geographies," p. 273.

57 Bell, "Reshaping Boundaries," p. 162; Matless, "Regional Surveys," pp. 464–80.

58 Ploszajska, "Constructing the Subject," pp. 388–98.

59 Matless, "Regional Surveys," p. 477.

60 Matless, "Visual Culture and Geographical Citizenship," p. 433.

61 Bell, "Reshaping Boundaries," pp. 161–2.

62 Driver, "Moral Geographies," p. 281.

63 Ibid., pp. 276–82.

64 Bell, "Reshaping Boundaries," p. 163.

65 Matless, "Regional Surveys," p. 472. Joel Outtes illustrated this use of town planning in Brazil and in Argentina as planners suggested an environmental transformation as an answer to social problems. "Disciplining Society through the City: The Genesis of City Planning in Brazil and Argentina (1894–1945)," *Bulletin of Latin America* 22(2), 2003, 148.

66 M. Dehaene, "Survey and the Assimilation of a Modernist Narrative in Urbanism," *The Journal of Architecture* 7, 2002, 33–55.

67 Ibid., p. 44. Patrick Abercrombie, claims Dehaene elsewhere, followed Geddes addressing both themes, that of civic survey and education of the public. However, he claims, the transformative cycle, which in the case of Geddes' vision led citizen and city to ever new horizons, in the context of Abercrombie's work is stabilized and broken down into a number of consecutive and relative autonomous phases. M. Dehaene, "Urban Lessons for the Modern Planner: Patrick Abercrombie and the Study of Urban Development," *Town Planning Review* 75(1), 2004, 1–30.

68 O. Söderström, "Paper Cities: Visual Thinking in Urban Planning," *Ecumene* 3(3), 1996, 249–81.

69 Ibid., p. 252. Söderström too uses the term "immutable mobiles" adapted from Latoure, meaning representations which can be detached from the place (or object which they represent), "whilst remaining immutable so that they may be moved in any direction without distortion, loss or additional corruption;" Latour, *Science in Action*, 1987, pp. 227, 236–37, quoted in Söderström, "Paper Cities," p. 253.

70 Ibid., pp. 277–8.

9 The Cities and Town Planning Exhibition: Success and Failure

1   "The Itinerant Cities Exhibition," *The Sociological Review* 4, 1911, 146–7, T-GED 23/3/3.8.

2   Both Lord and Lady Aberdeen were Scottish; they were also the parents-in-law of Lord Pentland. H. Meller, *Patrick Geddes: Social Evolutionist and City Planner*, London: Routledge, 1990, p. 199 (ref. 95).

3   "The Cities Exhibition," *The Sociological Review* 4, 1911, 342–3, T-GED 23/3/3.9.

4   P. Geddes, *Town Planning in Nagpur: A Report to the Municipal Council*, Nagpur: printed at the Municipal Press, 1917, pp. 7–8.

5   Meller, *Patrick Geddes*, p. 199 (ref. 95). "With a desire to enlighten municipal authorities and the public in general upon the subject of modern town planning and its relations to municipal administration and healthy conditions of life, the Government of Madras have under their consideration a proposal to invite Prof. Patrick Geddes of Edinburgh, director of the executive committee of the Cities and Town Planning Exhibition, 1914, to visit this presidency next cold weather and to deliver, after visiting a few typical municipalities, a series of lectures on the subject, illustrated by an extensive exhibition on town planning which he has collected." Memorandum no. 49–3/M/O, 22 July 1914, W. Frances to the Secretary to the Government of Bombay, General Department (and?) Bengal Municipal Department, Proceedings and Consultations, Municipal file 1914, OIOC.

6   "Can anyone go to Rotterdam, to Copenhagen . . . be sure to do what you can for Edinburgh; . . . send the Ramsay Garden perspective, happily not lost! . . . Can Norah get up any fresh exhibits of her garden, etc. in Dublin and Edinburgh and illustrate local detailed improvement which is needed here . . ." P. Geddes to his wife, 17 November 1914, NLS MS 10508/100. The exhibition which eventually made its way back to Britain is described by V. Welter, *Collecting Cities: Images from Patrick Geddes' Cities and Town Planning Exhibition* (researched and written for Collins Gallery, 15 May – 12 June 1999, 22 Richmond St. Glasgow). Seventy-five images are described under appropriate headings: "Surveying the City"; "Ancient and Antique Cities"; "Medieval Cities"; "Renaissance Cities"; "Cities of Gardens"; "Beautiful Cities"; "The Heart of the City". Indian images include: a map depicting the sacred geography of Allahabad Prayaga, and one of Ayodhya, both under Surveys; "Six Indian Miniature Paintings," photo sketch from the model of the design for the Victoria memorial gardens in Calcutta and three designs for an open space in another unidentified Indian city (probably Indore), as illustrations for Cities of Gardens; drawing of suggested war memorial, clock tower and fountain, for Indore and a proposed new series for Indore, both under Beautiful Cities; and finally, a perspective drawing of a design for a university at Indore, appropriately exhibited under "Heart of the City." The rest of the exhibits depict ancient and contemporary European cities.

7   "Professor Geddes and his work: The Town-Planning Exhibition. The Aims and Objects of a Great Movement," Newspaper cutting [n.d.] T-GED 1/7/25.

8   Ibid.

9   Order – no. 1431 M no. 19, dated 29 July 1914 (signed), W. Francis, Proceedings and Consultations, Municipal file 1914, OIOC; "Admission to the exhibition and the lectures will be by tickets for which application should be made to the president, Corporation of Madras, who is also the President of the Committee in charge of the arrangements connected with the exhibition and lectures of Prof. Geddes . . . The Government permit local bodies to pay a single second-class fare to Madras and back to each member of the local body visiting madras to attend the lectures." Order – no. 2411 M no. 3, dated 4 December 1914, W. Francis, Ag. Sec to Government, Proceedings and Consultations, Municipal file 1914, OIOC.

10 Various sources, T-GED 1/7/25. Similar themes were repeated throughout. Syllabus of the course of Special University Lectures to be delivered by Professor Patrick Geddes, from 1–6 February 1915, at the University of Madras, "Cities in Evolution," included the headings: "Cities in Growth: theories of the city from Aristotle and Plato to Rousseau and modern America"; "Cities in Development: products of this, in 'town,' and in 'school,' in 'people' and their immediate 'governing

class'"; "Cities in Development: arousal products of these in Cloister and of corresponding attainment"; "City of the Muses"; "Cities in Deterioration: unemployment, poverty and disease, ignorance, error and folly, vice and crime"; "Cities in Revivance and Renewal: the 'City Beautiful,' the 'University of the Future,'" examples from actual cities; and finally "Madras, the city around us, viewed from the various view-points of the present course," T-GED 1/1/4. The syllabus of lectures at the Civic Exhibition in Nagpur included: "Problems of Indian Cities"; "Cities of Antiquity"; "Medieval Cities"; "Renaissance Cities"; "Industrial and Railway Cities"; "Life Histories of Modern Capitals (Edinburgh, Glasgow, Oxford, London, Paris, Berlin)"; "Garden Cities and Garden Suburbs"; "Constructive Citizenship; Sanitation and Extension in Nagpur"; "Citizenship and Education in Nagpur"; and "The revival of Indian Crafts and Arts in Nagpur." T-GED 1/7/20.

11 "Civic Exhibition: Capital Cities," *The Indian Daily Telegraph*, 15 March 1916.

12 "Town Planning Lecture," *The Indian Daily Telegraph*, 22 March 1916.

13 "We particularly welcome the pleasing and wholesome presence of the Fountain; and though it is regrettable that its design should be of the very rudest in existence, this may the more easily be replaced some day by a work of art worthy of this central situation," *Town Planning in Jubbulpore*, p. 3. "Do I alarm any by these gentle, yet frankly defensive, interpretations of the Hindu Pantheon? I cannot see why those who respect and understand Western personifications, like the muses . . . should be such intolerant literalists to the gods of coeval." . . . "How may we understand the development of the Temple, and the Temple City? . . . 'it is natural for the European to admire Tanjore temple, since likest of all buildings perhaps in India to a Cathedral . . . [But in Srirangam] The incredible wealth of sculpture is lightly dismissed, as 'barbaric' . . ." P. Geddes, "The Temple Cities: A Town-Planning Lecture," reprinted from *The Modern Review*, March 1919, pp. 4–5, 12–13, T-GED 1/3/3.7.

14 "Town Planning: Professor Geddes' Lecture of Saturday the 11 March, 1916," *The Indian Daily Telegraph*, 16 March 1916; *The Indian Daily Telegraph*, 15 March 1916.

15 "There was a general lack of knowledge on the part of citizens of the cities to which they belonged . . . the city was open and should be known better; and this was primary education . . . boys should learn their geography and history from actual knowledge of their actual city. In this way the school boy would become a boy citizen, and, as the boy scouts are discovering the country, they would discover the town, and the next generation would be competent in their knowledge of their towns." Professor Geddes's Lecture dated the 22 March 1916 on "Citizenship and Education in Lucknow," *The Indian Daily Telegraph*, 26 March 1916.

16 "Editorial Notes," *The Advocates*, 2 March 1916, T-GED 1/7/25.

17 Meller, *Patrick Geddes*, p. 242.

18 P. Geddes to A. Defries, 9 December 1913, NLS MS10574/20–22.

19 P. Geddes, "The City of Jerusalem," *Garden Cities and Town Planning* (11)1921, 251–4; "Palestine in Renewal," *The Contemporary Review* (670)1921, 479–81; "Concerning Palestine: Jerusalem Old and New, Rhyme-Letter, from a Scotsman to his friend, a Jew", en route from Port Said to Jerusalem, 1925 (hand-written and typed, unpublished, 5 pp.) SUA T-GED 8/2/11. See also G. Biger, "Of Patrick Geddes and an Un-known Ode to 'the Return to Zion'," *Beeri* 1, 1988, 35–44 (Hebrew).

20 Hyman, "British Planners," p. 292.

21 P. Geddes, "Civics and Town Planning Exhibition, Jerusalem," *The Palestine Weekly* I(39), 1920, Special Town Planning Number, pp. 594–5.

22 Ibid., p. 597.

23 "[I]n Jerusalem he has attracted the serious attention only of a small band . . . That is an indictment that Britishers in Palestine should hasten to repudiate during the remaining 3 days of the exhibition. We confess to being greatly surprised that the opening of the exhibition to which all classes had been invited, was conspicuous by the lack of general support from the English community." "In Support of Professor Geddes", *The Palestine Weekly* I(39), 1920, Special Town Planning Number, p. 593.

24 Geddes, "Civics and Town Planning Exhibition, Jerusalem," ibid., p. 596.

25 P. Geddes to Louis Brandeis, 18 October 1920, NLS MS 10516/101. Earlier, Geddes differentiated, "while the eye is pre-eminently the organ of intellect, the ear is above all that of emotion." *The Masque of Learning and its Many Meanings, Devised and Interpreted by Patrick Geddes*. Edinburgh: Patrick Geddes and Colleagues, Outlook Tower and Chelsea, 1912, p. 64.

26 "[I]t has been said many times that the Jews with their world-wide experience will be able to bring to Palestine the best qualities of all nations amongst whom they lived . . . it does not apply to art, architecture and town planning." S. A. Van Vriesland, "Jews and Town Planning in Palestine," p. 598.

27 Ibid.

10 Surveys and Surgeries: Narratives of Old and New

1 H. Meller, *Patrick Geddes: Social Evolutionist and City Planner*, London: Routledge, 1990, pp. 237–8; G. Ferraro, *Rieducazione alla Speranza: Patrick Geddes Planner in India, 1914–1924*, Milano: Jaca Books, 1998, p. 29.

2 After a three-day survey in Jubbulpore he wrote: "Time has not permitted us to see anything of the Civil Station, beyond the appreciation of its unusually well planted character. We have concentrated our short stay upon the old city." *Town Planning in Jubbulpore: A Report to the Municipal Committee by Professor Geddes and H. V. Lanchester*, printed at the Hitkarini Press, Jubbulpore, 1917, p. 1; The Nagpur Report was "written after a visit of three days in October 1915 and a longer stay during the visit . . . of the Civic Exhibition between January and February 1916," In the Madras Presidency: "five cities to report on (averaging 50,000) in less than a fortnight;" P. Geddes, *Town Planning in Nagpur: A Report to the Municipal Council*, Nagpur: printed at the Municipal Press, 1917, p. 1.

3 "In these old Indian villages there is more of Peacedom than under great Cities of Wardom. So, despite all its cumulative martyrdoms and individual evils (that ruin of the peasant which is a midmost process of 'history,' 'government,' 'administration,' as of urban life, and most of what it thinks civilisation)." P. Geddes to family, "From Port Said . . . to Suez and Gulf of Suez," 1.10.1914, NLS MS10504/78–81.

4 Ferraro, *Patrick Geddes Planner in India*, p. 193.

5 Geddes, *Town Planning in Jubbulpore*, p. 8; see also Geddes, *Town Planning in Nagpur*, p. 12.

6 Ferraro, *Patrick Geddes planner in India*, pp. 191–2.

7 See also D. Goodfriend, "The Culturally Informed Town Planning of Patrick Geddes in India 1914–1924," *Human Organization* 38(4), 1979, 354.

8 P. Geddes, *Town Planning in Nagpur*, pp. 2–4, 17.

9 P. Geddes, *Report on the Towns in the Madras Presidency*, Tanjore, 1915, p. 17, quoted in *Patrick Geddes in India*, edited by J. Tyrwhitt, with an introduction by L. Mumford and a preface by H. V. Lanchester, London: Lund Humphries, 1947, p. 41; P. Geddes, *Report on the Towns in the Madras Presidency*, p. 23, quoted in ibid., p. 47; P. Geddes, *Town Planning in Balrampur: A Report to the Honourable the Maharajah Bahadur*, 1917, p. 41, quoted in *Patrick Geddes in India*, pp. 48–52.

10 P. Green, "Patrick Geddes," unpublished PhD thesis, University of Strathclyde, 1970, pp. 243–57.

11 P. Geddes, "Barra Bazar Improvement: A Report to the Corporation of Calcutta," Calcutta: printed at the Corporation Press, 1919, p. 5.

12 Ibid., p. 7. Similarly, in Nagpur, "Piercing of new main roads . . . with full regard to the cheap land which is still available in close proximity to the crowded centres of over population and highest values . . ." Geddes, *Town Planning in Nagpur*, p. 4; see similar description in Geddes, *Town Planning in Jubbulpore*, p. 9.

13 Geddes, "Barra Bazar Improvement," p. 13.

14 Ibid., pp. 22–3.

15 Ibid., p. 14.

16 The model he had in mind was an American one, which he described in detail. Ibid., pp. 16–17.

17 M. Beattie, "Sir Patrick Geddes and Barra Bazaar: Competing Visions, Ambivalence and Contradiction," *The Journal of Architecture* 9, 2004, 142. In Nagpur, Geddes suggested building new latrines upon similar considerations; *Town Planning in Nagpur*, p. 11. See also P. Geddes, "Town Planning in Colombo," papers laid before the Legislative Council of Ceylon during the year 1921, Colombo: H. R. Cottle, Government Printer, 1922, pp. 9–10.

18 Beattie, "Patrick Geddes and Barra Bazaar," p. 131.

19 "[A]ccording to Prof. Geddes' scheme about 50 percent of the houses would remain in their present condition without any improvement, that large blocks of insanitary areas would not be sufficiently opened up." *Report on the Municipal Administration of Calcutta for the Year 1919–1920*, Calcutta: Corporation Press, 1920, pp. 17–18, quoted in Beattie, *The Journal of Architecture* p. 145.

20 *Report on the Municipal Administration of Calcutta*, pp. 17–18, quoted in Beattie, ibid., pp. 145–6. Consequently, as Beattie witnessed, "the part north of Ratan Sarkar Garden Street proposed by Geddes is now a rubbish dump;" ibid.

21 Ibid., p. 146.

22 C. R. Ashbee (ed.), *Jerusalem 1918–1920: Being the Records of the Pro-Jerusalem Council during the period of the British Military Administration*, London: John Murray, 1921.

23 H. V. Lanchester, "Mr. Mclean's Plan Revised," *The Observer*, 12 July 1919. The article was attached to Geddes' report.

24 Lanchester, ibid.

25 Zionist Commission, Palestine to Inner Actions Committee, Zionist Organization, London, 15 May 1919, CZA Z4/1721.

26 A. Ruppin, London to Palestine Office, Jaffa, 5 September 1919, CZA S15/123c.

27 R. Fuchs and G. Herbert, "A Colonial Portrait of Jerusalem: British Architecture in Mandate-Era Palestine," in N. AlSayyad (ed.), *Hybrid Urbanism: On the Identity Discourse and the Built Environment*, Westport, CT and London: Praeger, 2001, pp. 83–108.

28 P. Geddes, *Jerusalem Actual and Possible: A Preliminary Report to the Chief Administrator of Palestine and Military Governor of Jerusalem on Town Planning and City Improvements*, November 1919, p. 2, CZA Z4/10202.

29 Ibid., p. 4.

30 Ibid., p. 6.

31 Ibid., p. 11.

32 Ibid., p. 30.

33 Ibid., pp. 11–12. Similar treatments were suggested for the Mount of Olives, commending to renew desolated and fallen terraces and planting. See ibid., p. 16; Damascus Gate was also to be exposed by removal of rows of shops and provided with an improved public place, ibid., p. 13.

34 Ibid., p. 11.

35 Ibid., pp. 4–5.

36 Ibid., pp. 23–4.

37 Ibid., pp. 10–11. For the plan see Hyman, "British Planners," p. 139, fig 3.6, CZA L4/770.

38 P. Geddes to R. Storrs, April 1930, NLS MS10518/73–4.

39 R. Storrs to P. Geddes, 16 April 1930, NLS MS10518/75. The plan is today kept amongst the papers of Charles Robert Ashbee, Jerusalem Municipal Archives.

40 P. Geddes to A. Ruppin, 10 October 1930, NLS MS10518/137.

41 A. Ruppin to P. Geddes, 3 December 1930, NLS MS10502/15b.

42 Ashbee was an Arts & Crafts Architect who worked in Jerusalem between 1918 and 1922. For more on his artistic urban theory and work in Jerusalem see N. Hysler-Rubin, "Arts & Crafts and the Great City: Charles Robert Ashbee in Jerusalem," *Planning Perspectives* 21(4), 2006, 347–68.

43 Geddes, *Jerusalem, Actual and Possible*, pp. 17–19.

44 Ibid., p. 16.

45 Ibid., pp. 20–1. A similar analysis of the relationship between the old and new, resulting in a complete separation between the historical core of the city and its modern development, is apparent in Geddes' report for the city of Tiberias, where Geddes was called in order to plan a new Jewish garden suburb. The report describes the ancient city walls, suggesting "some 'conservative surgery' . . . with moderate clearances accordingly." Geddes suggested repairing the ancient Castle rebuilding it and putting it into proper utilization which would be "*reasonable continuous*" with its past. Building around the fosse is to be restricted. The report then elaborates upon the dense and mixed Arab and Jewish population of the old city, calling for its thinning. Geddes fails to mention two neighborhoods already existing in close proximity to the old city, built haphazardly yet efficiently in order to relieve the existing congestion within. In fact, most of the report relates to the nearby hot springs which he suggested to revive and to bring, once again, health and wealth to the city dwellers "as in the days of Herods," and as part of the revival of the Jordan Valley. P. Geddes, "Tiberias and Neighbourhood," [n.d.] ATQ Tiberius file 184.

46 Geddes, *Jerusalem, Actual and Possible*, p. 1.

47 Ibid., p. 9.

48 Ibid., p. 13; see also Hyman, "British Planners," p. 132.

49 Geddes, *Jerusalem, Actual and Possible*, p. 18.

11 The Regional Analysis: Rehabilitating the Mediterranean Basin

1 "Cyprus and its Power to help the East, by Mr. and Mrs. Geddes," reprinted from the report of the International Conference on Armenian Aid, 1 May 1897, T-GED 1/8/22.

2 P. Geddes and V. Branford, "Rural and Urban Thought: A Contribution to the Theory of Progress and Decay," *The Sociological Review* 21(1), 1929 [presented to the Meeting of the International Association for the Improvement of Industrial Relations, held at Girton College, Cambridge], p. 8.

3 P. Geddes, "The Village World: Actual and Possible, *The Sociological Review* 19(2), 1927, 108–19. Geddes believed that the malaria in the Holy City defended it from repeat conquest. "The Second of the Talks from my Outlook Tower: Cities, and the Soils they Grow From," *The Survey*, 1925, 40–4, T-GED 23/3/9.1–5.

4 "The countless Indian intellectuals who now qualify as lawyers and politicians, both at home and in England, have as yet shown no policy in which forestry, irrigation or drainage appreciably figure." Geddes and Branford, "Rural and Urban Thought," p. 8.

5 P. Geddes, "Palestine in Renewal," *The Contemporary Review* 1921(670), 481.

6 P. Geddes, "Cities, and the Soils they Grow from," p. 43

7 P. Green, "Patrick Geddes," unpublished PhD thesis, University of Strathclyde, 1970, pp. 275–6. The reports relating directly to the regional treatment of Palestine are largely lost.

8 From "The Planning of Colonies." Note to the Zionist commission, typescript, p. 12, quoted in Green, "Patrick Geddes," p. 281; "Again, as in Cyprus a generation before, Geddes pointed to reforestation, improvement of water supply, and general revival of agriculture as the keys both to material prosperity in the Holy Land and to the solution of its internal conflicts." P. Boardman, *The Worlds of Patrick Geddes: Biologist, Town Planner, Re-educator, Peace-Warrior*, London, Henley and Boston: Routledge & Kegan Paul, 1978, p. 313.

9 Green, "Patrick Geddes," p. 276.

10 Ibid., pp. 282–3.

11 "Palestine in Renewal," 1921(670), p. 480; Green, "Patrick Geddes," p. 282.

12 Geddes also advocated a system of credit finance for the promotion of agricultural colonies, allowing for the utilization of Arab labour. Green, ibid., pp. 278–9. In doing so, Geddes was clearly also rebutting popular claim of the local Arab population regarding the capacity of the land: "The area of Palestine available for reclamation and improvement is vastly greater than its present too scanty population can overtake. This affords for immigration accompanied by increasing prosperity to the existing inhabitants." Geddes, "Palestine in Renewal," p. 479. For more about Geddes' perceived differences between Jews and Arabs see a series of lecture he delivered in Bombay

after having visited Palestine twice: "Civilisation: A Challenge, Patrick Geddes' Bombay Lectures (1922–23)."

13 Green, "Patrick Geddes," pp. 283–4.

14 Ibid., pp. 285–90. The reclamation of the country was clearly expressed in Geddes' report to the municipality of Haifa, pp. 6–7, 47–51, quoted in Green, ibid., pp. 292–5. In Haifa, Geddes advised the retention of run-off water by means of an extensive re-afforestation policy – for the purpose of supplying fuel for the population, to stabilize the sand dunes, and to act as a visual screen between parts of the industrial are and the town. Acre was incorporated in this local region of Haifa and had local roles of her own as the tourist and recreation town.

15 V. M. Welter, "The 1925 Master Plan for Tel-Aviv by Patrick Geddes," *Israel Studies*, 14(3), 2009, 100. Welter relates to Geddes' definition of the Conurbation, a regional development unit.

16 P. Geddes, *Town-Planning Report – Jaffa and Tel-Aviv*, 1925, p. 44.

17 R. Kallus, "Patrick Geddes and the Evolution of a Housing Type in Tel-Aviv," *Planning Perspectives* 12, 1997, 285–6.

18 B. Hyman, "British Planners in Palestine, 1918–1936," unpublished PhD thesis, London School of Economics and Political Science, 1994, pp. 203–4.

19 Ibid., pp. 290–306.

20 "With all respect to the ethnic distinctiveness and the civic individuality of Tel Aviv, as Township, its geographic, social and even fundamental economic situation is determined by its position as Northern Jaffa." Geddes, "Jaffa and Tel-Aviv," p. 1.

21 Geddes, *Jaffa and Tel-Aviv*, p. 58.

22 Ibid., p. 1.

23 Hyman, "British Planners," p. 315.

24 Geddes, *Jaffa and Tel-Aviv*, pp. 5–6.

25 Later on in the report, when Geddes discusses differentiation between housing conditions, he distinguishes between the "Old Town" and the "New Town," meaning the older, already built parts of Tel Aviv, and the planned extension. Ibid., p. 17.

26 Similar comparisons are offered in Geddes' report on the ancient hot springs nearby Tiberius, which Geddes recommending rehabilitating back to their old glory of Roman days. "The Hot Springs of Tiberius," [n.d.] CZA A107/825. See also Hyman, "British Planners," pp. 226–43.

27 Ibid., pp. 32–3.

28 Ibid., p. 35.

29 Ibid., pp. 8–9.

30 Ibid., p. 33.

31 Ibid., p. 32.

12 The Garden in the City: Civic Revival in Indore and Tel Aviv

1 See, for example, *Town Planning in Jubbulpore: A Report to the Municipal Committee* by Professor Geddes and H. V. Lanchester, printed at the Hitkarini Press, Jubbulpore, 1917; H. Meller, *Patrick Geddes: Social Evolutionist and City Planner*, London: Routledge, 1990, pp. 236–7, about town extension schemes providing workers' housing in Jamshedpur, 1920, '*in the wake of industrial unrest*'; and others.

2 The story of the Diwali was told in Geddes' "A Schoolboy's Bag and a City's Pageant: The first Talk from my Outlook Tower," *The Survey*, 1925, T-GED 23/3/9.1–5, and quoted in P. Boardman, *The Worlds of Patrick Geddes: Biologist, Town Planner, Re-educator, Peace-Warrior*, London, Henley and Boston: Routledge & Kegan Paul, 1978, pp. 295–7. Geddes had previously praised the traditional procession for helping to keep the streets clean, marking a future festival in Nagpur as an anticipated event: "For next Diwali something can be done: this will suggest more for next year, and so on. 'Nagpur 1920' may thus, by 1918, become a name to conjure with." P. Geddes, *Town Planning in Nagpur. A Report to the Municipal Council*, Nagpur: printed at the Municipal Press, 1917, p. 8.

3 "'Make me Maharaja for a day!' I cried. 'What do you mean?' asked the Minister. I explained; (and not without reference to precedents, such as Sancho Panza, and Christopher Sly). One main business of a prince is to be magnificent, and thus to head and express the ideals of his people . . . to arouse all alike to cleanliness, and good works complemental to such renewal and godliness." Geddes, "A Schoolboy's Bag," p. 528.

4 Ibid., pp. 529, 533.

5 Ibid., p. 553.

6 Ibid.

7 Ibid.

8 Geddes had witnessed this before in New York: "You may ask how all this bears on American cities? Well, my treatment of the sweepers was directly adapted from what I knew of the doings of Colonel Waring with his men in New York years before . . . The general idea goes further – that all cities, towns, even villages, and everywhere, are in need of such stir of show and festival to awake them from their daily routine; and from their depression, even stagnation, of civic thought and hope . . . though in Edinburgh we have made great pageants, we can do wonders with but a single piper. For children cannot but follow." Ibid., p. 554.

9 Ibid.

10 These include the plan for a new Jewish garden suburb outside the old city of Tiberias P. Geddes, *Tiberias and Neighbourhood*, ATQ Tiberius file 184, and five new estates upon garden city lines set within a natural park built for the Zionist Commission in Haifa, regarding which he wrote, "Here no doubt may be needed some education of the public in respect of natural life and beauty, but that is easy in the East . . ." P. Geddes, *Town Planning in Haifa: A Report to the Governor*, (typescript) 1920, quoted in B. Hyman, "British Planners in Palestine, 1918–1936," unpublished PhD thesis, London School of Economics and Political Science, 1994, p. 165; P. Geddes, "Zionist Commission's Carmel Estates," 1920, ibid., p. 165. See also P. Geddes, "A Garden City on Mount Carmel" [n. d.] 15 February 1921, CZA L51/875.

11 P. Geddes, "Town-Planning Report – Jaffa and Tel-Aviv," 1925.

12 Ibid., p. 19. This undoubtedly echoes a popular discussion at the time regarding the best way to design roads in the suburbs; see, for example, R. Unwin, *Town Planning in Practice*, London: T. Fisher, 1909. He also suggests new cheap building types as well as common building groups: "is this not a field in which Jewish Economic thought and activity should not lag but lead? And here in Tel Aviv of all places." Ibid., pp. 11–12.

13 Ibid., p. 47.

14 Ibid.

15 Ibid., pp. 6–7, 49.

16 Ibid., pp. 37–39, 49–50.

17 Ibid., p. 42.

18 "[W]hile the skilled scientific institution is providing for the increasing success of rural developments, these school gardens are in their own way no less important, by giving that touch of rural interest to the young city minds, which in most schools heretofore have been starved . . . it is thus very largely from lack of gardens that schools are so much condemned to a vicious circle of verbalistic and mechanistic conceptions." Ibid., p. 44.

19 Ibid., p. 46.

20 Ibid., p. 47.

21 Ibid., p. 44.

22 "Tel-Aviv assuredly may be – so surely must be – a living and contemporary evidence of this harmony of thought and action. And towards this in all directions, what better beginning than by spreading over this whole city, its verdant ad expanding banner, fruit-emblazoned in purple and gold." Ibid., p. 48.

23 Established already in 1909 on the 15th day of the Hebrew month of Shevat, the biblical beginning of the year of the trees. Ibid., p. 43.

24   Ibid., p. 51.
25   Ibid., p. 48.
26   Ibid., p. 56.
27   Ibid., p. 54.

13 Civic Centers and Cultural Institutes: Enhancing Local Traditions

1   Volker Welter illustrates this notion in Geddes' for an extension of the Indian town of Conjeevaram (Kanchipuram), where a new village is planned to surround a temple building "as a house of the spirit." In Tel Aviv, he shows the same principle, whereas here the gardens – or nature – substitute for the religious buildings. V. M. Welter, *Biopolis: Patrick Geddes and the City of Life*, Cambridge, MA: The MIT Press, 2002, pp. 241–3.

2   P. Geddes, *The Proposed University for Central India, at Indore*, a reprint from *Town Planning Towards City Development: A Report to The Durbar of Indore*, Indore: Holkar State Printing Press, 1918, p. 19.

3   P. Geddes, *A Report on the Development and Expansion of the City of Baroda*, printed at the "Lakshmi Vilas" Press, Baroda, 1916, pp. 29–30.

4   Ibid., p. 74.

5   Ibid., pp. 33–4.

6   Ibid., p. 25.

7   P. Geddes, *Jerusalem Actual and Possible: A Preliminary Report to the Chief Administrator of Palestine and Military Governor of Jerusalem on Town Planning and City Improvements*, November 1919, ATQ Jerusalem General file (78) [also CZM Z4/10.202], p. 19.

8   "We should be happy to think that many of those visiting the Exhibition were interested not merely in a short visit for the purpose of seeing some superficial beauty in pictures or antique city plans, but also interested in the principles and ideals underlying these plans which are of the most vital importance in the building up of this country into a beautiful national home of a happy Jewish nation enjoying life therein." Geddes, *Jerusalem Actual and Possible*, pp. 6, 12.

9   Similar themes were suggested later for the museum in Tel-Aviv; P. Geddes, *Town-Planning Report – Jaffa and Tel-Aviv*, 1925, p. 53.

10   Ibid., pp. 27–9.

11   A. T. Clay, *Notes on Mr. Geddes' Museum Plan*, 1919, ATQ, Jerusalem General File (78).

12   Geddes, *Jaffa and Tel-Aviv*, p. 59.

13   Ibid., p. 52.

14   Ibid.

15   "[I]s not then the discovery, the education and encouragement of artistic genius – so relatively frequent in Jewish populations and this despite all their past hardships – well worthy of the serious attention and the active encouragement ad support of their yet more numerous reflective and practical minds, and at the present period of Zionist initiative especially?" ibid.

16   "Is not now the time for architecture, when this and other cities are being rapidly built? The time too for furnishing each home with at least some worthy beginnings of that beauty of domestic furnishing, and of household 'goods' worthy of that name?" ibid., p. 53.

17   N. Hysler-Rubin, "Arts & Crafts and the Great City: Charles Robert Ashbee in Jerusalem," *Planning Perspectives* 21(4), 2006, 347–68.

18   Geddes, *Jaffa and Tel-Aviv*, p. 26.

19   Ibid., p. 27.

14 Cloisters between East and West: Incipient Universities in Indore and Jerusalem

1   "On Universities in Europe and in India: And a Needed Type of Research Institute, Geographical and Social, Five Letters to an Indian Friend," reprinted from *East and West*, September 1903, Madras: National Press, p. 33, T-GED 12/2/449.

2 "Fertilise his lotus-seedlet with our far-blown and strangely active Western pollen . . . returning to the study of India with the best Western evolutionary geography and anthropology and economics . . ." ibid., p. 16; "Modernise then your education by a wise use of the great opportunity now before you: Europeanise it in the best sense, and at the highest level," ibid., p. 20.

3 P. Geddes, "Cities in Evolution: Introductory Course of General Sociology," Winter Term 1919, University of Bombay, T-GED 1/1/5, included the following topics: cities present and past; the survey of cities; civic museums and observatories; cities as geographical and occupational developments; city origins generally; cities as historical developments; representative selection of historic cities; sociological interpretation of civic history; theories of progress and degeneration; social effects of cities; city and citizen; their essential life; the evils of cities; social pathology; the hopes of cities; civic therapeutics and hygiene; the incipient civic renascence; its needed policy; civic progress and its conditions. See also "Civilisation: A Challenge, Patrick Geddes' Bombay Lectures (1922–23)," summarised by Arthur Geddes (1923–4) edited by F. J. Adkins (1938) and foreword by L. Mumford ("never written"). Unpublished, NLS MS 10618/12–249, which presented familiar themes: Part I: Contemporary Civilization; Scotland, Wales, Spain and Portugal, Austria, Italy, Holland and Belgium, Turkey, Switzerland. Part II: Sociology, education outlooks, social changes: rural and mechanical, evolutionary interpretations of social life, sociology: its teaching and applications. Appendix A: the approach to citizenship through history and through regional surveys. Appendix B: what are regional and social surveys? "*Whether you agree with it or not, you must agree in the aim of the course – a review of the world and production of the best possible.*" Ibid., 127/8.

4 P. Geddes, *The Proposed University for Central India, at Indore*, a reprint from *Town Planning Towards City Development, A Report to The Durbar of Indore*, Indore: Holkar State Printing Press, 1918.

5 Ibid., p. 43.

6 Ibid., pp. 21, 23–4.

7 "Why not also the active criticism of the life of the day, like Moliere in his, or Ibsen, Brieux or Shaw in ours, or again the reopening idealism of the future, with Maeterlinck and Verhaeren? . . . and though Indore be yet in the day of smaller things, it has beginnings, which might be helped to grow. And is it not already twice as big as Athens at its greatness?" Ibid., p. 34. "Geddes suggested a group of buildings which would constitute the most unusual civic centre in the world. Although he credited the Maharajah with suggesting such a group, only P.G. could have crowded the whole of human history, science, and literature into the projected library, museum, and theatre." P. Boardman, *The Worlds of Patrick Geddes: Biologist, Town Planner, Re-educator, Peace-Warrior*, London, Henley and Boston: Routledge & Kegan Paul, 1978, p. 292.

8 *The Proposed University for Central India*, pp. 42–3.

9 "This, on the university side, would show the opening generation that they are part of an advancing community, and would also show that they can contribute to advance on the best lines and to avoid the pitfalls of the past. It would also indicate where mistakes are being made for lack of knowledge, and how to get the knowledge to avoid these mistakes. And it would make the University's greatest pride to be that it can help in the formation of a great community." *Committee on Collaboration between the Bombay University and the Bombay City*, Bombay: printed at the Government Central Press [n. d.] p. 1, T-GED 12/2/451.

10 "Of all the commissioners, with which I have been honored in this country, none do I appreciate more . . . than that of submitting plans for this coming university of Benares . . . on account of the beauty and associations of Benares and of the splendid opportunities which the city and the site afford and above all perhaps to the opportunity it opens towards the needed improvement of universities, not only in India but throughout the world . . . to arouse the world to the needs for modernizing, and reorganizing its education." "Professor Geddes on Town Planning in India, an interview," *The Leader* [?] T-GED 1/7/25.

11 V. M. Welter, *Biopolis: Patrick Geddes and the City of Life*, Cambridge, MA: The MIT Press, 2002, p. 22.

12 Zangwill supported Geddes' work and also encouraged the writing of his first biography. See, for example, I. Zangwill to P. Geddes, 23 August 1919, CZA A120–326.

13 D. Eder to P. Geddes, 16 July 1918, CZA L3/13/III.

14 "Is this new university to aim simply at being the latest – the 244th or thereby – upon the list of the world's universities?" *The Proposed Hebrew University of Jerusalem: Preliminary Report* by Patrick Geddes, Director of the City and Town Planning Exhibition, Professor of Sociology and Civics, University of Bombay, assisted by Captain Frank C. Mears. [Jerusalem] December 1919, p. 5, CZA L4/108.

15 Ibid., p. 3.

16 Ibid., p. 29; uniting humanities – grammar, logic and rhetoric (the traditional "Trivium") with the Sciences – Arithmetic, Geometry, and Astronomy (Quadrivium) culminated and centered in Music – this of course being understood not simply as the specific art of that name, but also as that "spirit of the Muses," who, for the Greek wisdom and culture, should not only crown all studies, but permeate and ennoble the whole life' as well as "harmony and unity in its highest human expression," p. 21; see also P. Geddes to Rabindranath Tagore, 17 May 1922, in B. Fraser (ed.), *The Tagore-Geddes Correspondence*, Kolkata: Visva-Bharati, 2004, pp. 65–6. On the symbolism of the "Magen David" and its use in Jerusalem: P. Geddes, "A Note on Graphic Methods, Ancient and Modern," *The Sociological Review* 15, 1923, pp. 230–1.

17 Geddes, "The Proposed Hebrew University of Jerusalem," pp. 27–8. Welter describes the Hebrew University as the cloister for Palestine as a city, and the great hall as "the temple of life for the region." V. M. Welter, "The Geddes Vision of the Region as City – Palestine as a 'Polis'," in J. Fiedler (ed.), *Social Utopias of the Twenties: Bauhaus, Kibbutz and the Dream of the New Man*, published for the Bauhaus Dessau Foundation and the Friedrich-Ebert Foundation, Tel Aviv. Wuppertal: Muller+Busmann Press, 1995, pp. 71–9.

18 Geddes, ibid., p. 5.

19 Ibid., p. 18. "What is this whole university scheme if not to be a worthy element of that renewed Jerusalem which is the undying hope of Israel? . . . And surely all the better earnest of all this, and of the wider fulfilment of these ancient hopes and aspirations a now more than ever renewing, if this be again also of world-wide appeal? May not that become the very highest function of the coming University?" Ibid., p. 29.

20 Ibid., pp. 18, 30.

21 The practical result, Meller claims, had been the restriction of any other development in the city, slowly causing its stagnation and eventually its resentment. After two months' tour in India in 1973 Meller concluded: "Patrick Geddes is well known by reputation still, but there is total ignorance about his planning ideas and his work." Letter to author, 5 April 1973, in Boardman, *The Worlds of Patrick Geddes*, pp. 436–7.

22 NLS MS/10517; CZM L12/39; Hebrew University Archives file 31.1.

23 M. Shapira, "The University and the City: Patrick Geddes and the First Master Plan for the Hebrew University, 1919," in S. Katz and M. Heyd (eds), *The History of the Hebrew University in Jerusalem: Roots and Beginnings*, Jerusalem: Magnes Publishers, 1997, p. 209. Green claims that this part in Geddes' work in Jerusalem was misunderstood, as Ashbee too believed that Geddes' prediction of the urban development toward Mount Scopus was far removed from the reality of the situation; P. Green, "Patrick Geddes," unpublished PhD thesis, University of Strathclyde, 1970, pp. 302–3.

15 Patrick Geddes and Colonial Town Planning

1 See, for example, P. Geddes, "Essentials of Sociology in Relation to Economics," *Indian Journal of Economics* 3, 1920, part 1, p. 5.

2 P. Geddes, "Civics: As Applied Sociology, Part I," *Sociological Papers*, Vol. I, published for the Sociological Society, London: Macmillan & Co., 1905, p. 109.

3 See, for example, A. Defries, *The Interpreter Geddes: The Man and his Gospel*, London: George Routledge & Sons, 1927, p. 261.

4   P. Geddes, *The Making of the Future: A Manifesto and a Project*, London: Sherrat & Hughes, 1917, reprinted from *The Sociological Review*, May 1917, p. 5.

5   A. King, *Urbanism, Colonialism, and the World-economy: Cultural and Spatial Foundations of the World Urban System*, The International Library of Sociology, University of Lancaster, London and New York: Routledge, 1990, p. 57; A. J. Christopher, "Urban Segregation Levels in the British Overseas Empire and its Successors in the Twentieth Century," *Transactions of the Institute of British Geographers* New Series 17, 1992, 95–107, and many others.

6   A. King, *Colonial Urban Development: Culture, Social Power and Environment*, London, Henley and Boston: Routledge & Kegan Paul, 1976; King, "Colonial Cities: Global Pivots of Change," in R. Ross and G. J. Telkamp (eds), *Colonial Cities: Essays on Urbanism in a Colonial Context*, Comparative Studies in Overseas History 5, Dordrecht and Lancaster: Martinus Nijhoff Publishers, 1985, pp. 7–32; J. M. Jacobs, *Edge of Empire: Postcolonialism and the City*, London and New York: Routledge, 1996; N. AlSayyad, "Urbanism and the Dominance Equation," in N. AlSayyad (ed.), *Forms of Dominance: On the Architecture and Urbanism of the Colonial Enterprise*, Aldershot: Avebury, 1992, p. 5. See also Z. Çelik, *Urban Forms and Colonial Confrontations, Algiers under French Rule*, Berkeley and Los Angeles, CA: University of California Press, 1997, p. 2.

7   D. Chakrabarty, *Provincializing Europe: Postcolonial Thought and Historical Difference*, Princeton, NJ: Princeton University Press, 2000, pp. 3–23; C. Nash, "Cultural Geography: Postcolonial Cultural Geographies," *Progress in Human Geography* 26(2), 2002, 220. See also R. Guha, "On Some Aspects of the Historiography of Colonial India," in *Subaltern Studies I: Writings on South Asian History and Society*, Delhi: Oxford University Press, 1982, pp. 1–8; G. Prakash, "Writing Post-orientalist Histories of the Third World: Perspectives from Indian Historiography," *Comparative Studies in Society and History* 32(1), 1990, 383–408; G. C. Spivak, "Can the Subaltern Speak?," in C. Nelson and L. Grossberg (eds), *Marxism and the Interpretation of Culture*, Urbana and Chicago, IL: University of Illinois Press, 1988, pp. 271–313; J. D. Sidaway, "Postcolonial Geographies: Survey-explore-review," in A. Blunt and C. McEwan (eds), *Postcolonial Geographies*, New York and London: Continuum, 2002, p. 13.

8   B. S. A. Yeoh, "Postcolonial Cities," *Progress in Human Geography* 25, 2001, 464; Yeoh, "Historical Geographies of the Colonised World," in C. Nash and B. Graham (eds), *Modern Historical Geographies*, Essex: Pearson Education, 2002, pp. 146–66; G. A. Myers, "Intellectual of Empire: Eric Dutton and Hegemony in British Africa," *Annals of the Association of American Geographers* 88(1), 1998, 5; M. S. Kumar, "The Evolution of Spatial Ordering," in A. Blunt and C. McEwan (eds), *Postcolonial Geographies*, p. 86; T. Ploszajska, "Historiographies of Geography and Empire," in C. Nash and B. Graham, *Modern Historical Geographies*, p. 122. See also T. Mitchell, *Colonising Egypt*, Berkeley and Los Angeles, CA: University of California Press, 1988 (2nd edn 1991), pp. 34–62.

9   B. S. A. Yeoh, *Contesting Space: Power Relations and the Urban Built Environment in Colonial Singapore*, Kuala Lumpur: Oxford University Press, 1996.

10 Yeoh, "Postcolonial Cities," pp. 457, 461; Jacobs, *Edge of Empire*, p. 21. Kong and Law defined *Contested Spaces* as a cultural notion opposing previously implicit assumptions of a unitary "culture" with unitary impacts on urban form, thus taking into account contestations between groups and opening landscapes to conflicts, contestations and negotiations. L. Kong and L. Law, "Introduction: Contested Landscapes, Asian Cities," *Urban Studies* 39, 2002, 1503–12.

11 Robert Home has provided a general review covering the whole period of British expansion overseas, emphasizing the contribution of individuals to the shaping of urban landscape in the tropics and the Third World: *Of Planting and Planning: The Making of British Colonial Cities*, Studies in History, Planning and the Environment, London: E. & F. Spon, 1997. Other examinations discuss the distribution of planning practices and regulation, plans and ideals and their influence upon specific cities or regions. See, for example Ross, and Telkamp, *Colonial Cities: Essays on Urbanism in a Colonial Context*; R. Home, "Town Planning and Garden Cities in the British Colonial Empire 1910–1940," *Planning Perspectives* 5(1), 1990, 23–37; Home, "Transferring British Planning Law

to the Colonies – The Case of the 1938 Trinidad Town and Regional-Planning Ordinance," *Third World Planning Review* 15(14), 1993, 397–410; P. R. Proudfoot, "The Symbolism of the Crystal in the Planning and Geometry of the Design for Canberra," *Planning Perspectives* 11, 1996, 225–57; A. Mabin and D. Smit, "Reconstructing South Africa's Cities? The Making of Urban Planning 1900–2000," *Planning Perspectives* 12, 1997, 193–223; M. Thompson-Fawcett, "Leon Krier and the Organic Revival within Urban Policy and Practice," *Planning Perspectives* 13, 1998, 167–94, and many others.

12 Blunt and McEwan, "Introduction," in Blunt and McEwan, *Postcolonial Geographies*, p. 9; L. Lees, "Rematerializing Geography: The 'New' Urban Geography," *Progress in Human Geography* 26(1), 2002, 101.

13 After E. Said, *Orientalism*, New York: Pantheon Books, 1978; M. Foucault, "Questions on Geography," in C. Gordon (ed.), *Power/Knowledge*, New York: Pantheon Books, 1972 (2nd edn 1980), pp. 63–77; Foucault, "Space, Knowledge and Power," in P. Rabinow (ed.), *The Foucault Reader*, London: Penguin Books, 1984 (2nd edn 1991), pp. 239–56. H. K. Bhabha, *The Location of Culture*, London and New York: Routledge, 1995.

14 J. T. Kenny, "Colonial Geographies: Accommodation and Resistance – An Introduction," *Historical Geography* 27, 1999, 1.

15 Jacobs, *Edge of Empire*, p. 20; King, *Urbanism, Colonialism, and the World-economy*, p. 9; P. Rabinow, *French Modern: Norms and Forms of the Social Environment*, Cambridge, MA, and London: The MIT Press, 1989; Rabinow, "Colonialism, Modernity: The French in Morocco," in N. AlSayyad, *Forms of Dominance*, pp. 167–82

16 A. King, "Exporting Planning: The Colonial and Neo-Colonial Experience," in G. Cherry (ed.), *Shaping an Urban World: Planning and the Environment in the Modern World*, vol. 2, London: Mansell Publishing, 1980, pp. 203–26; N. AlSayyad, "Introduction," in AlSayyad, *Forms of Dominance*, pp. 1–26; J. Hosagrahar, "City as Durbar: Theater and Power in Imperial Delhi," in ibid., pp. 83–106.

17 A. Loomba, *Colonialism/Postcolonialism*, London: Routledge, 1998, quoted in M. S. Kumar, "The Evolution of Spatial Ordering," in A. Blunt and C. McEwan, *Postcolonial Geographies*, p. 86.

18 Çelik, *Urban Forms and Colonial Confrontations*, pp. 1–8. See also G. Wright, *The Politics of Design in French Colonial Urbanism*, Chicago and London: The University of Chicago Press, 1991.

19 J. Nasr and M. Volait, "Introduction: Transporting Planning," in J. Nasr and M. Volait (eds), *Urbanism: Imported or Exported?* Chichester: Wiley-Academy, 2003, pp. xi–xxxviii. See also G. Myers, "Colonial Discourse and Africa's Colonized Middle: Ajit Singh's Architecture," *Historical Geography* 27, 1999, 27–55; N. AlSayyad, "Prologue," in N. AlSayyad, *Hybrid Urbanism*, p. 2; as manifested, for example, by R. Fuchs and G. Gilbert regarding the creation of local hybrid architectural style in Palestine: "A Colonial Portrait of Jerusalem: British Architecture in Mandate-Era Palestine," in ibid., pp. 83–108; or by A. King, treating the suburb as a hybrid modernity, in "Re-worlding the City," *Planning History* 22, 2000, 12. A similar theme is discussed by J. Hosagrahar in *Indigenous Modernities: Negotiating Architecture and Urbanism*, London: Routledge, 2005.

20 M. Dossal, "Limits of Colonial Urban Planning: A Study of Mid-nineteenth Century Bombay," *International Journal of Urban and Regional Research* 13(1), 1989, 19–22; S. Gupta, "Theory and Practice of Town Planning in Calcutta, 1817 to 1912: An Appraisal," *The Indian Economic and Social History Review* 30(1), 1993, 29–55; S. Hazareesingh, "Colonial Modernism and the Flawed Paradigms of Urban Renewal: Uneven Development in Bombay, 1900–1925," *Urban History* 28(2), 2001, 235–55; Kumar, "The Evolution of Spatial Ordering," in A. Blunt and C. McEwan, *Postcolonial Geographies*, pp. 85–98.

21 Yeoh, *Contesting Space*, p. 1; Z. Çelik, *Empire, Architecture, and the City: French-Ottoman Encounters, 1830–1914*, Seattle, WA: University of Washington Press, 2008.

22 M. LeVine, *Overthrowing Geography: Jaffa, Tel Aviv, and the Struggle for Palestine 1880–1948*. Berkeley and London: University of California Press, 2005.

23 P. Chatterjee and J. T. Kenny, "Creating a New Capital: Colonial Discourse and the Decolonization of Delhi," *Historical Geography* 27, 1999, 73–98; N. Perera, "Indigenising the Colonial City: Late 19th-century Colombo and its Landscape," *Urban Studies* 39(9), 2002, 1703–21; Perera, "Contesting Visions: Hybridity, Liminality and Authorship of the Chandigarh Plan," *Planning Perspectives* 19, 2004, 175–99.

24 A. D. King, "Colonial Architecture and Urban Development," *Lotus International* 34, 1982, 47, 57; AlSayyad, "Introduction," in N. AlSayyad, *Forms of Dominance*, p. 17.

25 J. Nasr and M. Volait, "Introduction," in J. Nasr and M. Volait, *Urbanism: Imported or Exported?* p. xiii.

26 Kenny, "Colonial Geographies," p. 3; Myers, "Ajit Singh's Architecture," pp. 27–55; Myers, "Intellectual of Empire," p. 4.

27 A. Lester, *Imperial Networks: Creating Identities in Nineteenth Century South Africa and Britain*, London and New York: Routledge, 2001, pp. 9–20; Lester, "British Settler Discourse and the Circuits of Empire," *History Workshop Journal* 54, 2002, 27–50.

28 After S. Daniels and C. Nash, "Life Paths: Geography and Biography," *Journal of Historical Geography* 30(3), 2004, 449–58.

29 D. Lambert and A. Lester, "Introduction: Imperial Spaces, Imperial Lives," in D. Lambert and A. Lester (eds), *Colonial Lives Across the British Empire: Imperial Careering in the Long Nineteenth Century*, Cambridge: Cambridge University Press, 2006, p. 24.

30 M. Fry, *The Scottish Empire*, Edinburgh: Tuckwell Press and Brilinn, 2001, p. 429.

31 Ibid., p. 92.

32 Ibid., pp. 87, 92–4.

33 Ibid., pp. 87–8.

34 Geddes "wished to show how, in the reunion of robust Scots intellect and the earthy Tamil spirituality, renewal could come by interaction of the world's marginalised cultures." Ibid., p. 430.

35 Ibid., p. 395.

36 Ibid., p. 399. Prominent figures such as Lawrence Oliphant and Arthur Wauchope made Palestine another Scottish stronghold. Ibid., pp. 389–91.

37 J. Nasr and M. Volait, "Introduction: Transporting Planning," in J. Nasr and M. Volait (eds), *Urbanism: Imported or Exported?* Chichester: Wiley-Academy, 2003, p. xi.

38 Kenny, "Colonial Geographies," p. 3.

39 A. Blunt and C. McEwan, "Introduction to Part I: Postcolonial Knowledge and Networks," in A. Blunt and C. McEwan (eds), *Postcolonial Geographies*, New York and London: Continuum, 2002, p. 9; C. Nash, "Cultural Geography: Postcolonial Cultural Geographies," *Progress in Human Geography* 26(2), 2002, 223.

40 J. T. Kenny, "Colonial Geographies: Accommodation and Resistance – An Introduction," *Historical Geography* 27, 1999, 2; Nash, "Cultural Geography," p. 220. See also G. A. Myers, "Intellectual of Empire: Eric Dutton and Hegemony in British Africa," *Annals of the Association of American Geographers* 88(1), 1998, 2.

41 Nash, "Cultural Geography," p. 222. See also J. Duncan and D. Ley, "Introduction," in J. Duncan and D. Ley (eds), *Place/Culture/Representation*, London and New York: Routledge, 1993, pp. 1–24.

42 A. Blunt and C. McEwan, "Introduction," in A. Blunt and C. McEwan, *Postcolonial Geographies*, p. 1; Duncan and Ley, "Introduction," p. 13.

43 B. S. A. Yeoh, "Postcolonial Cities," *Progress in Human Geography* 25, 2001, 456–68. See also Myers, "Intellectual of Empire," p. 4.

44 L. Lees, "Rematerializing Geography: The 'New' Urban Geography," *Progress in Human Geography* 26(1), 2002, 101, 109.

45 M. Dehaene, "Survey and the Assimilation of a Modernist Narrative in Urbanism," *The Journal of Architecture* 7, 2002, 42; "If planning duplicates the construction of a modern relationship between man and the world, between the subject and the environment that surrounds him, survey constructs the space in which planning unfolds." p. 47.

46 See S. Naylor and G. A. Jones, "Writing Orderly Geographies of Distant Places: Regional Survey Movement and Latin America," *Ecumene* 4(3), 1997, 273–99; O. Söderström, "Paper Cities: Visual Thinking in Urban Planning," *Ecumene* 3(3), 1996, 249–81, Part II above.

16 The Colonial Planning Gambit

1 H. E. Meller, "Conservation and Evolution: The Pioneering Work of Sir Patrick Geddes in Jerusalem, 1919–1925," *Planning History Bulletin* 9, 1987, 43.

2 Meller, *Patrick Geddes: Social Evolutionist and City Planner*, London: Routledge, 1990, p. 217.

3 G. Ferraro, *Rieducazione alla Speranza: Patrick Geddes Planner in India, 1914–1924*, Milano: Jaca Books, 1998, pp. 65, 191–5.

4 D. Goodfriend, "Nagar Yoga: The Culturally Informed Town Planning of Patrick Geddes in India 1914–1924," *Human Organization* 38(4), 1979, 355.

5 The conclusion seems unavoidable: "In examining the ten-year range of Geddes' work in south Asia, one is struck with a contradictory conclusion. While Geddes' planning recommendations each seem uniquely suited to their context, there is little change in the basic operating principles and solutions from one report to another. This is as true across diverse subcultural areas as it is across the temporal perspective." D. Goodfriend, "Nagar Yoga: The Culturally Informed Town Planning of Patrick Geddes in India 1914–1924," *Human Organization* 38(4), 1979, p. 354.

6 As described, for example, in one of Geddes' earliest letters home: "One concrete idea begins to come up, like a distant isle on the horizon, that of all times and places where the Kingdom has Come, and Peacedom had its day, one of the greatest, most significant, most truly classic – perhaps biblical – in significant and value (and even portent and suggestive guidance?) is that of Asoka . . . Akbar too had some considerable vision of this . . . For Peacedom is no continuing State or City, the great thing is that we should see that it has at times existed – that here and there for a season, its Kingdom has actually come." P. Geddes to family, 1 October 1914, NLS MS10504/78–81.

7 Meller, *Patrick Geddes*, p. 283.

8 M. Beattie, "Sir Patrick Geddes and Barra Bazaar: Competing Visions, Ambivalence and Contradiction," *The Journal of Architecture* 9, 2004, 131.

9 Quoted in P. Boardman, *The Worlds of Patrick Geddes: Biologist, Town Planner, Re-educator, Peace-Warrior*, London, Henley and Boston: Routledge & Kegan Paul, 1978, p. 287 [33]. Geddes further enquired why the Indians have merely copied "the customary and orderly ritual of every British Congress" when there were other examples in the West, such as Highland gatherings.

10 Ibid., p. 288 [34].

11 First letter: Ibid., p. 288–90 [35]. Ferraro claims that the differences between their separate sets of values was apparent, thus preventing any cooperation. Geddes' relationships with other prominent Indians, he claims, were just as futile. *Patrick Geddes Planner in India*, p. 65.

12 A. Ponte, "The Geddes Myth," *Lotus International* 34, 1982, 119. Following in Geddes' steps in the 1990's Sofia Leonard reported of a similar memory of Geddes' attitude toward planning in India; "Finding Geddes Abroad," in W. Stephen (ed.), *Think Global, Act Local: The Life and Legacy of Patrick Geddes*, Edinburgh: Luath Press, 2004, p. 51.

13 Geddes' soft eugenics is rarely discussed, as are the Zionist social aims in Palestine. On the obvious eugenic intentions of the Zionist endeavour, see R. Falk, "Settling the Land as a Eugenic Practice," *Alpayim* 23, 2002, 179–98 (Hebrew).

14 Mark LeVine described the role of Geddes' plan for Tel Aviv in the facilitation of purchase and parcelization of adjacent Arab lands as part of his examination of the role played by the discourse of town planning and development in the drive by the leaders of Tel Aviv in particular to expand the territorial limits of the city and by the Zionists in general, in its attempts to expand its urban territorial base. M. LeVine, "Conquest Through Town Planning: The Case of Tel Aviv, 1921–1948," *Journal of Palestine Studies* 27(4), 1998, 36–52.

15 R. Fuchs and G. Herbert, "A Colonial Portrait of Jerusalem: British Architecture in Mandate-Era Palestine," in N. AlSayyad (ed.), *Hybrid Urbanism: On the Identity Discourse and the Built Environment*, Westport, CT, and London: Praeger, 2001, pp. 101–2.

16 "Without stating it in so many words," claims Hyman, Geddes regarded the local Arabs "as the conservative and passive element in Palestine." B. Hyman, "British Planners in Palestine, 1918–1936," unpublished PhD thesis, London School of Economics and Political Science, 1994, p. 302.

17 Meller, *Patrick Geddes*, p. 278; Hyman, "British Planners," p. 306.

18 Fuchs and Herbert, "A Colonial Portrait of Jerusalem," in AlSayyad, *Hybrid Urbanism*, p. 85.

19 Ibid., p. 99.

20 "Geddes was a great supporter of Zionism, but the Zionism he supported was a Zionism sublimated and reinterpreted to fit his own conceptions . . . the re-Hebraization of the world ended thus in the Orientalizaiton of Zionism." Ibid., p. 102. In a letter to Mrs. Fels (by then the widow of Joseph Fels, an American Jewish philanthropist who previously supported Geddes in Scotland), Geddes described and justified his design for the Hebrew University: "you all agree that Zionists are not only Jews, with an ideal in common, but also very deeply impressed with the culture . . . of the various nations and countries from which they come. Thus the Americans are very American, the Germans very German, the French very French, the English very English, and so on. All Westerns so far and not yet re-Orientalised (which may take 40 years) and all this in architecture as much as other things." P. Geddes, 6 July 1920, CZM J15/7206.

21 C. R. Ashbee (ed.), *Jerusalem 1920–1922: Being the Records of the Pro-Jerusalem Council during the First Two Years of the Civil Administration*, London: John Murray, 1924, pp. 11–4.

22 Kallus, "Building Types," 295–8.

23 Ibid., pp. 314–15.

24 Ibid.

Conclusion: The Historiography of Town Planning, a Postcolonial Reading

1 Consequently, when Geddes returned to Britain after years of imperial experience, his work in the colonies was not incorporated into his writings. Other than his work concerning physical regional rehabilitation in Palestine, Geddes hardly wrote about his work outside Britain; the reports were not described anywhere. Geddes hardly used Indian and Palestinian plans or miniscule accomplishments as illustrations for further teaching, as he constantly returned to his earlier British experiences. The Edinburgh survey was described and published again as part of his contemporary crusade. It therefore seems as if Geddes' theory, rather than develop and evolve, became repetitive, perpetual and eventually doomed for stagnation. See, for example, P. Geddes, "Beginnings of a Survey of Edinburgh," *The Scottish Geographical Magazine* 35, 1919, 298–327.

2 See, for example, Geddes' failure to relate to the renewal of Jaffa's port; B. Hyman, "British Planners in Palestine, 1918–1936," unpublished PhD thesis, London School of Economics and Political Science, 1994, p. 315.

3 M. Beattie, "Sir Patrick Geddes and Barra Bazaar: Competing Visions, Ambivalence and Contradiction," *The Journal of Architecture* 9, 2004, 146.

4 D. Goodfriend, "Nagar Yoga: The Culturally Informed Town Planning of Patrick Geddes in India 1914–1924," *Human Organization* 38(4), 1979, 354–5.

5 See, for example, N. Shepherd, *Ploughing Sand: British Rule in Palestine 1917–1948*, London: John Murray, 2000; A. Almog, "Focus on Detail: The Critical Role of Architectural Elements in Representational Architecture: The Case of British Buildings in Jerusalem, (1849–1939)," unpublished PhD thesis, York University, 1996; D. B. Monk, *An Aesthetic Occupation: The Immediacy of Architecture and the Palestine Conflict*, Durham, NC: Duke University Press, 2002.

6 M. Hebbert, "Retrospect on the Outlook Tower," in *Patrick Geddes: A Symposium*, 1 March 1982, Special Occasional Paper in Town and Regional Planning, Duncan of Jordanstone College of Art/University of Dundee, p. 61.

7   V. M. Welter, *Biopolis: Patrick Geddes and the City of Life*, Cambridge, MA: The MIT Press, 2002, p. 1.

8   C. Mercer, "Geographies for the Present: Patrick Geddes, Urban Planning and the Human Sciences," *Economy and Society* 26(2), 1997, 211; his biography is a valuable book despite its tendency to hagiography. "Reviews: The day Patrick Geddes blew his top," *Town and Country Planning* 52(2), 1983, 58–59; the fact that two of his posthumous biographies have been written by ex-students has helped to sustain the hagiographic aura with which he has become surrounded; M. Hebbert, "Patrick Geddes Reconsidered," *Town and Country Planning*, January 1980, p. 16.

9   See, for example, L. Andersson, *Mellan Byrakrati och Laissez Faire: En Studie av Camillo Sittes och Patrick Geddes Stadsplaneringsstrategier* [Beyond bureaucracies and laissez faire: a study of Camillo Sitte's and Patrick Geddes' city planning strategies], unpublished PhD thesis, Gothenburg: Acta Universitatis Gothoburgensis [Swedish], 1989.

10 Welter, *Biopolis*, p. 20; 131; 138; H. E. Meller, *Patrick Geddes: Social Evolutionist and City Planner*, London: Routledge, 1990, pp. 40–3 and more, as illustrated in Part II.

11 J. Hasselgren, "What is Living and What is Dead in the Work of Patrick Geddes?" in *Patrick Geddes: A Symposium*, p. 46.

12 M. C. Sies and C. Silver, introduction to Sies and Silver (eds), *Planning the 20th Century American City*, 1996, pp. 9–12; see also J. Holston, "Spaces of Insurgent Citizenship," in L. Sandercock (ed.), *Making the Invisible Visible: A Multicultural Planning History*, Berkeley and London: University of California Press, 1998, p. 38.

13 L. Sandercock, "Framing Insurgent Historiographies for Planning," in Sandercock, *Making the Invisible Visible*, pp. 1–36.

14 O. Kramsch, "Tropics of Planning Discourse: Stalking the 'Constructive Imaginary' of Selected Urban Planning Histories," in ibid., p. 164.

15 A. King, "Introductory Comments: The Dialectics of Dual Development," *City and Society* 12(1), 2000, 9, quoted in J. Nasr and M. Volait (eds), *Urbanism: Imported or Exported?* Chichester: Wiley-Academy, 2003, p. xxiii.

16 J. S. Duncan, "Notes from the Archive," *Historical Geography* 27, 1999, 119–28.

17 J. Nasr and M. Volait, "Introduction," in J. Nasr and M. Volait, *Urbanism: Imported or Exported?* p. xxx; B. S. A. Yeoh, *Contesting Space: Power Relations and the Urban Built Environment in Colonial Singapore*, Kuala Lumpur: Oxford University Press, 1996, pp. 18–20; Duncan, "Notes from the Archive."

18 See, for example, F. Driver and D. Gilbert (eds), *Imperial Cities: Landscape, Display and Identity*. Manchester and New York: Manchester University Press, 1999.

19 A. King, *Urbanism, Colonialism, and the World-Economy: Cultural and Spatial Foundations of the World Urban System*, The International Library of Sociology, University of Lancaster, London and New York: Routledge, 1990, p. 7.

20 J. M. Jacobs, *Edge of Empire: Postcolonialism and the City*, London and New York: Routledge, 1996, pp. 20–1.

21 See, for example, C. Booth, *Life and Labour of the People in London*, London: Macmillan, 1892. William Booth drew direct parallels between slums at home and jungles abroad; *In Darkest England*, London: International Headquarters of the Salvation Army, 1890; F. Driver, "Moral Geographies: Social Science and the Urban Environment in Mid-nineteenth Century England," *Transactions of the Institute of British Geographers* New Series 13, 1988, 275–87.

Appendix: Geddes' Urban Scheme: A comprehensive reading

*   All sources to this part, unless otherwise stated, are Geddes' writings; however, as Geddes referred to the various components of his theory repeatedly in his writings, I generally referred either to the first place where they are mentioned or to the source in which they are best elaborated.

1 Geddes' elaboration of the meaningful relationship is presented, for example, in "Civics: As Concrete and Applied Sociology, Part II," *Sociological Papers* II, published for the Sociological Society, London: Macmillan & Co., 1906, pp. 70–3. The components of the notation received various definitions. As *Place, Work, Folk*, for example, in "The Influence of Geographical Conditions on Social Development," *The Geographical Journal* 12(6), 1898, 584; as *organism, function, or environment*, for example, in *Syllabus of a Course of Ten Lectures on Evolution in Life, Mind, Morals and Society*, University of London, 1910, pp. 3–4; *People, Affairs and Places* in "Civics: As Concrete and Applied Sociology," p. 68; and finally, *Environment-Condition-Organism = region-occupation-family type* – ibid., p. 70. The notation similarly denotes the unity of the sciences; see, for example, "A Proposed Co-ordination of the Social Sciences," *The Sociological Review* 16, 1924, 58–61; *On Universities in Europe and in India: And a Needed Type of Research Institute, Geographical and Social, Five Letters to an Indian Friend*, reprinted from *The Pioneer* (14 August 1901) and from *East and West* (September 1903), Madras: National Press, T-GED 12/2/449, p. 16 and many other sources.

2 "Every movement – moral or social, industrial or spiritual – sooner or later takes architectural embodiment . . . And as in things both social and natural, small types serve as well as great." Geddes, "The Scots Renascence," *Evergreen*, 1895, in *Essays*, Akros, pocket classics series no. 30, Edinburgh: Akros, 1995, p. 17. Geddes supplied examples from political and economic activity.

3 *Cities in Evolution: An Introduction to the Town Planning Movement and to the Study of Civics*, London: Williams & Norgate, 1915, p. 102. Geddes supplied many examples for the relations between society and environment, including the evolvement of the game of golf in St Andrews, Scotland, due to the unique landscape, and photography as an upshot of Viking legacy of exploratory sea-bearing. "City Deterioration and the Need of City Survey," reprinted from *The Annals of the American Academy of Politician and Social Science*, July 1909, publication of the American Academy of Political and Social Science no. 579, Philadelphia: The American Academy of Political and Social Science, T-GED 1/6/48, p. 63. Other examples included the reflection of the present capitalist drive in contemporary banking, "A Banker's Part in Reconstruction," *The Sociological Review* 9, 1917, 149–50; or the relationship between governments occupied with war and peace with forts and battlefields, P. Geddes and V. Branford, *Our Social Inheritance*, London: Williams & Norgate, 1919, p. 24; "The Movement Towards Synthetic Studies, and its Educational and Social Bearings," *The Sociological Review* 10(3), 1928, 224–5, T-GED 1/6/30.

4 "Civics: As Concrete and Applied Sociology," pp. 64, 68.

5 *Syllabus of a Course of Ten Lectures on Evolution in Life, Mind, Morals and Society*, University of London, 1910, pp. 1, 9.

6 "The Geddes Diagram," in *Cities in Evolution*, edited by the Outlook Tower Association, Edinburgh and The Association for Planning and Regional Reconstruction, London: Williams & Norgate, 1949, p. 195. By defining everyday active as "out-world," and placing thoughts and dreams in an "in-world," Geddes added a spiritual dimension to his global analysis. "The World Without and the World Within: Sunday Talks with my Children," 1905, T-GED 12/2/171.

7 "An Analysis of the Principles of Economics" (read before the Royal Society of Edinburgh, 17 March, 7 April, and 7 July 1884), London and Edinburgh: Williams and Norgate, 1885, p. 30, T-GED 2/2/1.

8 Described by Geddes in a paper quoted by Amelia Defries in 1927. A. Defries, *The Interpreter Geddes: The Man and his Gospel*, foreword by Rabindranath Tagore, introduction by Israel Zangwill. London: George Routledge & Sons, 1927, pp. 123–40; "The Notation of Life," in *Cities in Evolution*, 1949, pp. 194–9.

9 "Civics: As Concrete and Applied Sociology," p. 73; "Ten Lectures on Evolution in Life," p. 12; "The Twofold Aspect of the Industrial Age: Paleotechnic and Neotechnic," *Town Planning Review* 3(3), 1912, 183.

10 "Society around us . . . presents not only a phantasmagoria of events, but a succession of phases, with survivals and continued growths of these;" *Observation and Method in Sociological Studies*,

Notes

Synopsis of a Course of Lectures for the Second Term, School of Sociology and Social Economics, Spring 1904, p. 5, T-GED 3/5/49; "A Schoolboy's Bag and a City's Pageant: The First of the Talks from My Outlook Tower," *The Survey*, 1925, 565, T-GED 23/3/9.1.

11 *The Masque of Learning and its Many Meanings, Devised and Interpreted by Patrick Geddes*. Edinburgh: Patrick Geddes and Colleagues, Outlook Tower and Chelsea, 1912, p. vi.

12 "Evolution in Life, Mind, Morals and Society," p. 17; see also, for example, "Papers for the Present – Introduction to Series" [issued for the Cities Committee of the Sociological Society] in *The Modern Midas*, Papers for the Present, Letchworth: Garden City Press, [1918?] T-GED 2/3/6 p. iii.

13 "Country and Town: In Development, Deterioration, and Renewal," [n.d.], p. 27, T-GED 3/7/37.

14 "A City Survey for Disoriented Citizens," in Geddes and Branford, *Our Social Inheritance*, pp. 131–293.

15 "Country and Town," p. 25; *Cities in Evolution*, 1949, pp. 168–70.

16 "An Analysis of the Principles of Economics" (read before the Royal Society of Edinburgh 17 March, 7 April, and 7 July 1884), London and Edinburgh: Williams and Norgate, 1885, p. 21, T-GED 2/2/1; another definition was "the pride of pedigree"—"In an Old Scots City," *Contemporary Review* 82, January–June 1903, 563.

17 "Civics: As Concrete and Applied Sociology."

18 Geddes elaborated widely on the relationship between Geography and History and their importance to each other: "The historical table is perpendicular to each region as representing the layer of dust above (a geological strata)." "Paper on Geographic Survey," 1894, T-GED 1/5/1.

19 *The Making of the Future: A Manifesto and a Project*, reprinted from *The Sociological Review*, May 1917, 5.

20 "The Influence of Geographical Conditions on Social Development," *The Geographical Journal* 12(6), 1898, 581; "We may take up the standpoint of our own immediate region and use it as the centre around which to group our ideas," "Nature Study and Geographical Education," *Scottish Geographical Magazine* 18, 1902, 526.

21 "The Valley Section is a general and introductory outline towards fuller anthropological and historical studies, region by region and age by age, up to our own land and day; also the very essence of the social survey that is needed for every region and every city; finally if we see to work our way towards regional betterment and development, towards town improvement and city design. From these few and seemingly simple occupations, all others have developed. To trace these developments is thus to unravel the explanation of the individuality, the uniqueness, of each of the towns and cities of men; and yet also to understand their manifold similarities, region by region." *Cities in Evolution*, 1949, p. xxvi.

22 "From the forest we may emerge upwards up on the higher pastures . . . beginning with cattle in Switzerland, sheep in Scotland, goats in Cyprus . . . with its characteristic associated type of man – Swiss heardman, highland shepherd, and Moslem goatherd, with their widely divergent families and societies, ideas and ideals . . . the loamy forest glade . . . the progress of forest-clearing and pasture and agriculture, urban and maritime construction . . . the Mediterranean . . . similarly the fisher – Norway, Dundee, Yarmouth, Newfoundland . . . each is a definite type with characteristic family relations and social outcomes . . . note the skipper with his definite subordinate hierarchy, whence has come no small element in the strong governments of Western peoples . . . compare this with the weak government of the patriarchal East, which, from the very nature of its pastoral tradition, never succeeds in forming an organization of Western type – or at least in giving it permanence of succession." "The Influence of Geographical Conditions on Social Development," p. 583. The Valley Section was also repeatedly realized through history, manifesting different stages of evolution; for example "we thus re-interpret the vicissitudes of history in more general terms, those of the differentiation, progress or degeneracy of each occupational and social type, and the ascending and descending oscillations of these types." "Civics: As Concrete and Applied Sociology," p. 60.

23 "Country and Town"; *Syllabus of a Course of Ten Lectures on: Contemporary Social Evolution*, University of London (University Extension Lectures), W. Bishop [Hampton & Co.], 1906, T-GED 3/2/34.

24 "A Rustic View of War and Peace," *The Sociological Review* 10(1), 1918, 8–9.

25 *The Making of the Future: A Manifesto and a Project*, reprinted from *The Sociological Review*, May 1917, 5; P. Geddes and V. Branford, "Rural and Urban Thought: A Contribution to the Theory of Progress and Decay," *The Sociological Review* 21(1), 1929, presented to the Meeting of the International Association for the Improvement of Industrial Relations, held at Girton College, Cambridge, pp. 4–5.

26 For example, the rural miner as the urban steam train driver; "A Course of Three Lectures on Inland Towns and Cities" [n.d.]; "Edinburgh Summer Meeting (August 1–27, 1904)," *The Geographical Teacher*, p. 229.

27 "Our modern city, with its familiar capitalists and labourers, is still only the ancient one, save that its miners, smiths, and weavers have multiplied out of all proportion to the rest; so that the higher craftsmen are now an unnoticed few, and those half starving, and mostly out of employment." *Co-operation versus Socialism*, reprinted from *The Co-operative Wholesale Societies Annual* for 1888, Manchester: Co-operative Printing Society, p. 22; *Cities in Evolution*, 1949), pp. xix–xxv.

28 Illustration of the role of the natural occupations in war and peace in: "A Rustic View of War and Peace," pp. 8–14; "In a sense these six rustic types . . . are the long sought missing links of evolution," ibid., p. 6.

29 *The Masque of Learning and its many Meanings, Devised and Interpreted by Patrick Geddes*. Edinburgh: Patrick Geddes and Colleagues, Outlook Tower and Chelsea, 1912, p. vi.

30 *The Masque of Learning*, pp. 12, 74–5; "The Twofold Aspect of the Industrial Age," pp. 176–87.

31 *The Masque of Learning*, pp. 11–12. Geddes also found in Indian mythology the basis for every great (evolutionary) movement, involving "first the destroyer of the outworn past, next the breath of a new creation, then the power of conservation also – the work of Siva, of Brahma, and of Vishnu. And of their three-fold spirit, applied to past, to present, and future, what three moderns have had a more decisive share?" ibid., pp. 57–8. Working in India alongside with his father, Arthur Geddes suggested a "corresponding picture, symbol or diagram for India" demonstrating similar notions as the Occidental Tree. The drawing of the Indian "tree" is centered on a palm tree, "symbolic of its people's life." The beginning of history is symbolized with the hunter's bow. Follow a description of the main periods in India's history, topped by the introduction of European culture and the contribution of missionary and Humanitarian thinkers to an Indian Renascence. Thus, "a new contribution to the old arts and the old wisdom of life in India . . . and. Last of all . . . re-grouping for vigorous and renewed temporal life, of people and chief, of planters and builders, chasas and mistris, united by leadership." Similarly, the singer and thinker, "Expressional and Intellectual," are symbolized by the vibrating sitar, and the book of ancient wisdom renewed . . . followed by Imperial Administration. Arthur Geddes, "Suggestion Towards a Visual & Symbolic Presentment of History for India" [n.d.] T-GED 4/3/8.

32 P. Geddes and G. Slater, *Ideas at War*, London: Williams & Norgate, 1917, p. 28.

33 "A Suggested Plan for a Civic Museum (or Civic Exhibition) and its Associated Studies," read at a Research Meeting of the Sociological Society, at the School of Economics and Political Science (University of London) 19 March, 1906, James Oliphant, Esq., in the Chair. *Sociological Papers* III published for the Sociological Society, London: Macmillan & Co., 1907, pp. 219–21.

34 Geddes connected the temporal powers with politics, business and industry, and the spiritual powers with religion, science and academic research. "Civics: As Concrete and Applied Sociology," 1906, p. 109; Temporals are barons and slaves in one age, capitalists and labourers in another; spiritual history describes priests, legislators and poets. "Country and Town," p. 11. Current manifestations: Gladstone, Bismarck, Rothschild, Kelvin. "The Higher Uses of Geography" [n.d.].

35 A full description of the process is provided in Geddes' final article about Civics (1906).

36 "The Higher Uses of Geography," p. 7.

Notes

37 This is a direct illumination of Geddes' on-going and elaborate criticism of contemporary education. See, for example, "University Systems, Past and Present," *The Fortnightly Review* 322 new series, October 1893, 524–38.

38 "'Country and Town," p. 21.

39 Geddes, *The Returning Gods*, London: [n.p.], 1914, p. 3, quoted in V. M. Welter, *Biopolis: Patrick Geddes and the City of Life*, Cambridge, MA: The MIT Press, 2002, pp. 233–5. See also "Theory of Town and City." Significance of school, college and university, cloister, cathedral, acropolis, etc. civic education. *Syllabus of a Course of Ten Lectures on: Contemporary Social Evolution*, 1906, p. 9.

40 Temple schemes, explains Welter, evolve "round the theme of knowledge and its synthesis, or temples dedicated to the phenomenon of life itself." Two early examples are a sketch for a temple of life, based on Greek gods and goddesses (192–9) and a Garden for the nine Greek muses both developed 1907. These two reinterpretations of Greek mythology are conceptually linked, based upon the fourth quadrant of the notation of life. Welter lists 17 such temples, including the Nature Palace of Dunfermline and the Hall of Vision built upon at the Conference on Some Living Religions within the Empire, London, 1924; Welter, *Biopolis*, pp. 199–200.

Bibliography

Archives and special collections

Geddes Manuscripts, National Library of Scotland, Edinburgh [NLS]
Geddes Collection, Strathclyde University Archives, Glasgow [T-GED]
Oriental and India Office Collection (British Library, London) [OIOC]
Central Zionist Archive, Jerusalem [CZM]
Israel Antiquities Authority, Jerusalem [ATQ]
Hebrew University of Jerusalem Archives [HUA]
Jerusalem Municipal Historical Archives [JMHA]

Geddes' writings in chronological order

"A Course of Three Lectures on Inland Towns and Cities: Their Main Origins," Royal Geographical
    Society [n.d.] T-GED 1/5/25.
"Athens, Notes," [n.d.] T-GED 1/6/26/1a.
"Committee on Collaboration Between the Bombay University and the Bombay City," Bombay: printed
    at the Government Central Press, [n.d.] T-GED 12/2/451.
"Country and Town: In Development, Deterioration, and Renewal," [n.d.] T-GED 3/7/37.
"Paper on the Power of Sight, the Art of Seeing and the Camera Obscura," [n.d.] T-GED 7/4/5.
"The Cities Exhibition," *The Sociological Review* [n.d.], pp. 342–3, T-GED 23/3/3.9.
"The Higher Uses of Geography: A Course of Lectures," The Outlook Tower [n.d.], p. 1, T-GED 13/1/17.
"The Hot Springs of Tiberius," [n.d.] CZA A107/825.
"The Itinerant Cities Exhibition," *The Sociological Review*, pp. 146–7, T-GED 23/3/3.8.
"Tiberias and Neighbourhood," [n.d.] ATQ Tiberius file 184.
"What a Local Museum Might Be," [n.d.] T-GED 5/1/7.
"An Analysis of the Principles of Economics," Read Before the Royal Society of Edinburgh 17 March,
    7 April, and 7 July 1884, London and Edinburgh: Williams and Norgate, 1885, T-GED 2/2/1.
Every Man his Own Art Critic at the Manchester Exhibition, Manchester and London: John Heywood,
    1887, T-GED 5/3/1.
Every Man his Own Art Critic: Glasgow Exhibition, 1888, Edinburgh: William Brown, and Glasgow:
    John Menzies, 1888.
Co-operation versus Socialism, reprinted from *The Co-operative Wholesale Societies Annual* for 1888,
    Manchester: Co-operative Printing Society.
"The Outlook Tower as an Embryonic School and College: On the Tower's Aim of Training Students
    as Social Minders and Socialised Men and the Women of Action," 24/12/02, 1892, T-GED 7/4/8.
"University Systems, Past and Present," *The Fortnightly Review* 322, new series, October 1893,
    pp. 524–38.
"Paper on Geographic Survey," 1894, T-GED 1/5/1.
"The Scots Renascence," *The Evergreen: A Northern Seasonal* 1895, in *Essays*, Akros: Pocket Classics
    Series no. 30, Edinburgh, 1895, pp. 12–20.

Bibliography

"Cyprus and its Power to Help the East, by Mr. and Mrs. Geddes," reprinted from *The Report of the International Conference on Armenian Aid*, 1 May 1897, T-GED 1/8/22.

"The Influence of Geographical Conditions on Social Development," *The Geographical Journal* 12(6), 1898, 580–6.

"Lecture Notes by Patrick Geddes on the Synthetic Approach to Study, Especially History," 15 May 1900 [Paris] T-GED 6/2/1.

"Nature Study and Geographical Education," *Scottish Geographical Magazine* 18, 1902, 525–36.

"On Universities in Europe and in India: And a Needed Type of Research Institute, Geographical and Social, Five Letters to an Indian Friend," reprinted from *The Pioneer*, 14 August 1901, and from *East and West*, September 1903, Madras: National Press, T-GED 12/2/449.

"Note on Draft Plan for Institute of Geography," *Scottish Geographical Magazine* 18, 1902, 142–4.

"Edinburgh and its Region, Geographic and Historical," *Scottish Geographical Magazine* 18, 1902, 302–12.

[Letter] to the Secretary, Scotch Education Department, 5 March 1903, T-GED 5/3/55.

"In an Old Scots City," *The Contemporary Review* 82, January–June 1903, 559–68.

"Edinburgh Summer Meeting (August 1–27, 1904)," *The Geographical Teacher*, 229–30.

"Observation and Method in Sociological Studies, Synopsis of a Course of Lectures for the Second Term," *School of Sociology and Social Economics*, Spring 1904, T-GED 3/5/49.

"City Development, a Study of Parks, Gardens, and Culture-Institutes, a Report to the Carnegie Dunfermline Trust," Edinburgh: Geddes and Company, Outlook Tower, Westminster, and Birmingham: The Saint George Press, Bournville, 1904.

"The World Without and the World Within: Sunday Talks with my Children," 1905, T-GED 12/2/171.

Syllabus of a Course of Ten Lectures on Evolutionary Ethics, Based on Natural Science and Sociology, University of London (University Extension Lectures), London: W. Bishop [Hampton & Co.], 1905, T-GED 3/6/5.

"Civic Education and City Development," *The Contemporary Review* 87, 1905, 413–26.

"Civics: As Applied Sociology, Part I," *Sociological Papers* I, published for the Sociological Society, London: Macmillan & Co., 1905, 103–44.

"Introduction," in L. R. Latter, *School Gardening for Little Children*, London: Swan Sonnenschein & Co., 1906, pp. xiii–xiv.

"Civics: As Concrete and Applied Sociology, Part II," *Sociological Papers* II, published for the Sociological Society, London: Macmillan & Co., 1906, 57–119.

"University Studies and University Residence: An Address to the University Extension Students' Guild," at the University of London, South Kensington, February 1906, in P. Geddes, W. Seton, J. W. Graham, A. C. Ward, W. McDougall and T. B Whitson, *Halls of Residence for University Students*, with extract from reports by Inter-Universities Halls of Residence Committee. Edinburgh: Geddes and Colleagues, 1906, pp. 9–23.

Syllabus of a Course of Ten Lectures on: Contemporary Social Evolution, University of London (University Extension Lectures), W. Bishop [Hampton & Co.], 1906, T-GED 3/2/34.

"A Suggested Plan for a Civic Museum (or Civic Exhibition) and its Associated Studies," read at a Research Meeting of the Sociological Society, at the School of Economics and Political Science (University of London) 19 March 1906, James Oliphant, Esq., in the Chair, *Sociological Papers* III, published for the Sociological Society, London: Macmillan & Co., 1907, 199–240.

"The Museum and the City: A Practical Proposal," read at the Dundee Conference, 1907, reprinted from *The Museums Journal*, 1908, pp. 371–82, T-GED 5/3/26.

"Town Planning and City Design – in Sociology and in Citizenship," 1908, T-GED 3/6/7.

"The Town Planning Bill," *Garden Cities and Town Planning* 3(28), May–June 1908, 69–72.

"The Survey of Cities," *The Sociological Review* 1, 1908, 74–9.

"Chelsea, Past and Possible," in D. Hollins (ed.), *Utopian Papers*, London: Masters and Co., 1908, pp. 6–16.

"City Deterioration and the Need of City Survey," reprinted from *The Annals of the American Academy of Politician and Social Science*, July 1909, publication of the American Academy of Political and

Social Science no. 579, Philadelphia: The American Academy of Political and Social Science, T-GED 1/6/48.

Syllabus of a Course of Ten Lectures on Evolution in Life, Mind, Morals and Society, University of London, 1910.

"A Symposium on Town-Planning," Supplement to the *New Age* 8(1), 1910, T-GED 1/6/53.

"City Surveys for Town Planning: And the Greater Cities," a paper read at the Birkenhead Congress, 1910, Edinburgh: Geddes and Colleagues, 1911, T-GED 1/6/52.

"The City Survey: A First Step: I, II, II," *Garden Cities and Town Planning* 1, 1911, 18–19, 31–3, 56–8.

"The Civic Survey of Edinburgh," *Transactions of the Town Planning Conference London 10–15 October 1910*, London: Royal Institute of British Architects, 1911, 538–68.

"Sociological Society – Cities Committee, Memorandum on the Need of City Survey Preparatory to Town Planning," February 1911, T-GED 1/6/34.

The Masque of Learning and its Many Meanings, Devised and Interpreted by Patrick Geddes. Edinburgh: Patrick Geddes and Colleagues, Outlook Tower and Chelsea, 1912.

"The Twofold Aspect of the Industrial Age: Paleotechnic and Neotechnic," *Town Planning Review* 3(3), 1912, 176–87.

The Masque of Medieval and Modern Learning and its Many Meanings: A Pageant of Education from Medieval to Modern Times, Devised and Interpreted by Patrick Geddes, The Outlook Tower, Edinburgh: Patrick Geddes and Colleagues, 1913.

"Two Steps in Civics: 'Cities and Town Planning Exhibition' and the 'International Congress of Cities,'" Ghent International Exhibition, 1913, T-GED 1/5/40.

Syllabus of a Course of Five Lectures on the History of Learning, at Crosby Hall, Cheyne Walk, Chelsea, London: University of London Press, 1913.

"Programme of Conference on Regional Survey during the Easter 1915 at the Outlook Tower," Provisional Committee for the Development of Regional Survey, 2–5 April, T-GED 1/6/42.2.

Cities in Evolution: An Introduction to the Town Planning Movement and to the Study of Civics, London: Williams & Norgate, 1915 (2nd edn, 1949, edited by the Outlook Tower Association, Edinburgh, and the Association for Planning and Regional Reconstruction, London, new and revised edition, London: Williams & Norgate).

A Report on the Development and Expansion of the City of Baroda, Baroda: printed at the "Lakshmi Vilas" Press, 1916.

"A Banker's Part in Reconstruction," *The Sociological Review* 9, 1917, 149–75.

With G. Slater, *Ideas at War*, London: Williams & Norgate, 1917.

With H. V. Lanchester, *Town Planning in Jubbulpore: A Report to the Municipal Committee*, Jubbulpore: printed at the Hitkarini Press, 1917.

The Proposed University for Central India, at Indore, a reprint from *Town Planning Towards City Development*, a report to The Durbar of Indore, Indore: Holkar State Printing Press, 1918.

"The Making of the Future: A Manifesto and a Project," reprinted from *The Sociological Review* 9, May 1917, 3–8.

Town Planning in Nagpur: A Report to the Municipal Council," Nagpur: printed at the Municipal Press, 1917.

"The Joint Secretaries of the Cities Committee, The Doctrine of Civics," *The Sociological Review* 10(1), 1918, 60–4.

"A Rustic View of War and Peace," *The Sociological Review* 10(1), 1918, 1–24.

"The Modern Midas," Papers for the Present, Letchworth: Garden City Press, 1918, T-GED 2/3/6.

"Education for Citizenship: The Outlook Tower," Edinburgh, 1918, T-GED 7/8/42.

With V. Branford, *Our Social Inheritance*, London: Williams & Norgate, 1919.

—— *The Coming Polity, The Making of the Future*, Westminster: Le Play House Press, 1919.

"Beginnings of a Survey of Edinburgh," *The Scottish Geographical Magazine* 35, 1919, 298–327.

"Cities in Evolution: Introductory Course of General Sociology," Winter Term 1919, University of Bombay, T-GED 1/1/5.

Bibliography

"The Temple Cities: A Town-Planning Lecture," reprinted from *The Modern Review*, March 1919, T-GED 1/3/3.7.

Barra Bazar Improvement: A Report to the Corporation of Calcutta, Calcutta: printed at the Corporation Press, 1919.

Jerusalem Actual and Possible: *A Preliminary Report to the Chief Administrator of Palestine and Military Governor of Jerusalem on Town Planning and City Improvements*, November 1919, ATQ Jerusalem General File (78) [also CZM Z4/10.202].

The Proposed Hebrew University of Jerusalem, preliminary report by Patrick Geddes, Director of the City and Town Planning Exhibition, Professor of Sociology and Civics, University of Bombay, assisted by Captain Frank C. Mears [Jerusalem] December, 1919, CZA L4/108.

"Essentials of Sociology in Relation to Economics," *Indian Journal of Economics* 3, 1920, Parts 1 and 3.

"Civics and Town Planning Exhibition, Jerusalem," *The Palestine Weekly* 1(39), 1920, Special Town Planning Number, 594–5.

"Programme of Conference on Regional Survey During the Easter Vacation at the Outlook Tower," The Regional Association, 6–13 April 1920, T-GED 1/6/42.1.

"Regional and City Surveys as Affording Policy and Theory for Town Planning and City Design," in *Town Planning Institute Papers and Discussions* III, 1920–1, pp. 119–31.

"A Garden City on Mount Carmel," [n.d.] 15 February 1921, CZA L51/875.

"The City of Jerusalem," *Garden Cities and Town Planning* 11, 1921, 251–4.

"Palestine in Renewal," *The Contemporary Review* 670, 1921, 479–81.

"Town Planning in Colombo," Papers laid before the Legislative Council of Ceylon during the year 1921, Colombo: H. R. Cottle, Government Printer, 1922, pp. 5–25.

"Civilisation: A Challenge, Patrick Geddes' Bombay Lectures (1922–23)," summarized by Arthur Geddes (1923–4) edited by F. J. Adkins (1938) and foreword by L. Mumford ("never written"), unpublished, NLS MS 10618/12–249.

"A Note on Graphic Methods, Ancient and Modern," *The Sociological Review* 15, 1923, 230–1.

"A Proposed Co-ordination of the Social Sciences," *The Sociological Review* 16, 1924, 54–63.

"Concerning Palestine: Jerusalem Old and New, Rhyme-Letter, from a Scotsman to his friend, a Jew", en route from Port Said to Jerusalem, 1925 (hand-written and typed, unpublished, 5 pp.) SUA T-GED 8/2/11.

"Industries of the University: Further Talk with Professor Geddes," *The Palestine Weekly*, 10 April 1925.

"Talks from My Outlook Tower," *The Survey Graphic* 53–55, 1925, T-GED 23/3/9.1–5, 525–9.

"A Schoolboy's Bag and a City's Pageant" (The first of the talks from the Outlook Tower), *The Survey Graphic* 1925, 523–9; 553–4.

"Cities, and the Soils They Grow From" (The second of the talks from the Outlook Tower), *The Survey Graphic*, April 1925, 40–4.

"The Valley Plan of Civilization" (The third of the talks from the Outlook Tower), *The Survey Graphic*, June 1925, 288–90; 322–3; 325.

"The Valley in the Town" (The fourth of the talks from the Outlook Tower), *The Survey Graphic*, July 1925, 396–400; 415–6.

"Our City of Thought" (The fifth of the talks from the Outlook Tower), *The Survey Graphic*, August 1925, 487–90; 504.

Town-Planning Report – Jaffa and Tel-Aviv, 1925.

"The Hebrew University of Jerusalem," *Sunday School Chronicle and Times*, 21 May 1925.

"Town-Planning in Palestine," *Garden Cities and Town Planning* 15(11), 1925, 267–8.

"The Making of Our Coal Future" [Part I of "Coal: Ways to Reconstruction," Ways of Approach I. The Regional Planner's Way.] *The Sociological Review* 18(3), 1926, 178–85.

"The Charting of Life," *The Sociological Review* 19(1), 1927, 40–62.

"The Village World: Actual and Possible," *The Sociological Review* 19(2), 1927, 108–19.

"The Movement Towards Synthetic Studies, and its Educational and Social Bearings," *The Sociological Review* 20(3), 1928, 223–32, T-GED 1/6/30.

With V. Branford, "Rural and Urban Thought: A Contribution to the Theory of Progress and Decay," *The Sociological Review* 21(1), 1929, 1–19. Presented to the Meeting of the International Association for the Improvement of Industrial Relations, held at Girton College, Cambridge.

"Ways of Transition: Towards Constructive Peace," *The Sociological Review* 22(1), 1930, 22.

"Scouting and Woodcraft – Present and Possible," *The Sociological Review* 22(3), 1930, 274–7.

"Talent and Genius," *The Sociological Review* 23, 1931, 131–4.

Patrick Geddes in India, edited by J. Tyrwhitt, with an introduction by L. Mumford and a preface by H. V. Lanchaster, London: Lund Humphries, 1947.

"Geddes on Letchworth" (Originally published November 1905), *Town and Country Planning* 23(126), October 1954, 518.

"Geddes on Dispersal" (Originally published April 1906), *Town and Country Planning* 23(126), October 1954, 524.

"Geddes on Suburbs" (Originally published August 1906), *Town and Country Planning* 23(126), October 1954, 526.

General literature

Abercrombie, P. "Geddes as Town Planner," in A. Defries, *The Interpreter Geddes: The Man and his Gospel*, foreword by Rabindranath Tagore and introduction by Israel Zangwill, London: George Routledge & Sons, 1927, pp. 322–5.

—— *Town and Country Planning*, London: Thorntom Butterworth, 1933.

Abercrombie, P. and Matthew, R. H. *The Clyde Valley Regional Plan 1946: A Report*, Edinburgh: HMSO, 1946.

Adshead, S. D. "Town Planning Conference of the Royal Institute of British Architects," *Town Planning Review* 1(3), 1910, 177–91.

Almog, A. "Focus on Detail: The Critical Role of Architectural Elements in Representational Architecture; The Case of British Buildings in Jerusalem, 1849–1939," unpublished PhD thesis, York University, 1996.

AlSayyad, N. "Urbanism and the Dominance Equation," in N. AlSayyad (ed.), *Forms of Dominance: On the Architecture and Urbanism of the Colonial Enterprise*, Aldershot: Avebury, 1992, pp. 1–26.

AlSayyad, N. (ed.), *Hybrid Urbanism: On the Identity Discourse and the Built Environment*, Westport, CT, and London: Praeger, 2001.

Andersson, L. "Mellan Byrakrati och Laissez Faire: En Studie av Camillo Sittes och Patrick Geddes Stadsplaneringsstrategier" [Beyond bureaucracies and laissez faire: a study of Camillo Sitte's and Patrick Geddes's city planning strategies], unpublished PhD thesis, Acta Universitatis Gothoburgensis [Sweden], 1989.

"ARTIFEX," "Sir Patrick Geddes: Town Planner, Scientist, and Social Reformer," *The Irish Builder and Engineer* 7 May, 1932.

Ashbee C. R. (ed.), *Jerusalem 1918–1920: Being the Records of the Pro-Jerusalem Council During the Period of the British Military Administration*, London: John Murray, 1921.

—— *Jerusalem 1920–1922: Being the Records of the Pro-Jerusalem Council During the First Two Years of the Civil Administration*, London: John Murray, 1924.

C. R. A., [C. R. Ashbee?] "Sir Patrick Geddes," *The Times*, 21 April 1932.

Ashworth, W. *The Genesis of Modern British Town Planning: A Study in Economic and Social History of the Nineteenth Century*, London: Routledge & Kegan Paul, 1954.

Aves, E. Review of *City Development: A Study of Parks, Gardens, and Culture-Institutes, A Report to the Carnegie Dunfermline Trust*, by Patrick Geddes, *The Economic Journal* 16(2), 1906, 243–6.

Azrayahu, M. *Tel Aviv: Ha'ir Ha'Amitit* (*Tel Aviv: Mythography of a City*) Beer Sheva: Ben Gurion University of the Negev, 2005.

Bibliography

Bannon, M. J. "The Making of Irish Geography, III: Patrick Geddes and the Emergence of Modern Town Planning in Dublin," *Irish Geography* 11, 1978, 141–9.

—— "The Genesis of Modern Irish Planning," in M. J. Bannon (ed.), *A Hundred Years of Irish Planning Vol. I: The Emergence of Irish Planning 1880–1920,* Dublin: Turoe Press, 1985, pp. 189–265.

—— "Dublin Town Planning Competition: Ashbee and Chettle's 'New Dublin: A Study in Civics,'" *Planning Perspectives* 14, 1999, 145–62.

Barker, G. B. "Plan for Central and South East Scotland," *Town and Country Planning* 17(65), 1949, 40–3.

Beattie, M. "Sir Patrick Geddes and Barra Bazaar: Competing Visions, Ambivalence and Contradiction," *The Journal of Architecture* 9, 2004, 131–50.

Beauregard, R. A. "Subversive Histories: Texts from South Africa," in L. Sandercock (ed.), *Making the Invisible Visible: A Multicultural Planning History*, Berkeley and London: University of California Press, 1998, pp. 184–97.

Bell, G. and Tyrwhitt J. (eds), *Human Identity in the Urban Environment,* Baltimore, MD: Penguin, 1972.

Bell, M. "Reshaping Boundaries: International Ethics and Environmental Consciousness in the Early Twentieth Century," *Transactions of the Institute of British Geographers* New Series 23, 1998, 151–75.

Bell, M., Butlin, R. and Heffernan M. (eds), *Geography and Imperialism 1820–1940*, Studies in Imperialism, New York: Manchester University Press, 1995.

Ben-Arieh, Y. "The Planning and Conservation of Jerusalem During the Mandate Period in Israel 1917–1926: A Land Reflected in Its Past," in R. Aharonsohn and H. Lavsky (eds), *Studies in [the] Historical Geography of Israel*, Jerusalem: Magnes Press, Yad Ben-Zvi Press, 2001, pp. 441–93 (Hebrew).

"Better Indian Cities: Sir P. Geddes Dead," *Times of India*, 19 April 1932.

Bhabha, H. K. *The Location of Culture*, London and New York: Routledge, 1995.

Biger, G. "Of Patrick Geddes and an Un-known Ode to 'the Return to Zion,'" *Beeri* 1, 1988, 35–44 (Hebrew).

—— "A Scotsman in the First Hebrew City: Patrick Geddes and the 1926 Town Plan for Tel Aviv," *The Scottish Geographical Magazine* 108, 1992, 4–8.

Blunt, A. and McEwan, C. (eds), *Postcolonial Geographies*, New York and London: Continuum, 2002.

Boardman, P. *Esquisse de l'Oeuver educatrice de Patrick Geddes*, Montpellier: Imprimerie de la Charite, 1936.

—— *Patrick Geddes: Maker of the Future*, Chapel Hill: University of North Carolina Press, 1944.

—— "Not Housing But Home-Building: The Life-centered Approach of Patrick Geddes," reprinted from *Teknisk Ukeblad* (no. 30), Kronprinsensgt 17 Oslo Norway, 1948.

—— *The Worlds of Patrick Geddes: Biologist, Town Planner, Re-educator, Peace-Warrior*, London, Henley and Boston: Routledge & Kegan Paul, 1978.

Booth, C. *Life and Labour of the People in London*, London: Macmillan, 1892.

Booth, W. *In Darkest England,* London: International Headquarters of the Salvation Army, 1890.

Borden, I., Rendell, J. and Thomas, H. "Knowing Different Cities: Reflections on Recent European Writings on Cities and Planning History," in L. Sandercock (ed.), *Making the Invisible Visible: A Multicultural Planning History,* Berkeley and London: University of California Press, 1998, pp. 135–49.

Boyer, M. C. *The City of Collective Memory: Its Historical Imagery and Architectural Entertainments*, Cambridge, MA, and London: The MIT Press, 1994; 2nd edn, 1998.

S. B. "The Hebrew University in Jerusalem," *Nature* 115(2897), 1925, 681–2.

Breheny, M. J. "In Search of Survey-Analysis-Plan," *The Planner* 75(6), 1989, 21–3.

Brine, J. "Ramsay Gardens, Patrick Geddes Centre," *Planning History* 11(3), 1989, 25.

Brown, R. N. Rudnose. "Scotland and Some Trends in Geography: John Murray, Patrick Geddes and Andrew Herbertson," (Abridged from The Herbertson Memorial Lecture delivered to the Royal

Scottish Geographical Society and the Edinburgh Branch of the Association on 5 March 1948) *Geography* 33, 1948, 107–16.

Bryce, J. "Proposed National Institute of Geography," *The Scottish Geographical Magazine* 18, 1902, 217.

Burgess, P. "Should Planning History Hit the Road? An Examination of the State of Planning History in the United States," *Planning Perspectives* 11, 1996, 201–24.

C. B. F., Review of *Patrick Geddes in India*, edited by Jacqueline Tyrwhitt, *The Geographical Journal* 115(1–3), 1947, 115–16.

Carter, H. "The Garden of Geddes," *The Forum* 54, October 1915, 455–71.

—— "The Garden of Geddes," *The Forum*, November 1915, 588–95.

Carr, E. H. *What is History?* Harmondsworth: Penguin, 1965.

Çelik, Z. *Urban Forms and Colonial Confrontations, Algiers under French Rule*, Berkeley and London: University of California Press, 1997.

—— *Empire, Architecture, and the City: French-Ottoman Encounters, 1830–1914,* Seattle: University of Washington Press, 2008.

Chabard, P. "Towers and Globes: Architectural and Epistemological Differences Between Patrick Geddes' Outlook Towers and Paul Otlet's Mundaneums," in B. Rayward (ed.), *European Modernism and the Information Society, Informing the Present, Understanding the Past*, London: Ashgate, 2008, pp. 105–26.

—— "Competing Scales in Transnational Networks: The Impossible Travel of Patrick Geddes' Cities Exhibition to America, 1911–1913," *Urban History* 36(2), 2009, 202–22.

Chakrabarty, D. *Provincializing Europe: Postcolonial Thought and Historical Difference*, Princeton, NJ: Princeton University Press, 2000.

Chapman, D. "The Common Sense of Patrick Geddes", *Town and Country Planning* 13(52), 1945–6, 161–2; 181.

Chatterjee, P. and Kenny, J. T. "Creating a New Capital: Colonial Discourse and the Decolonization of Delhi," *Historical Geography* 27, 1999, 73–98.

Cherry, G. "Biographies and Planning History," in G. Cherry (ed.), *Pioneers in British Planning*, London: The Architectural Press, 1981, pp. 1–18.

—— "George Pepler 1882–1959," in G. Cherry, *Pioneers in British Planning*, London: The Architectural Press, 1981, pp. 131–49.

—— "Today's Issues in a 20th Century Perspective," *The Planner*, 11 January 1991, 7–11.

—— *Town Planning in Britain Since 1900*, Making Contemporary Britain Series, Oxford and Cambridge, MA: Blackwell, 1996.

Christopher, A. J. "Urban Segregation Levels in the British Overseas Empire and its Successors, in the Twentieth Century," *Transactions of the Institute of British Geographers* New Series 17, 1992, 95–107.

"Civic Exhibition, Dublin," *Town Planning Review* 5(3), 1914, 249.

Clavel, P. "Ebenezer Howard and Patrick Geddes: Two Approaches to City Development," in Parsons, K. C. and Schuyler, D. (eds), *From Garden City to Green City: The Legacy of Ebenezer Howard*, Baltimore and London: Johns Hopkins University Press, 2000, pp. 39–57.

Clay, A. T. *Notes on Mr. Geddes Museum Plan*, 1919, ATQ Jerusalem General File 78.

Cohen, S. E. "Greenbelts in London and Jerusalem," *Geographical Review* 84(1), 1994, 74–89.

Confurius, G. "Tel Aviv und die Transportfähigkeit der Moderne" (Tel Aviv and the Transportability of the Modern Movement), *Daidalos* 54, 15 December 1994, 52–61.

Cosgrove, D. and Daniels, S. (eds), *The Iconography of Landscape: Essays on the Symbolic Representation, Design and use of Past Environments*, Cambridge: Cambridge University Press, 1988.

Cosgrove, D. and Domosh, M. "Author and Authority," in J. Duncan and D. Ley (eds), *Place/Culture/Representation*, London and New York: Routledge, 1993, pp. 25–38.

Cowan, R. "Planners, Gardeners and Patrick Geddes," *Town and Country Planning* 45(7–8), 1977, 348–51.

Bibliography

Cuthbert, M. "The Concept of the Outlook Tower in the Work of Patrick Geddes," unpublished thesis, University of St. Andrews, 1987.

Daniels, S. and Nash, C. "Life Paths: Geography and Biography," *Journal of Historical Geography* 30(3), 2004, 449–58.

"Death of Famous Scotsman, Sir Patrick Geddes; Distinguished Work in Many Spheres," *Glasgow Herald*, 18 April 1932.

Defries, A. *The Interpreter Geddes: The Man and his Gospel*, London: George Routledge & Sons, 1927.

Dehaene, M. "Survey and the Assimilation of a Modernist Narrative in Urbanism," *The Journal of Architecture* 7, 2002, 33–55.

—— "Urban Lessons for the Modern Planner: Patrick Abercrombie and the Study of Urban Development," *Town Planning Review* 75(1), 2004, 1–30.

Dix, G. "Patrick Abercrombie 1879–1957," in G. Cherry, *Pioneers in British Planning*, London: The Architectural Press, 1981, pp. 103–30.

Dolev, D. "The Architectural Master Plans of the Hebrew University, 1918–1948," in S. Katz and M. Heyd (eds), *The History of the Hebrew University in Jerusalem: Roots and Beginnings*, Jerusalem: Magnes Publishers, 1997, pp. 257–80 (Hebrew).

—— "Architecture and Nationalist Ideology: The Case of the Architectural Master Plans for the Hebrew University in Jerusalem (1919–1974) and their Connections With Nationalist Ideology," unpublished PhD thesis, University College: London, 2001.

Dossal, M. "Limits of Colonial Urban Planning: A Study of Mid-nineteenth Century Bombay," *International Journal of Urban and Regional Research* 13(1), 1989, 19–22.

Driver, F. "Moral Geographies: Social Science and the Urban Environment in Mid-nineteenth Century England," *Transactions of the Institute of British Geographers* New Series 13, 1988, 275–87.

—— "Geography, Empire and Visualization," Department of Geography Working Paper no. 1, Royal Holloway, University of London, 1994.

—— *Geography Militant: Cultures of Exploration in the Age of Empire*, Oxford: Blackwell, 2001.

Driver F. and Gilbert, D. (eds), *Imperial Cities: Landscape, Display and Identity*, Manchester and New York: Manchester University Press, 1999.

Driver, F. and Maddrell, A. M. C. "Geographical Education and Citizenship: Introduction," *Journal of Historical Geography* 22(4), 1996, 371–2.

Driver, F. and Rose, G. "Introduction," in F. Driver and G. Rose (eds), *Nature and Science: Essays in the History of Geographical Knowledge*, Historical Geography Research Series 28, London: Institute of British Geographers, 1992, pp. 1–7.

"Dublin Competition and Exhibition," *Town Planning Review* 5(2), 1914, 172–3.

Duncan, J. S. *The City as Text: The Politics of Landscape Interpretation in the Kandy Kingdom*, Cambridge: Cambridge University Press, 1990.

—— "Sites of Representation," in J. Duncan and D. Ley (eds), *Place/Culture/Representation*, London and New York: Routledge, 1993, pp. 39–56.

—— "Notes from the Archive," *Historical Geography* 27, 1999, 119–28.

Duncan, J. and Ley, D. "Introduction," in J. Duncan and D. Ley (eds), *Place/Culture/Representation*, London and New York: Routledge, 1993, pp. 1–24.

Dunevitz, N. *Holot SheHayu LeKrach* (Sands which have turned into City), Jerusalem and Tel Aviv: Shocken, 1959.

Earley, J. "Sorting in Patrick Geddes' Outlook Tower," *Places* 7(3), 1991, 64–71.

Eder, D. "In Palestine," *The Sociological Review* 24, 1932, 376–8.

"Editorial Notes," *The Advocate*, 2 March 1916.

Edwards, B. "Edinburgh Debates Mumford's Distortion of Geddes' Ideas," *Architects' Journal* 16 November 1995, 16.

Efrat, E. "British Town Planning Perspectives of Jerusalem in Transition," *Planning Perspectives* 8, 1993, 377–93.

Falk, R. "Settling the Land as a Eugenic Practice," *Alpayim* 23, 2002, 179–98 (Hebrew).

Ferraro, G. "Il gioco del piano. Patrick Geddes in India 1914–1924," *Urbanistica* 103, 1995, 136–52.

—— "Patrick Geddes, *Cities in Evolution*," *Urbanistica* 108, 1997, 157–61.

—— *Rieducazione alla Speranza: Patrick Geddes Planner in India, 1914–1924*, Milano: Jaca Books, 1998.

Ferreira, J. J. and Jha, S. S. (eds), *The Outlook Tower: Essays on Urbanization in Memory of Patrick Geddes*, Department of Sociology, University of Bombay [upon the Golden Jubilee of the Department of Sociology 1969], Bombay: Popular Prakashan, 1976.

Fleure, H. J. "Patrick Geddes (1854–1932)," *The Sociological Review* New Series 1(2), December 1953, 5–13.

Foucault, M. "Questions on Geography," in C. Gordon (ed.), *Power/Knowledge*, New York: Pantheon Books, 1972; 2nd edn, 1980.

—— "Space, Knowledge and Power," in P. Rabinow (ed.), *The Foucault Reader*, London: Penguin, 1984; 2nd edn, 1991, pp. 239–56.

Fowle, F. and Thomson, B. (eds), *Patrick Geddes: The French Connection*, Oxford: White Cockade, 2004.

Fraser, B. (ed.), *The Tagore-Geddes Correspondence,* Calcutta: Visva-Bharati, 2004.

Freestone, R. "Learning from Planning's Histories," in R. Freestone, *Urban Planning in a Changing World*, London: E. & F.N. Spon, 2000, pp. 1–19.

F. R. S., "The Relevance of Geddes To-day," *Journal of the Town Planning Institute* 11(8), 1954, 209–11.

Fry, M. *The Scottish Empire*, Edinburgh: Tuckwell Press and Brilinn, 2001.

Fuchs, R. and Herbert, G. "A Colonial Portrait of Jerusalem: British Architecture in Mandate-Era Palestine," in N. AlSayyad (ed.), *Hybrid Urbanism: On the Identity Discourse and the Built Environment*, Westport, CT, and London: Praeger, 2001, pp. 83–108.

Fuller, S. "A Path Better Not to Have Been Taken," *The Sociological Review* 55(4), 2007, 805–15.

G. G. C., Review of *Cities in Evolution: An Introduction to the Town Planning Movement and to the Study of Civics*, by Patrick Geddes. *The Geographical Journal* 47(4), 1916, 309–11.

Gardiner, G. *Pillars of Society*, London: James Nisbet & Co., 1913.

Gavrieli, T. "Hatochnit Ha'estratgit leTel Aviv-Yafo: Ekronot, Tahalich, Matrot Tichnun, Yissum" (The Strategic Plan for Tel Aviv-Jaffa: Principles, Process, Plan Targets, Implementation), in B. A. Kipnis (ed.), *Tel Aviv-Yafo: Me'ir Ganim le'ir Olam: Mea Hashanim Harishonot (Tel Aviv-Yafo: from a garden city to a world city. The first one hundred years)*, Tel Aviv: Pardes Publishing, 2008, pp. 467–76.

Geddes, A. "Suggestion Towards a Visual & Symbolic Presentment of History for India," [n. d.], T-GED 4/3/8.

—— "Patrick Geddes as a Sociologist" [from a lecture given at the Outlook Tower to the Sociological Group in December 1933, edited by Mrs. J. Geddes from a single manuscript] in J. J. Ferreira, and S. S. Jha (eds), *The Outlook Tower: Essays on Urbanization in Memory of Patrick Geddes*, Department of Sociology, University of Bombay [upon the Golden Jubilee of the Department of Sociology 1969] Bombay: Popular Prakashan, 1976, pp. 14–19.

—— "The Life and Work of Professor Sir Patrick Geddes: His Indian Reports and their Influence," *Journal of the Town Planning Institute* 26, 1940, pp. 191–4.

—— "Geography, Sociology, and Psychology: A Plea for Coordination, with an Example from India," *Geographical Review* 38(4), 1948, 590–7.

—— "Introduction," in P. Mairet, *Pioneer of Sociology: The Life and Letters of Patrick Geddes,* London: Lund Humphries, 1957, pp. xvii–xx.

Gillion, K. L. *Ahmedabad: A Study in Indian Urban History*, Berkeley and Los Angeles: University of California Press, 1968.

Glass, R. "Urban Sociology in Great Britain: A Trend Report," *Current Sociology (La Sociologie Contemporaine)* 4(4), 1955, 5–19.

—— "The Evaluation of Planning: Some Sociological Considerations," *UNESCO International Social Science Journal* 11(3), 1959, 393–409.

Bibliography

Glikson, A. *Regional Planning and Development. Six Lectures Delivered at the Institute of Social Studies, at the Hague*, Leiden: A. W. Sijthoff's Uitgeversmaatschappij, 1953, p. 63, quoted in V. Welter, M. "Arthur Glikson, Thinking-Machines, and the Planning of Israel," in V. M. Welter and J. Lawson (eds), *The City after Patrick Geddes*, Bern: Peter Lang, 2000, pp. 211–26.

Godlewska, A. "Napoleon's Geographers (1797–1815): Imperialists and Soldiers of Modernity," in A. Godlewska and N. Smith (eds), *Geography and Empire*, Oxford and Cambridge, MA: Blackwell, 1994, pp. 31–54.

Goist, P. D. "Patrick Geddes and the City," *Journal of American Institute of Planners* 40(1), January 1974, 31–7.

Goldman, L. "Foundations of British Sociology 1880–1930: Contexts and Biographies," *The Sociological Review* 55(3), 2007, 431–40.

Goodfriend, D. "Nagar Yoga: The Culturally Informed Town Planning of Patrick Geddes in India 1914–1924," *Human Organization* 38(4), 1979, 343–55.

Green, P. "Patrick Geddes," unpublished PhD thesis, University of Strathclyde, 1970.

—— Review of *Cities in Evolution* (3rd edn) by Patrick Geddes, *Town Planning Review* 41(3), July 1970, 293.

—— "Patrick Geddes – Pioneer of Social Planning (1854–1932)," *Journal of Indian History* Golden Jubilee Volume, 1973, Department of History, University of Kerala, 847–62.

Greenhalgh, P. *Ephemeral Vistas: A History of the Expositions Universelles, Great Exhibitions and World's Fairs, 1851–1939*, Manchester: Manchester University Press, 1988.

Guha, R. "On Some Aspects of the Historiography of Colonial India," in R. Guha (ed.), *Subaltern Studies I: Writings on South Asian History and Society*, Delhi: Oxford University Press, 1982, pp. 1–8.

Gupta, N. *Delhi Between Two Empires 1803–1931: Society, Government and Urban Growth*, Delhi: Oxford University Press, 1981.

—— "A Letter from India," in W. Stephen (ed.), *Think Global, Act Local: The Life and Legacy of Patrick Geddes*, Edinburgh: Luath Press, 2004, pp. 117–9.

—— "Twelve Years on: Urban History in India," *Urban History Yearbook*, 1981, 76–9.

Gupta, S. "Theory and Practice of Town Planning in Calcutta, 1817 to 1912: An Appraisal," *The Indian Economic and Social History Review* 30(1), 1993, 29–55.

"Haifa's Future, Vision of the Town Beautiful: Interview with Prof. Geddes," *The Egyptian Gazette* [15 September 1920] CZM L18/80-11.

Hall, P. *Cities of Tomorrow: An Intellectual History of Urban Planning and Design in the Twentieth Century*, Oxford and New York: Basil Blackwell, 1988.

—— "The Centenary of Modern Planning," in R. Freestone (ed.), *Urban Planning in a Changing World: The Twentieth Century Experience*, London: E. & F.N. Spon, 2000, pp. 20–39.

Halliday, R. J. "The Sociological Movement, the Sociological Society and the Genesis of Academic Sociology in Britain," *The Sociological Review* New Series 16, 1968, 377–98.

"Happy Birthday, Patrick Geddes," *Town and Country Planning,* September 1979, 181.

Haraway, D. *Primate Visions*, London: Verso, 1989.

Harley, J. B. "Maps, Knowledge and Power," in D. Cosgrove and S. Daniels, (eds), *The Iconography of Landscape: Essays on the Symbolic Representation, Design and Use of Past Environments*, Cambridge: Cambridge University Press, 1988, pp. 279–312.

Hasselgren, J. A. "What is Living and What is Dead in the Work of Patrick Geddes?" in *Patrick Geddes: A Symposium*, Special Occasional Paper in Town and Regional Planning, Duncan of Jordanstone College of Art/University of Dundee (an event organized by the Department of Town and Regional Planning to celebrate the Centenary of the foundation of the university), 1 March 1982, pp. 26–46.

Hazareesingh, S. "Colonial Modernism and the Flawed Paradigms of Urban Renewal: Uneven Development in Bombay, 1900–1925," *Urban History* 28(2), 2001, 235–55.

Hebbert, M. "Retrospect on the Outlook Tower," in *Patrick Geddes: A Symposium,* Special Occasional

Paper in Town and Regional Planning, Duncan of Jordanstone College of Art/University of Dundee, 1 March 1982, pp. 49–63.

—— "Patrick Geddes Reconsidered," *Town and Country Planning*, January 1980, 15–17.

Heinonen, S. "Slow Housing: Competitive Edge for Innovative Living Environments," *Fennia* 184(1), 2006, 91–104.

Herbert, G. and Sosnovsky, S. *Bauhaus on the Carmel and the Crossroads of Empire: Architecture and Planning in Haifa during the British Mandate*, Jerusalem: Yad Yizhak Ben-Zvi, 1993.

Holford, Sir W. "Foreword," in P. Mairet, *Pioneer of Sociology: The Life and Letters of Patrick Geddes*, London: Lund Humphries, 1957, pp. xi–xvi.

Holston, J. "Spaces of Insurgent Citizenship," in L. Sandercock (ed.), *Making the Invisible Visible: A Multicultural Planning History*, Berkeley and London: University of California Press, 1998, pp. 37–56.

Home, R. "Town Planning and Garden Cities in the British Colonial Empire 1910–1940," *Planning Perspectives* 5(1), 1990, 23–37.

—— "Transferring British Planning Law to the Colonies: The Case of the 1938 Trinidad Town and Regional-Planning Ordinance," *Third World Planning Review* 15(14), 1993, 397–410.

—— *Of Planting and Planning: The Making of British Colonial Cities*, Studies in History, Planning and the Environment, London: E. & F.N. Spon, 1997.

Hosagrahar, J. "City as Durbar: Theater and Power in Imperial Delhi," in N. AlSayyad (ed.), *Forms of Dominance: On the Architecture and Urbanism of the Colonial Enterprise*, Aldershot: Avebury 1992, pp. 83–106.

—— *Indigenous Modernities: Negotiating Architecture and Urbanism*, London: Routledge, 2005.

"Humanity and Town Planning," *The Birmingham Post* quoted in "Notes and News," *Garden Cities and Town Planning* 12(4), 1932, 113.

Hyman, B. *British Planners in Palestine, 1918–1936*, unpublished PhD thesis, The London School of Economics and Political Science, 1994.

Hysler-Rubin, N. "Arts & Crafts and the Great City: Charles Robert Ashbee in Jerusalem," *Planning Perspectives* 21(4), 2006, 347–68.

"In Support of Professor Geddes", *The Palestine Weekly* I(39), 1920, Special Town Planning Number.

Jacobs, J. *The Death and Life of Great American Cities*, Harmondsworth: Penguin Books in association with Jonathan Cape, 1994 [1961].

Jacobs, J. M. *Edge of Empire: Postcolonialism and the City*, London and New York: Routledge, 1996.

Jerusalem Master Plan, 1968, Jerusalem: Municipality of Jerusalem, 1972.

Jones, B. "European Modernism and the Information Society: Review Article," *Australian Academic & Research Libraries* 39(3), 2008, 207–13.

Kallus, R. "Patrick Geddes and the Evolution of a Housing Type in Tel-Aviv," *Planning Perspectives* 12, 1997, 281–30.

Kauffman, R. "Planning of Jewish Settlements in Palestine," *The Town Planning Review* 22(2), 1926, 93–116.

Kendall, H. *Jerusalem the City Plan: Preservation and Development During the British Mandate, 1917–1948*, London: HMSO, 1948.

Kenny, J. T. "Colonial Geographies: Accommodation and Resistance – An Introduction," *Historical Geography* 27, 1999, 1–4.

King, A. *Colonial Urban Development: Culture, Social Power and Environment*, London, Henley and Boston: Routledge & Kegan Paul, 1976.

—— "Exporting Planning: The Colonial and Neo-Colonial Experience," in G. Cherry (ed.), *Shaping an Urban World: Planning and the Environment in the Modern World*, vol. 2, London: Mansell Publishing, 1980, pp. 203–26.

—— "Colonial Architecture and Urban Development," *Lotus International* 34, 1982, 47.

—— "Colonial Cities: Global Pivots of Change," in R. Ross and G. J. Telkamp (eds), *Colonial Cities: Essays on Urbanism in a Colonial Context*, Comparative Studies in Overseas History, Publications of the Leiden Centre for the History of European Expansion no. 5, Dordrecht, Boston and Lancaster: Martinus Nijhof Publishers, 1985, pp. 7–32.

—— *Urbanism, Colonialism, and the World-Economy: Cultural and Spatial Foundations of the World Urban System*, The International Library of Sociology, University of Lancaster, London and New York: Routledge, 1990.

—— "Re-Worlding the City," *Planning History* 22, 2000, 5–15.

—— "Introductory Comments: The Dialectics of Dual Development," (first published *City and Society* 12(1), 2000, 9), in J. Nasr and M. Volait (eds), *Urbanism: Imported or Exported?* Chichester: Wiley-Academy, 2003, p. xxiii.

Kitchen, P. *A Most Unsettling Person: An Introduction to the Ideas and Life of Patrick Geddes*, London: Victor Gollancz, 1975.

Kobayashi, A. "Multiculturalism: Representing a Canadian institution," in J. Duncan and D. Ley (eds), *Place/Culture/Representation*, London and New York: Routledge, 1993, pp. 205–31.

Kong, L. and Law, L. "Introduction: Contested Landscapes, Asian Cities," *Urban Studies* 39, 2002, 1503–12.

Kramsch, O. "Tropics of Planning Discourse: Stalking the 'Constructive Imaginary' of Selected Urban Planning Histories," in L. Sandercock (ed.), *Making the Invisible Visible: A Multicultural Planning History*, Berkeley and London: University of California Press, 1998, pp.163–83.

Krueckeberg, D. A. "Between Self and Culture or What are Biographies of Planners About?" *Journal of the American Planning Association* 59(2), Spring 1993, 217–21.

—— "Planning History's Mistakes," *Planning Perspectives* 12, 1997, 269–79.

Kumar, M. S. "The Evolution of Spatial Ordering," in A. Blunt and C. McEwan (eds), *Postcolonial Geographies,* New York and London: Continuum, 2002, pp. 85–98.

Lambert, D. and Lester, A. "Introduction: Imperial Spaces, Imperial Subjects," in D. Lambert and A. Lester (eds), *Colonial Lives Across the British Empire: Imperial Careering in the Long Nineteenth Century*, Cambridge: Cambridge University Press, 2006, pp. 1–32.

Lanchester, H. V. "Mr. Mclean's Plan Revised," *The Observer*, 12 July 1919.

—— "Town Planning in India," *The Sociological Review* 24, 1932, 370–1.

Landa, M. and Oesemnik, A. (eds), *Our City Tel Aviv*, Tel Aviv: Jaffa Municipality, 1959 (Hebrew).

Lasker, B. Review of *Patrick Geddes in India*, edited by J. Tyrwhitt, *Pacific Affairs* 21(1), 1948, 74–5.

"The Late Sir Patrick Geddes: Report on Town Planning in Colombo," *Times of Ceylon*, 25 April 1932.

Latour, B. "Centres of Calculations," in *Science in Action: How to Follow Scientists and Engineers Through Society*, Cambridge, MA: Harvard University Press, 1987, pp. 215–57.

Law, A. "The Ghost of Patrick Geddes: Civics as Applied Sociology," *Sociological Research Online* 10(2), 2005. Available at: http://www.socresonline.org.uk/10/2/law.html (accessed May 2010).

Learmonth, A. T. A. "Urban Improvements: A Strategy for Urban Works. Observations of Sir Patrick Geddes with Reference to Old Lahore" (Book Review), *The Geographical Journal* 132(4), 1966, 538.

Lees, L. "Rematerializing Geography: The 'New' Urban Geography," *Progress in Human Geography* 26(1), 2002, 101–12.

Leonard, S. "Patrick Geddes Centre For Planning Studies," *Planning History* 10(1), 1988, 26.

—— "The Regeneration of the Old Town of Edinburgh by Patrick Geddes," *Planning History* 21(2), 1999, 33–47.

—— "The Context and Legacy of Patrick Geddes in Europe," in V. M. Welter and J. Lawson (eds), *The City after Patrick Geddes*, Bern: Peter Lang, 2000, pp. 71–90.

—— "Finding Geddes Abroad," in W. Stephen (ed.), *Think Global, Act Local: The Life and Legacy of Patrick Geddes*, Edinburgh: Luath Press, 2004, pp. 41–60.

Lesser, W. "Patrick Geddes: The Practical Visionary," *Town Planning Review* 45(3), 1974, 311–27.

Lester, A. *Imperial Networks: Creating Identities in Nineteenth Century South Africa and Britain*, London and New York: Routledge, 2001.

—— "British Settler Discourse and the Circuits of Empire," *History Workshop Journal* 54, 2002, 27–50.

LeVine, M. "Conquest Through Town Planning: The Case of Tel Aviv, 1921–1948," *Journal of Palestine Studies* 27(4), 1998, 36–52.

—— *Overthrowing Geography: Jaffa, Tel Aviv, and the Struggle for Palestine 1880–1948*, Los Angeles and London: University of California Press, 2005.

Lilley, K. D. "On Display: Planning Exhibitions as Civic Propaganda or Public Consultation?" *Planning History* 25(3), 2003, 3–8.

Livingstone, D. N. "Never Shall Ye Make the Crab Walk Straight: An Inquiry into the Scientific Sources of Racial Geography," in *Nature and Science: Essays in the History of Geographical Knowledge*, Historical Geography Research Series no. 28, London: Institute of British Geographers, 1992, pp. 37–48.

Mabin, A. and Smit, D. "Reconstructing South Africa's Cities? The Making of Urban Planning 1900–2000," *Planning Perspectives* 12, 1997, 193–223.

Macdonald, M. "Understanding the European City Around 1900: The Contribution of Patrick Geddes," in V. M. Welter and J. Lawson (eds), *The City after Patrick Geddes*, Bern: Peter Lang, 2000, pp. 55–70.

McGee, T. G. "Planning the Asian City: The Relevance of 'Conservative Surgery' and the Concept of Dualism," in J. Ferreira and S. S. Jha (eds), *The Outlook Tower: Essays on Urbanization in Memory of Patrick Geddes*, Department of Sociology, University of Bombay [upon the Golden Jubilee of the Department of Sociology 1969], Bombay: Popular Prakashan, 1976, pp. 266–81.

McGegan, E. "Geddes as a Man of Action," *The Sociological Review* 24, 1932, 355–7.

—— "The Life and Work of Professor Sir Patrick Geddes: Biographical," *Journal of the Town Planning Institute* 26, 1940, 189–91.

McLoughlin, J. B. *Urban and Regional Planning – A Systems Approach*, London: Faber and Faber, 1969.

Maddrell, A. M. C. "Empire, Emigration and School Geography: Changing Discourses of Imperial Citizenship, 1880–1925," *Journal of Historical Geography* 22(4), 1996, 373–87.

Mairet, P. *Pioneer of Sociology: The Life and Letters of Patrick Geddes*, London: Lund Humphries, 1957.

Marom, N. *Ir im Conceptsia: Metachnenim et Tel-Aviv (A City with a Concept: Planning Tel-Aviv)*, Tel Aviv: Babel, 2009.

Matless, D. "Ordering the Land: The 'Preservation' of the English Countryside, 1918–1939," vol. I, unpublished PhD thesis, University of Nottingham, 1990.

—— "Regional Surveys and Local Knowledges: The Geographical Imagination in Britain, 1918–39," *Transactions of the Institute of British Geographers* New Series 17(4), 1992, 464–80.

—— "Visual Culture and Geographical Citizenship: England in the 1940s," *Journal of Historical Geography* 22(4), 1996, 424–39.

—— "Forms of Knowledge and Forms of Belonging: Regional Survey and Geographical Citizenship," in V. M. Welter and J. Lawson (eds), *The City After Patrick Geddes*, Bern: Peter Lang, 2000, pp. 91–112.

Mavor, J. *My Windows on The Street of the World*, vol. I, London: J. M. Dent & Sons; New York: E. P. Dutton & Co., 1923, pp. 213–16.

Mears, F. "The Life and Work of Professor Sir Patrick Geddes: Geddes Contribution to Planning in Evolution," *Journal of the Town Planning Institute* 26, 1940, 194–5.

Meller, H. E. "Patrick Geddes: An Analysis of his Theory of Civics, 1880–1914," *Victorian Studies* 16(3), 1973, 291–315.

—— *Leisure and the Changing City 1870–1914*, London, Henley and Boston: Routledge & Kegan Paul, 1976.

—— "Introduction" *The Ideal City*, edited with an introduction by Helen E. Meller, Leicester: Leicester University Press, 1979, pp. 9–46.

—— "Note to Civics: As Applied Sociology," *The Ideal City*, edited with an introduction by Helen E. Meller, Leicester: Leicester University Press, 1979, pp. 67–74.

—— "Urbanization and the Introduction of Modern Town Planning Ideas in India, 1900–1925," in K. N.

Chaudhuri and C. J. Dewey (eds), *Economy and Society Essays in Indian Economic and Social History*, Delhi: Oxford University Press, 1979, pp. 330–50.

—— "Patrick Geddes 1854–1932," in G. Cherry (ed.), *Pioneers in British Planning*, London: The Architectural Press, 1981, pp. 46–71.

—— "Cities and Evolution: Patrick Geddes as an International Prophet of Town Planning Before 1914," in A. Sutcliffe (ed.), *British Town Planning: The Formative Years*, Leicester: Leicester University Press, 1981, pp. 199–219.

—— "Geddes and his Indian Reports," in *Patrick Geddes: A Symposium*, Special Occasional Paper in Town and Regional Planning, Duncan of Jordanstone College of Art/University of Dundee (an event organised by the Department of Town and Regional Planning to celebrate the Centenary of the Foundation of the University), 1 March 1982, pp. 4–21.

—— "Conservation and Evolution: The Pioneering Work of Sir Patrick Geddes in Jerusalem, 1919–1925," *Planning History Bulletin* 9, 1987, 42–9.

—— *Patrick Geddes: Social Evolutionist and City Planner*, London: Routledge, 1990.

—— "Philanthropy and Public Enterprise: International Exhibitions and the Modern Town Planning Movement, 1889–1913," *Planning Perspectives* 19, 1995, 295–310.

—— *Towns, Plans and Society in Modern Britain*, prepared for the Economic History Society, Cambridge: Cambridge University Press, 1997.

—— "Understanding the European City Around 1900: The Contribution of Patrick Geddes," in V. M. Welter and J. Lawson (eds), *The City after Patrick Geddes*, Bern: Peter Lang, 2000, pp. 35–54.

Mercer, C. "Geographies for the Present: Patrick Geddes, Urban Planning and the Human Sciences," *Economy and Society* 26(2), 1997, 211–24.

Miller, M. "Raymond Unwin 1863–1940," in G. Cherry, *Pioneers in British Planning*, London: The Architectural Press, 1981, pp. 72–102.

Mitchell, D. *Cultural Geography: A Critical Introduction*, Oxford and Malden, MA: Blackwell, 2000.

Mitchell, T. *Colonising Egypt,* Berkeley, Los Angeles and Oxford: University of California Press, 1988; 2nd edn, 1991.

Mitchell, W. J. T. *Iconology: Image, Text, Ideology*, Chicago and London: The University of Chicago Press, 1986.

Monk, D. B. *An Aesthetic Occupation: Architecture, Politics, and the Menace of Monuments in Mandate-Era Palestine, 1917–1929*, unpublished PhD dissertation, Princeton University, 1995.

Morton, P. A. *Hybrid Modernities: Architecture and Representation at the 1931 Colonial Exposition*, Paris, Cambridge, MA, and London: The MIT Press, 2000.

Mukerjee, R. "In India," *The Sociological Review* 24, 1932, pp. 374–5.

Muller, J. "From Survey to Strategy: Twentieth Century Developments in Western Planning Method," *Planning Perspectives* 7(2), 1992, 125–55.

—— "Although God Cannot Alter the Past, Historians Can: Reflections on the Writing of Planning Histories," *Planning History* 21(2), 1999, 11–19.

Mumford, E. *The CIAM Discourse on Urbanism, 1928–1960*, Cambridge, MA, and London: The MIT Press, 2000.

Mumford, L. "Who is Patrick Geddes?" *The Survey*, New York, pp. 1–7, T-GED 23/3/9.1.

—— "Introduction," in *Patrick Geddes in India*, edited by J. Tyrwhitt, with an introduction by L. Mumford and a preface by H. V. Lanchaster, London: Lund Humphries, 1947, p. 7.

—— "Mumford on Geddes," *The Architectural Review* 108, July 1950, 81–7.

—— "The Disciple's Rebellion: A Memoir of Patrick Geddes," *Encounter* 27(3), 1966, 11–24.

—— "The Geddesian Gambit," in F. G. Novak, Jr. (ed.), *Lewis Mumford and Patrick Geddes: The Correspondence*, London and New York: Routledge, 1995, pp. 353–72.

Myers, G. A. "Intellectual of Empire: Eric Dutton and Hegemony in British Africa," *Annals of the Association of American Geographers* 88(1), 1998, 1–27.

—— "Colonial Discourse and Africa's Colonized Middle: Ajit Singh's Architecture," *Historical Geography* 27, 1999, 27–55.

Nash, C. "Cultural Geography: Postcolonial Cultural Geographies," *Progress in Human Geography* 26(2), 2002, 219–30.

Nash, C. and Graham B. (eds), *Modern Historical Geographies*, Essex: Pearson Education, 2002.

Nasr, J. and Volait, M. "Introduction: Transporting Planning," in J. Nasr and M. Volait (eds), *Urbanism: Imported or Exported?* Chichester: Wiley-Academy, 2003, pp. xi–xxxviii.

"The New University at Jerusalem," *The Graphic* [London] 16, 2884, 1925.

"The New University at Jerusalem," *The Observer*, 1 March 1925.

Naylor, S. and Jones, G. A. "Writing Orderly Geographies of Distant Places: Regional Survey Movement and Latin America," *Ecumene* 4(3), 1997, 273–99.

Novak, F. G. "Introduction," in F. G. Novak, Jr. (ed.), *Lewis Mumford and Patrick Geddes: The Correspondence*, London and New York: Routledge, 1995, pp. 1–36.

"Obituary: Professor Sir Patrick Geddes," *Journal of Town Planning Institute* 18(7), 1932, 184.

Odum, H. W. "Patrick Geddes' Heritage to 'The Making of the Future,'" *Social Forces* 22(3), 1944, 275–81.

Ogen, Y. (ed.), *Asher Haya*, Tel Aviv: Ahdut, 1959.

"One Who Loved His Fellow-men: Sir Patrick Geddes, a Long Life of Doing Good for Each and All," *Children's Newspaper,* 27 April 1932.

Osborne, T., Rose, N. and Savage, M. "Editors' Introduction Reinscribing British Sociology: Some Critical Reflections," *The Sociological Review* 56(4), 2008, 519–34.

Outtes, J. "Disciplining Society through the City: The Genesis of City Planning in Brazil and Argentina (1894–1945)," *Bulletin of Latin America* 22(2), 2003, 137–64.

Painter, J. and Philo, C. "Spaces of Citizenship: An Introduction," *Political Geography* 14(2), 1995, 107–20.

Payton, N. I. "The Machine in the Garden City: Patrick Geddes' Plan for Tel Aviv," *Planning Perspectives* 19(4), 1995, 359–81.

Pentland, M. "An Ideal Rising from the Real," *The Sociological Review* 24, 1932, 368–9.

Pepler, G. "Geddes' Contribution to Town Planning," *Town Planning Review* 26, 1955–6, 19–24.

Perera, N. "Indigenising the Colonial City: Late 19th-century Colombo and its Landscape," *Urban Studies* 39(2), 2002, 1703–21.

—— "Contesting Visions: Hybridity, Liminality and Authorship of the Chandigarh Plan," *Planning Perspectives* 19, 2004, 175–99.

Petruccioli, A. "Patrick Geddes in Indore: Alcune questioni di metodo" (Some Questions of Method), *Lotus International* 34, 1982, 106–15.

Pinkerton, R. "Patrick Geddes Hall: Scotland's First Hall of Residence," [n.p.], 1978.

Ploszajska, T. "Constructing the Subject: Geographical Models in English Schools, 1870–1944," *Journal of Historical Geography* 22, 1996, 388–98.

—— "Historiographies of Geography and Empire," in C. Nash and B. Graham (eds), *Modern Historical Geographies*, Essex: Pearson Education, 2002, pp. 121–42.

Ponte, A. "Arte civica o sociologia applicata? P. Geddes e T. H. Mawson: due progetti per Dunfermline" (Civic Art or Applied Sociology? P. Geddes and T. H. Mawson: Two Plans for Dunfermline), *Lotus International* 30, 1981, 91–8.

—— "The Geddes Myth," *Lotus International* 34, 1982, 118–19.

Prakash, G. "Writing Post-Orientalist Histories of the Third World: Perspectives from Indian Historiography," *Comparative Studies in Society and History* 32(1), 1990, 383–408.

Pratt, M. L. *Imperial Eyes: Travel Writing and Transculturation*, London: Routledge, 1992.

Price, D. "At Montpellier," *The Sociological Review* 24, 1932, 379.

"Professor Geddes on Town-Planning in India, an Interview," *The Advocate*, 1–2 March 1916.
"Professor Patrick Geddes on the Site and Design," *The Scotsman*, May 1925.

Proudfoot, P. R. "The Symbolism of the Crystal in the Planning and Geometry of the Design for Canberra," *Planning Perspectives* 11, 1996, 225–57.

Rabinow, P. *French Modern: Norms and Forms of the Social Environment*, Cambridge, MA, and London: The MIT Press, 1989.

Bibliography

—— "Colonialism, Modernity: The French in Morocco," in N. AlSayyad (ed.), *Forms of Dominance: On the Architecture and Urbanism of the Colonial Enterprise*, Aldershot: Avebury, 1992, pp. 167–82.

"A Radio Broadcast was Devoted to Sir Geddes, The Father of Modern Town Planning, a Centenary Tribute to a Practical Visionary," BBC, November 1954, NLS MS10608/62–89.

Ratcliffe, S. K. "A Light that Lighted other Minds," *The Sociological Review* 24, 1932, 366–7.

Ravetz, A. *The Government of Space: Town Planning in Modern Society*, London: Faber and Faber, 1986.

Razi, T. *Yaldei Hahefker: Hechatzer Ha'achorit shel Tel Aviv HaMandatorit (Forsaken Children: The Backyard of Mandatory Tel-Aviv)*, Tel Aviv: Am Oved, 2009, pp. 126–7.

Reilly, J. P. "The Early Social Thought of Patrick Geddes," unpublished PhD thesis, Columbia University, 1972.

Renwick, C. and Gunn, R. C. "Demythologizing the Machine: Patrick Geddes, Lewis Mumford, and Classical Sociological Theory," *Journal of the History of the Behavioral Sciences* 44(1), 2008, 59–76.

"Reviews: The Day Patrick Geddes Blew his Top," *Town and Country Planning* 52(2), 1983, 58–9.

Reynolds, J. P. Review of *The Genesis of Modern British Town Planning* by William Ashworth, *Town Planning Review* 25(3), 1954, 231.

Robson, B. T. "Geography and Social Science: The Role of Patrick Geddes," in D. R. Stoddart (ed.), *Geography, Ideology and Social Concern*, London: Blackwell, 1981, pp. 186–207.

Rose, G. "Geography as a Science of Observation: The Landscape, The Gaze and Masculinity," in *Nature and Science: Essays in the History of Geographical Knowledge,* Historical Geography Research Series 28, London: Institute of British Geographers, 1992, pp. 8–18.

Ross, R. and Telkamp, G. J. (eds), *Colonial Cities: Essays on Urbanism in a Colonial Context*, Comparative Studies in Overseas History, Publications of the Leiden Centre for the History of European Expansion 5, Dordrecht, Boston and Lancaster: Martinus Nijhof Publishers, 1985.

Ryan, J. R. "Visualizing Imperial Geography: Halford Mackinder and the Colonial Office Visual Instruction Committee, 1911," *Ecumene* 1(2), 1994, 157–76.

Sacher, H. "The Hebrew University at Jerusalem, to be Opened on April 1: Working out a Great Idea," *Manchester Guardian*, 16 March 1925.

Said, E. *Orientalism*, New York: Pantheon Books, 1978.

Saint, A. "Ashbee, Geddes, Lethaby and the Rebuilding of Crosby Hall," *Architectural History* 34, 1991, 206–17.

Sandercock, L. "Introduction: Framing Insurgent Historiographies for Planning," in L. Sandercock (ed.), *Making the Invisible Visible: A Multicultural Planning History*, Berkeley and London: University of California Press, 1998, pp. 1–33.

—— *Cosmopolis II: Mongrel Cities in the 21st Century*, London and New York: Continuum, 2003.

Sandwich, 9th Earl of, Lord Lieutenant of Hunts, "The Saving of Crosby Hall," *The Sociological Review* 24, 1932, 362–4.

Searby, P. "'A Dreamer of Dreams': Patrick Geddes 1854–1932," Hughes Hall, Cambridge, the Wood Memorial Lecture 1985, delivered in Hughes Hall on Saturday, 5 October 1985, pp. 1–20.

Shapira, M. "The University and the City: Patrick Geddes and the First Master Plan for the Hebrew University, 1919," in S. Katz and M. Heyd (eds), *The History of the Hebrew University in Jerusalem: Roots and Beginnings*, Jerusalem: Magnes Publishers, 1997, pp. 201–35 (Hebrew).

Shapiro, S. "Planning Jerusalem: The First Generation, 1917–1968," in D. Amiran, A. Shachar and I. Kimhi (eds), *Urban Geography of Jerusalem: A Companion Volume to the Atlas of Jerusalem*, Jerusalem: Massada Press, 1973.

Shepherd, N. *Ploughing Sand: British Rule in Palestine 1917–1948*, London: John Murray, 2000.

Shillan, D. "Biotechnics: The Practice of Synthesis in the Work of Patrick Geddes," New Atlantis Foundation, Sixteenth Foundation Lecture, Richmond: New Atlantis Foundation, 1972.

Shoshkes, E. "Jaqueline Tyrwhitt: A Founding Mother of Modern Urban Design," *Planning Perspectives* 21, April 2006, 179–97.

Sidaway, J. D. "Postcolonial Geographies: Survey-Explore-Review," in A. Blunt and C. McEwan (eds), *Postcolonial Geographies*, New York and London: Continuum, 2002, pp. 11–26.

Sies, M. C. and Silver, C. "Introduction," in M. C. Sies and C. Silver (eds), *Planning the 20th Century American City*, Baltimore, MD, and London: Johns Hopkins University Press, 1996, pp. 1–34.

Silver, C. "American Planning and Planners: A Review of Two Books in Planning History," *Journal of Planning Education and Research* 3(2), 1984, 129.

Simmons, H. G. "Patrick Geddes: Prophet without Politics," *Studies in Modern European History and Culture* 2, 1976, 159–88.

"Sir Patrick Geddes: Biology and Town Planning," *The Times*, 18 April 1932.

Sir Patrick Geddes Centenary Celebrations, report of a symposium held in the Edinburgh College of Art on Friday, 1 October 1954, Heriot-Watt University.

"Sir Patrick Geddes: Noted Scot's Death in France, Town Planning Pioneer," *The Scotsman*, 18 April 1932.

Slater, G. "Illuminations . . . as by Flashes of Lightning," *The Sociological Review* 24, 1932, 372–3.

Söderström, O. "Paper Cities: Visual Thinking in Urban Planning," *Ecumene* 3(3), 1996, 249–81.

Spivak, G. C. "Can the Subaltern Speak?," in C. Nelson and L. Grossberg (eds), *Marxism and the Interpretation of Culture*, Urbana and Chicago: University of Illinois Press, 1988, pp. 271–313.

"Staff and Board of Survey Associates, From New York," *The Sociological Review* 24, 1932, 380.

Stephen, W. (ed.), *Think Global, Act Local: The Life and Legacy of Patrick Geddes*, Edinburgh: Luath Press, 2004.

Stevenson, R. "The Social Reformer," *The Sociological Review* 24, 1932, 353–4.

Stevenson, F. R. Review of *Pioneer of Sociology: The Life and Letters of Patrick Geddes*, by Philip Mairet, *Journal of the Town Planning Institute* 44, 1957–8, 20.

Stevenson, W. I. "Patrick Geddes and Geography: Biobibliographical Study," Occasional Papers 27, 1975, Department of Geography, University College, London.

Studholme, M. "Patrick Geddes and the History of Environmental Sociology in Britain," *Journal of Classical Sociology* 8(3), 2008, 367–91.

Studholme, M., Scott, J. and Husbands, C. "Dopplegängers and Racists: On Inhabiting Alternative Universes. A Reply to Steve Fuller's 'A path better not to have been taken,'" *The Sociological Review* 55(4), 2007, 816–22.

Sutcliffe, A. "Why Planning History?" *Built Environment* 7(1), 1981, 65–7.

Szmuk, N. *Tel-Aviv's Modern Movement: The White City of Tel Aviv, A World Heritage Site* ("Living on the Dunes" Exhibition Catalogue, Tel Aviv Museum) Tel Aviv: Municipality of Tel Aviv-Yafo, 2004.

Talen, E. "Beyond the Front Porch: Regionalist Ideals in the New Urbanism Movement," *Journal of Planning History* 7(1), 2008, 20–47.

Teggart, F. K. Review of *Science and Politics: The Coming Polity: A Study in Reconstruction*, by Patrick Geddes and Victor Branford, *Geographical Review* 9(4), 1920, 366.

T. F. L., "Outlook Towers," *Journal of the Town Planning Institute* 11(6), 1954, 145–6.

Thomson, Sir A. "Obituary: Sir Patrick Geddes," *The Times*, 19 April 1932.

Thompson-Fawcett, M. "Leon Krier and the Organic Revival Within Urban Policy and Practice," *Planning Perspectives* 13, 1998, 167–94.

Toppin, J. "History of Working Abroad," *The Architects' Journal* July 1982, 28–35.

"A Town Plan for Dublin," *Town Planning Review* 5(1), 1914, 68.

Trietsch, D. "Garden Cities for Palestine," *Garden Cities and Town Planning* 13(1), 1923, 11–12.

Troen, I. "Tel Aviv: Vienna on the Mediterranean," in *Imagining Zion: Dreams, Designs, and Realities in a Century of Jewish Settlement Zion*, New Haven, CT: Yale University Press, 2003, pp. 85–111.

Turnbull, P. "Patrick Geddes and the Planning Unit Today," reprinted from *Quarterly Journal of the R.I.A.S.*, 1947, T-GED 1/6/45.

Tyrwhitt, J. "Introduction," in *Cities in Evolution by Patrick Geddes*, edited by the Outlook Tower Association, Edinburgh, and the Association for Planning and Regional Reconstruction, London. New and revised edition, London: Williams & Norgate, 1949, pp. vi–xxx.

Bibliography

UNESCO, *Decision 27COM 8C.23 – White City of Tel-Aviv: The Modern Movement (Israel)*, 2003 Available at: http://whc.unesco.org/en/decisions/718 (accessed 15 March 2010).

Unwin, R. *Town Planning in Practice*, London: T. Fisher, 1994 [1909].

Urban Improvements: A Strategy for Urban Works, Government of Pakistan Planning Commission (Physical Planning & Housing Section), Study no. P. P. & H. 21, June 1965.

Van Vriesland, S. "Jews and Town Planning in Palestine," *The Palestine Weekly* 1(39), 1920, Special Town Planning Number, pp. 598–601.

Vardi, A. (ed.), *The City of Wonders*, Tel Aviv: Lema'an Hasefer, 1959 (Hebrew).

Ward, C. "The Outlook Tower, Edinburgh: Prototype for an Urban Studies Centre," *Bulletin of Environmental Education* 32, 1973.

—— "Old Prophets of New City-Regions," *Town and Country Planning* December 1990, 329–30.

Weill-Rochant, C. "Tel-Aviv des années trente: béton bland sur la terre promise," *l'architecture d'aujourd'hui* 293, June 1994, 41–7.

—— "Myths and Buildings of Tel Aviv," *Bulletin du Centre de recherché francais de Jerusalem* 12, 2003, 159.

Welter, V. M. "The Return of the Muses: Edinburgh as a *Museion*," in M. Giebelhausen (ed.), *The Architecture of the Museum: Symbolic Structures, Urban Contexts*, Manchester and New York: Manchester University Press, 1993, pp. 144–59.

—— "The Geddes Vision of the Region as City: Palestine as a 'Polis,'" in J. Fiedler (ed.), *Social Utopias of the Twenties: Bauhaus, Kibbutz and the Dream of the New Man*, published for the Bauhaus Dessau Foundation and the Friedrich-Ebert Foundation, Tel Aviv, Wuppertal: Muller+Busmann Press, 1995, pp. 71–9.

—— "History, Biology and City Design: Patrick Geddes in Edinburgh," *Architectural Heritage* 6, 1995, 61–82.

—— "Stages of an Exhibition: The Cities and Town Planning Exhibition of Patrick Geddes," *Planning History* 20(1), 1998, 25–35.

—— "Arcades for Lucknow: Patrick Geddes, Charles Rennie Mackintosh and the Reconstrucion of the City," *Architectural History* 42, 1999, 316–32.

—— "Arthur Glikson, Thinking-Machines, and the Planning of Israel," in V. M. Welter and J. Lawson (eds), *The City after Patrick Geddes*, Bern: Peter Lang, 2000, pp. 211–26.

—— *Biopolis: Patrick Geddes and the City of Life*, Cambridge, MA: The MIT Press, 2002.

—— "The 1925 Master Plan for Tel-Aviv by Patrick Geddes," *Israel Studies* 14(3), 2009, 94–119.

Welter, V. M. and Lawson, J. (eds), *The City After Patrick Geddes*, Bern: Peter Lang, 2000.

Wheeler, K. "A Note on the Valley Section of Patrick Geddes," *Bulletin of Environmental Education* 33, 1974, 126.

Whyte, I. B. "The Spirit of the City," in V. M. Welter and J. Lawson (eds), *The City after Patrick Geddes*, Bern: Peter Lang, 2000, pp. 15–32.

Wilson, P. "French Dressing," *Building Design* 12 March 2004, 18.

Withers, C. *Geography, Science and National Identity: Scotland since 1520* (Cambridge Studies in Historical Geography), Cambridge: Cambridge University Press, 2006.

Wright, G. *The Politics of Design in French Colonial Urbanism*, Chicago and London: The University of Chicago Press, 1991.

Yaari-Polskin, Y. *Meir Dizengoff – His Life and his Deeds*, Tel Aviv: Yishuv Publications, 1963.

Yiftachel, O. "Planning and Social Control: Exploring the Dark Side," *Journal of Planning Literature* 12(4), 1998, 395–406.

Yeoh, B. S. A. *Contesting Space: Power Relations and the Urban Built Environment in Colonial Singapore*, Kuala Lumpur: Oxford University Press, 1996.

—— "Postcolonial Cities," *Progress in Human Geography* 25, 2001, 456–68.

—— "Historical Geographies of the Colonised World," in C. Nash and B. Graham (eds), *Modern Historical Geographies*, Essex: Pearson Education, 2002, pp. 146–66.

Yosskovitz, B. "Tichnun vePituach Tel Aviv-Yaffo" (Planning and Development of Tel Aviv – Yaffo), *Tichnun Svivati* 57, 1999, 60–4.

Zandberg, E. "Halbinu et Ha'ir HaLevana" (Bleach the White City), *Haaretz (The Country)* 14 February 1999, Gallery section, quoted in Y. Shavit and H. Biger, *Ha'historya shel Tel Aviv 1: Leydata shel ir (1909–1936) (The History of Tel Aviv Vol. 1: The Birth of a Town (1909–1936))*, Tel Aviv: Ramot Press, Tel Aviv University, 2001, p. 34.

Zangwill, I. "Without Prejudice," (first published in *Pall Mall Magazine* February 1895), in A. Defries, *The Interpreter Geddes: The Man and his Gospel*, London: George Routledge & Sons, 1927, pp. 315–16.

"The Zionist University," *The Sociological Review* 17, 1925, 223–4.

Zueblin, C. "The World's First Sociological Laboratory," *The American Journal of Sociology* 4(5), March 1899, 577–92.

Works of Patrick Geddes

Note: page numbers in **bold** refer to figures

Index

Note: page numbers in **bold** refer to figures

Index